Praise for Travesty in Haiti

"This book is by far the most insightful, educating, and rewarding work on Haiti -- and indeed on the entire field of overseas charitable operations. Anyone interested in Haiti or in charities should read it."

Paul M. Gahlinger, M.D., Ph.D., M.P.H
Professor of Medicine at the University of Utah,
Author, and Winner of the American Association
for the Advancement of Science prize in Philosophy
of Science

"Anyone on the way to join the rebuilding of Haiti, or to write about it, must put this book in her bag. It's a tour de force -- a searing expose of what bad foreign aid and trade policies have wrought in Haiti, a gripping and moving account of hamlet life, and a rollicking, hilarious read. Beyond Haiti, it's a must read for anyone who wants to understand international development as actually practiced. It belongs on the shelf next to Paul Collier, Bill Easterly and other smart "mend it don't, end it" critics of foreign aid."

Ken Dilanian, Investigative Reporter, LA Times

". . . painfully personal, shockingly revealing, intensely honest. .In addition to the enlightening content, Schwartz's lyrical and lapidary prose maintains the reader's attention throughout.
I invite all those with ideas of saving the world to study this work."

Robert Lawless, Ph.D. Author of Haiti's Bad Press
Chairman Department of Anthropology, Wichita
State

"An excellent & illuminating piece of work, and very well written to boot.. Does a great deal to show how forms of behaviour that are regularly denounced by observers as 'irrational & backward' (having large numbers of children, adopting a 'predatory' approach to foreign aid, drug smuggling, etc.) make perfect sense within the desperate constraints and economic insecurity that people face."

> Peter Hallward, Author of Damming the Flood:
> Professor of Modern European Philosophy at Middlesex University in the UK

". . . bracingly honest and unflinching analysis of Haiti's charity industry – food aid, orphanages, religious missions, foreign non-government organizations (NGOs) . . . essential reading for anyone seeking to understand the true effects and role of international aid to Haiti."

> Kim Ives, Editor, Haiti Liberte

"Timothy T. Schwartz makes the complex and weighty topic of foreign aid to Haiti, Christian missions and the impact of "charitable" works interesting, humorous and readily understandable. With this book, he has made a significant contribution to the plight of the Haitian people. . . . . . a must read for anyone interested in hearing the truth about Haiti."

> Marguerite Laurent
> Playwright, performance poet, lawyer, and
> founder of Haitian Lawyers Leadership Network

Travesty
in
Haiti

A true account of
Christian missions, orphanages,
fraud, food aid, and
drug trafficking

By

Timothy T. Schwartz, Ph.D.

All that is necessary for the triumph of evil
is that good men do nothing.

Edmund Burke

For my father and my editor
H.L. Schwartz III
who helped teach me to hate lies,
and to love writing.

CHAPTERS

Chapter One
Death, Destruction, and Development

Five black peasant men walked down the dusty Village street. Their clothes were torn; their hands were bound; their heads were bowed. A jeering mob trailed. From amidst the mob emerged a thin young man. His shirt was open and his wiry torso glistened with sweat. In one hand he carried a cudgel. He lunged at one of the bound men, swung the cudgel, and with a sickening thud crushed the man's skull. Another of the bound men was smashed in the knees with a pole. He crumpled to the ground where a machete sunk halfway through his neck. The mob fell on the remaining three and hacked and beat them to death. Several men then dragged the bodies to the crossroad in the middle of the Village and heaved them one on top of the other. A moment later a fat middle aged woman came waddling quickly up the street. In her hands she carried a dirty white bucket of gasoline. She poured the gas on the pile, scattering it so that all the bodies were soaked. The local domino champion lit a match, tossed it on the pile, and the corpses exploded into a blaze. Soon the pile began to sizzle and crackle and the sickly smell of burning flesh wafted through the street.

Officially 139 men were killed that day. Some say it was more like thousands. The leader of the massacre claimed before a journalist's video camera that he had organized the killing of 1,042 "communists."

They were not communists in the traditional sense of the word. They were members of a Catholic development cooperative funded by the Church and a Swiss charity advocating land reform. Throats were slit, heads cut off, one man had his bound hands tied to a log and then, screaming, watched as they were chopped off.

Most aid workers subsequently left the area. But others soon replaced them. The projects started again and when I first arrived in the area three years later they were in full swing. This is the inside story of those projects and the impact on the people they were meant to help. It is largely a story of fraud, greed, corruption, apathy, and political agendas that permeate the industry of foreign aid. It is a story of failed agricultural, health, and credit projects; violent struggles for control over aid money; corrupt orphanage owners, pastors, and missionaries; the nepotistic manipulation of research funds; economically counterproductive food relief programs that undermine the Haitian agricultural economy; and the disastrous effects of economic engineering by foreign governments and international aid organizations such as the World Bank and USAID and the multinational corporate charities that have sprung up in their service, specifically, CARE International, Catholic Relief Services, World Vision, and the dozens of other massive charities that have programs spread across the globe, moving in response not only to disasters and need, but political agendas and economic opportunity. It is also the story of the political disillusionment and desperation that has led many Haitians to use whatever means possible to better their living standards, most recently drug trafficking; and how in the service of international narcotraffickers and money launderers, Haiti has become a failed State.

The accounts I present in the pages that follow come from my own experiences while living, researching, and working in Haiti over a period of ten years. The stories are entirely factual. Anecdotes are based on real events, dialogues on real conversations, and statistical and archival information is accurate to the best of my ability as a researcher. Sources not referenced in the text are summarized in chapter by chapter appendices. I have, however, blended two towns. I have also changed names of people and places.

The reason that I have made an effort to disguise people and places is because what I hope to accomplish is not to embarrass or denounce individuals or to attack specific charities. Nor do I aim to damage the industry of charity. What I hope to do is call attention to the need for accountability for I believe that the disaster we call foreign aid—'disaster,' at least, in the case of Haiti—comes from the near total absence of control over the distribution of money donated to help impoverished people in the country.

At the level of individuals and nongovernmental organizations (NGOs), the lack of fiscal accountability is manifest in the enrichment of the custodians of the money—pastors and directors of NGOs, schools, and orphanages—and the redirection of charity toward middle and upper class Haitians for whom it was not intended. At the level of governments, the absence of accountability invites subversion of a different sort: Charity is manipulated to serve political ends. In both cases lack of accountability allows the aid to be distorted into something that arguably does more harm than good. I hope that this book in some way contributes toward correcting the problem and redirecting the millions of dollars that well-meaning citizens of developed countries annually donate to the people it was originally intended: the poorest of the poor in Haiti. In the following chapter I begin the account with my return to Haiti in 1995 and the impoverished people whom I lived with. It is they who originally motivated me to write this book.

Chapter Two
The Hamlet, Witch Doctors, and Sorcery

My story begins in a remote area of Haiti. There is a bay. Toward the back of the bay, deep blue water encircles the ivory sands of a beachhead. An orderly line of rowboats rest on the sand and just beyond the high-water mark, the huts of a small fishing hamlet retreat haphazardly back toward the desert scrub. The huts are made of thatch, sticks, rocks, and mud. Behind them are built smaller thatch and stick structures. These are kitchens where food is cooked over smoky wood fires. On the sides of the houses and the kitchens, nets are slung, waiting to be mended. In the yards, bamboo weirs lie strewn about. On frail pole racks, fish hang to dry in the sun.

The Hamlet is located in the back of the bay where even during the wildest storm the little thatch-roofed huts go unmolested. But on the bay itself it is not always so calm. On a typical day, as noon approaches, the air in the desert valley behind the Hamlet heats up and rises up the slopes of a desolate and wind-sheared mountain. The rising air sucks the easterly trade winds in from the *gran mar,* the Big Sea. By afternoon the wind rips across the water, churning up whitecaps and whipping them past the beachhead.

Approaching midnight, long after most of the fisherfolk have gone to sleep, the air on the mountain cools and the wind falls off again. Inside the little thatch and stick houses the mosquitoes come down from the rafters to feed. People slap at the pests, pull sheets over their heads, and sweat. At daybreak the air is dead still. The bay is smooth as glass. Women and children come out from their huts soaping their faces and brushing their teeth. Fires are started and the smell of coffee wafts through the Hamlet. The men are already on the water, rowing across the bay, raising fish traps and nets. But the catch these days is almost always meager, for marine life has been disappearing. The silt that washes down from the deforested and eroding mountains smothers the reefs. They are dying. Today, instead of thousands of teaming tropical fishing, colors, and sea fans waving in the current, one more often finds white skeletons of dead corral, barren, like swimming among gravestones. Porpoises, whales, and sharks no longer visit the bay. Turtles have become a rare delicacy. In the autumn the migratory fish still come but they are fewer every year.

I arrived in the Hamlet in 1995. I had come to conduct research on marriage and child rearing practices, the final hurdle in attaining my doctorate in cultural anthropology from the University of Florida. Equipped with three years of graduate school and a grant from the National Science Foundation, I was supposed to do what is called participant observation, meaning that I was to live in the community, take part in the lives of the people there, live as they live, interfering as little as possible so that I could learn about their culture and how impoverished Haitians deal with problems of daily survival. When I was done, after I had written my dissertation, I would be qualified to join the ranks of foreign aid experts who work for charitable organizations such as CARE International, experts who design and carry out farm, commerce, and health projects meant to help the poor in their struggle to overcome hunger and disease.

I thought that desire, that will to help, would give me a special status among the people living in the Hamlet, a status of respect and appreciation. I also expected to pass the year in close and relatively comfortable association with nature, with the sea and the natural environment.

It didn't work out that way, on either account.

To begin with, adapting to life in the Hamlet was not easy. Simple luxuries did not exist. There were no toilets, no running water or appliances or gas stoves. And the natural environment was anything but comfortable. The first few months were especially miserable. I detested the food. Typical meals consisted of huge portions of rice and beans, and tiny portions of small, bony, and oil-drenched fish. For most of the year I was sick with intestinal infections, making the trudge into the thorny, cactus-ridden brush to relieve myself that much more onerous. Often the Hamlet spigot was dry and I had to walk half an hour to get clean fresh water. Brushing my teeth, bathing, getting my clothes cleaned, all these tasks were drudgeries. The afternoon winds made sure that sand penetrated everything I owned, my books, my clothes, my laptop.

Another problem was mosquitoes. I had first chosen the Hamlet because, unless there had been a recent rain, there were few mosquitoes. Not long after I arrived the International Red Cross came and changed that. An official of the organization visited, saw the people deprived of comfortable and hygienic latrines and decided to do something about the problem. Experts, materials, and money arrived. Household heads who wished to have a toilet agreed to dig a five-foot pit behind their home. The people dug. But when the digging reached two or three feet below the surface the pits filled with fresh water. Undaunted, eager to modernize, and never seeming to realize the boon that the fresh water offered in other respects, the directors of the project ordered the digging to continue. The pits were then covered with cement platforms that had round toilet holes perforated through the middle. The project was heralded a success. The Red Cross erected a large sign on the nearby dirt road announcing to the few people who passed that way—the few who could read—that it had aided the Hamlet with thirty new latrines. The experts departed.

Soon, in the depths of the water-filled privies, mosquito larvae began to hatch.

Sleeping became hell. At night I would wake to people cursing and slapping at the blood suckers. Babies would scream. In the morning people wandered about the Hamlet complaining about the lack of sleep, about the curse that had befallen them. A malaria epidemic hit the Hamlet. To escape the mosquitoes some of us took to sleep aboard the rowboats moored in the bay. To my knowledge, no one ever used any of the toilets, but no one could tolerate the idea of undoing this significant step in the modernization of the Hamlet. Eventually the toilets began to cave in because the sides of the holes, dug in the sand, had never been reinforced. But for several years, until the last toilet collapsed, the problem lingered.

Another thing that made me miserable was the very people I had come to study. They turned out to be annoying in ways I never anticipated. Among the annoyances was the begging. First, there were the children.

The Hamlet covered an area not much larger than a football field and there lived in this space a total population of 253 people, 79 of whom were under the age of ten. Whenever I emerged from the hut where I was staying, these little people came running from every quarter of the Hamlet. Usually naked and covered with dirt, they would plead for *sinkant kob* (about 3 U.S. cents at the time) to buy a piece of bread or a small pouch of sugar. How do you say no to a hungry child? Giving made the begging worse.

And then there were the adults.

Scrawny underfed mothers, infants at breast, would pull me to their houses, whispering desperately, pointing to sick children.

Old men, young men, teenage girls, even officials, judges, policemen, and politicians came by the Hamlet to beg from me. People literally asked me for everything I owned. If someone saw me using a pocket knife they would ask to have it. When I slept in a tent, the "cloth house" awed the locals and they came from far around to ask me if I would give it to them. People with whom I was only dimly acquainted would present me with carefully prepared lists of personal gifts to purchase for them on my next trip to town or overseas. The more money someone had, the bigger the items they wanted. Important men, men who were older than me and for whom I would take pains to demonstrate respect would ply me with food, rum, and coconuts and then pester me to buy expensive items for them.

The begging, I would learn, was one legacy of half a century of foreign aid, but there were also aspects of my behavior that perhaps invited annoyance and begging, or at least made me seem stupid and easy to manipulate. I was, for instance, linguistically and socially inept when I arrived. I had been to Haiti on earlier research and I had studied Creole at the university, but actually speaking with anything near functional fluency was something that came neither easily nor quickly. There was also the issue of cultural competency. I knew about *voudou* and I knew about Haitian folklore. But local versions turned out to be vastly different than what I had studied. Farming, fishing, and rearing livestock were also subjects and skills I knew little about. The local plants and animals were strange to me. Any Hamlet child could identify a dozen different types of mango trees while I had difficulty remembering the difference between the leaves of a mango and those of an avocado tree. I considered myself athletic, but the people of the Hamlet were far more skilled in their environment. They were agile when walking in the mountains and when boating and swimming among the reefs. Even the girls could make me look clumsy. One time en route from a market I followed a train of Hamlet women and girls down the face of a cliff so steep and precarious that a single misstep would have meant plunging to a certain death on the sharp and jagged lime rock below. My female companions walked down the precipice perfectly upright while expertly balancing cumbersome loads of produce and wares on their heads. To the intense amusement of the women, I, empty handed, crab-crawled backward.

Nor did I know about the social status of people around me, a shortcoming that significantly enhanced my apparent idiocy. It was not uncommon during those first few months for me to inadvertently snub someone to whom I should have been showing great respect while respecting someone to whom I should have been paying no attention at all. One incident comes to mind where I spent a good ten minutes ardently trying to converse in broken Creole with a woman who the laughing villagers later told me was insane.

So in turn, during that early period of my research, I got little respect from my hosts. An eight-year-old girl neatly summed up the attitudes among the people of the Hamlet. I was sitting on a straw mat in a thatch-roofed kitchen and the girl's mother reprimanded her for poking and pulling on me, *uh ohhh, pitit, fe respè a gran moun, tande.* "Uh ohhh, child, respect adults, you hear."

"But *manman,*" the child responded, "it is not a big person that Timotè is, *non.* He's a *blan.*"

I was an especially easy target for bored young men who as a cultural rule in Haiti—and perhaps the world over—take great pride in being obnoxious. There were times when I had to decide on the spur of a moment and in a state of blinding anger if I was expected to fight or if fighting would get me killed. I never did fight and it happily turned out that fighting was not expected. In fact, it might have gotten me killed. But, as I soon learned, if I was to get any respect at all I sometimes had to act like I would fight.

Nevertheless, during those first few months I was unsure how to deal with the annoyances and begging. I did not want to abandon my research. But I was desperate for a solution. The way I eventually evaded the pestering and begging was by going to live in the house of a *bokor* (shaman).

In September 1973, a boat came to the Hamlet to buy charcoal. It was a large sailing vessel from the capital, Port-au-Prince. On the boat was Ram, thirty-four years old at the time and a *bokor* or, if you prefer, shaman or witch doctor. It was his first sea voyage. On board he worked as a mariner, a grunt brought along to help keep watch and to do menial jobs. But Ram did not know the sea and he did not like it. He could not swim and when the sea was rough he got sick. No one is quite sure why he had boarded the vessel in the first place. Some say he was running from the revenge of families of people he had killed with sorcery. His wife and children say he was simply trying to make a living, *cheche lavi* (looking for life). In any case, Ram got off the boat in the Hamlet and never got back on. Nor did he ever return to wherever it was he came from.

Twenty-two years later, when I returned to Haiti and began research in the Hamlet, Ram was a foul-mouthed and sour-faced man. He was ugly, almost six feet tall, deep dark black with flaring nostrils, pursed lips, bushy sideburns, and a raggedy beard. His hair was not the tight kinky curls like the other African descendents of the Hamlet, but a scraggly mop of never-combed curls that dangled down to his shoulders in a form resembling dreadlocks. His body was lean and impressively rippled with muscles, a feature almost comical in the way it contradicted his fifty-six years of age and his crabby demeanor.

The first time I met Ram, I had come to the Hamlet looking for Givme, a conch diver who I had befriended. But Givme was already out on the bay so I parked my little all-terrain pick-up truck—one of the few vehicles that could reach the Hamlet—and took advantage of the time to change the oil and check for loose bolts. Ram came over from the neighboring house—his own—and pretended to help me. Squatting by the truck as I grunted and groaned underneath, Ram gave me annoying advice on things about which he knew nothing—Ram, like most people in the Hamlet, had never turned a wrench in his life and might not know what one was if he found it on the ground. "Don't hold that thing like that, *non*, son" he said, punctuating his advice with affirmatives and negatives as Haitians do. "Turn the screw like this, *oui*." I wished he would go away. When I was ready to leave he tried to get me to pay him for his annoyances.

The next time I met Ram was different. It was late, close to midnight. Givme and I were returning from a bout of drinking in another hamlet when our attention was drawn to a ceremony at Ram's. There was drumming and singing, people were spilling out of the doors, others cramming to get inside. We managed to push our way through, whereupon someone seized my arm and seated me in the middle of the activity.

Ram sat in a corner by a table covered with white linen on which rested cola bottles and candles. There was no trace of the beggar I met weeks before. From where he sat Ram commanded a room full of disciples, dancers, and onlookers. He held a wooden drum between his legs, expertly beat out a rhythm on the drum, sang a couple lines, and then the entire room would respond in exquisite chorus. After each song, Ram sent around a bottle of *klerin* (moonshine). Occasionally a *lwa*, or spirit, possessed someone. The person would fall to the floor jerking, then stand up and greet *la societe*. Several times Ram himself was possessed. He passed around the room, going from person to person, greeting them, shaking hands, still holding on to the first hand, he would cross his arms and shake the other. He would then pass back around the room spraying us with Right Guard underarm deodorant and rubbing our faces with a silk scarf.

I had no idea what was going on. I was treated well, but the entire scene—my ignorance of what was expected of me and the *bokor* negotiating that ignorance while trying to make me comfortable—bordered on the ridiculous, or, at least, seemed ridiculous to me at the time. Every now and then the *bokor* would stand and give a speech that invariably concluded with a long repetition of how happy he was that I was there. A direct translation would have gone something like, "It's happy that we are happy, happy, happy, happy, happy that you've come here to make a little visit with us." At the appropriate moment Givme would nudge me and I'd get up and in broken Creole, slightly drunk and unsure of what was expected, say, "It's happy happy that I'm happy, happy, happy, happy, happy, that it's happy that you're happy that I'm here to make a little visit with you." Then the rum would be sent around, all the adults would get a chug, we would all get another spray in the face with Right Guard deodorant, and the singing would begin again.

And so, as I mentioned earlier, I eventually came to live in the house of Ram the *bokor*. And there were very good reasons. Most importantly, to escape the gaggle of begging children and wisecracking teenage boys who followed me everywhere in the Hamlet, for I discovered that as I approached the house of the *bokor* these pests would drop away like fanned flies until I would arrive at the door alone.

Ram always received me well, gave me a place to sit, rum to drink, and cigarettes to smoke. There were no wild little children or crying babies in the house. There was only Ram and his wife, Sadi, their two teenage daughters Lili and Albeit, and their brother Robè, then a quiet, athletic fifteen-year-old who became my fishing buddy. No member of the house was permitted to pester me. No member of the Hamlet ever dared come looking for me while I was there. Sadi would cook fish, conch, and lobster that I caught. I was at peace.

And there was another reason I enjoyed the house of the *bokor*: Rather peculiarly, the mosquitoes didn't bite. They were there, millions of them. I would lie in the corner of the hut on a bed of wooden sticks lashed together and made soft with old used cloths and listen to them buzzing in the thatch roof, a low hum of a million tiny wings. But they were not a problem. In the house of the *bokor* they simply did not bite.

I never unraveled the mystery of the mosquitoes. Perhaps the old man had some herb that he used like a repellent. I never knew. But life was unquestionably more pleasant for me in his house.

So I eventually moved in with the *bokor* and his family and while I couldn't have cared less about spirits and *voudou*, subjects I thought anthropologists and travel writers before me had overworked—all too frequently using *voudou* to sensationalize Haitian culture and sell books—I nevertheless began to learn about sorcery. I would lie at night in the corner of the hut, on the bed of wooden sticks and discarded used clothes, and from there quietly watch the *bokor* perform his divinations.

Visitors, usually older men, would come, always after dark, and Ram would burn candles for them, divine their wishes and fears, and set magical traps for their enemies. I can still see him there, sitting on a rickety wooden chair in the dimly lit corner of his crumbling mud-and-thatch house, by his side a small table cluttered with magical paraphernalia: a candle, a half dozen bottles of Haitian cola, an ancient colonial dagger, a 1967 Introduction to Hygiene book, and a dog-eared deck of playing cards.

The *bokor* would light the candle, stab the dagger into the ground, and methodically lay the cards down, one by one, silently, intently interpreting their meanings to himself. The *lwa* named *Ogoun*, the spirit of iron and war, would enter his head and clarify what he was seeing. Then he would explain to the client what he had learned and he would offer remedies or retributions.

Once I burned a candle with him. I was visiting at Givme's house when someone stole money from my book bag. And so at the urgings of Ram I sought to discover the culprit through divination. I put seven *goud* (50 cents) on the floor, Ram lit a candle, stuck the ancient dagger into the dirt, laid out his dog-eared cards, and pretending to read from his Introduction to Hygiene book, he began to see things that came from the other world.

In his possessed state Ram divined the thieves who took my money. And he did a poor job of it. He misdivined the sum of money stolen. I had told everyone it was 500 *goud* ($33). In reality it was 1,000 ($66). As expected, Ram divined 500. As for the hygiene book, I assumed the book was a way of impressing clients who were mostly, like Ram, illiterate, for he held the book upside down. He ended his performance asking what I wanted to do, force the culprits to get caught in the act of stealing from someone else or kill them? Prompted by the urging of his two young daughters, Lili and Albeit—who had sat watching and listening the whole time and whispered, "don't kill"—I opted for forcing the thieves to get caught.

Ram then instructed me to go off in pursuit of an assortment of items needed to perform the magic, including a series of plants for which I would have had to climb the dry, stony 2,400-foot mountain that rose up behind the Hamlet. At the time, I simply could not have cared less about the *lwa*, divination, sorcery, or even the money I had lost, and I sure as hell was not going to climb a mountain for a laundry list of weeds. I let the whole thing go.

But no matter what opinion I had of Ram, his determination, mystical demeanor, and occasional success as a *bokor* convinced others of his spiritual powers, something that brought him a certain degree of wealth and prestige. And I came to respect Ram for something else. Whether a bluffer or not, Ram helped the neediest people in the area.

When I did my first census of the Hamlet, I began at Ram's house, where he lived with his principal wife, Sadi, a buxom woman with smooth skin and a harsh demeanor. Sadi was forty-two years old.

I then headed next door to Sadi's sister's house. Ram ran out ahead of me and stood in the doorway. Perplexed, I told him, "if you wouldn't mind," that I needed to speak to the man or the woman of the house. Beaming, Ram assured me that he was the man of the house. He was the husband of his wife Sadi's buck-toothed, slightly retarded younger sister, Kwaku.

About an hour later, after visiting a half dozen other households, I approached a hut on the far side of the Hamlet. Arriving at the front door I hollered, as is customary, *oné* (honor). A man inside hollered, *respè* (respect). The door opened and there stood Ram holding a broom and wearing an apron—quite a joke for rural Haitian men. He was, he assured me, the husband of Janette who lived in the house. And so it went. All told Ram had seven wives, five in the Hamlet, one on the mountain, and one in another fishing settlement up the coast. He had nineteen children between the ages of one and twenty-one whom he cared for and not all of whom were his genetic progeny.

There were many people who depended on the *bokor*. Had I known more the night that I attended the *gombo* in Ram's house I would have recognized that the people around him, those who attended his ceremonies and who depended on him, had come to the Hamlet out of desperation. His wives and children, many of whom were adopted, were a collection of misfits, survivors of disease, and the remains of families that death and economic misfortune had shattered.

Sadi, for instance, was the child of a destitute peasant family on the mountain. Her father had died and her mother was unable to care for her. At eleven years of age she had been sent to live and work as a servant with a family in the Village near the Hamlet. When she was sixteen she became the common-law wife of a fisherman named Chesnel with whom she had nine children. All but two boys died. The older of the boys was named Tiyol and the other was called Robè. After the birth of Robè, Sadi fell ill with some kind of lingering uterine infection. Chesnel the fisherman took her to several *bokor* but none was able to successfully treat her and he eventually brought her to Ram, where she spent a year living in his sacred home and being treated spiritually and with the herbal teas and baths that Ram made for her. Ram fed and cared for her and drove off the spirits that were making her ill. In the end neither she nor her husband could pay for the treatment. Chesnel did not seem to care and had taken another wife, so Ram kept Sadi, along with the baby, Robè, and the older son Tyol. She had two more children with Ram, Albeit and Lili. Both lived in the house when I arrived.

Sadi loved all of her children profoundly. Perhaps as compensation for the seven she had lost, she spoiled them. She doted over the girls, performing little chores that for any other female child of the Hamlet would have been considered their duties. Lili responded by becoming a bitter girl who complained and cursed at the slightest inconvenience. Albeit was spoiled as well, but she was a happy and sweetly manipulative girl who, instead of lashing out angrily, would say things to her mother such as one time that stands out in my memory. Her mother had been pestering her to fetch a bucket of water.

"*Manman*," Albeit whined, "I don't want to."

"*Non*, you don't want to, but you have no choice. Go or I will whip you," Sadi threatened.

"But *manman*, you don't love me?" Albeit's voice was small.

"But, *oui,* I love you, *cherie*," Sadi forgot what she was doing and looked at her youngest daughter.

"You would love me if my face was burnt by fire?"

Sadi kissed Albeit on the forehead, picked up the bucket, and headed off to get water herself.

Sadi was harder on the boys, but in a good way. She pushed the two boys in school and made every sacrifice to get them educated. She scrounged the money for tuition and school supplies; she sold fish in the market and she specialized in selling *dous*, hard sugar candies. The money from these activities went to cover the costs of the boys' education. What happened appeared to everyone in the Hamlet a miracle: The boys turned out to be star pupils. From the very beginning they were the brightest in their classes. They had begun school together and they competed with each other, driving one another and leaving the other Hamlet children behind. At first the other Hamlet families were jealous; the children of the lowliest outsiders in the Hamlet were getting better grades than their own children. But when the boys arrived in school in the Village and proceeded to surpass the Village children, the people in the Hamlet were proud. The boys were representatives of the Hamlet, proof that their children there were as good as any other. But, as the people in the Hamlet say, *Lè ké ti poul kontan, malfini pa lwenn.* "When the little chicken is happy, the hawk is not far behind."

When Tiyol was twelve and Robè was nine, a severe drought hit Jean Makout County. Making matters worse for the people of the Hamlet, the migratory fish did not come that year. The people had no money. Sadi's market activities suffered. The business of sorcery suffered. Ram had no income and was forced to go deeper into the *kadas*, the semi-desert scrub that surrounds the Hamlet, to cut bushes and cacti, hacking them into piles of sticks, covering them with dirt and leaves and smoldering them into charcoal that could be sold to ships destined for the city. With the money earned from the charcoal he was able to purchase just enough meager rations of rice and beans to keep himself and his miserable dependents alive.

Then a typhoid epidemic hit the Hamlet. The nearest government clinic was swamped with patients. Children were hit especially hard. More than thirty of them died. Tiyol and Lili, children of Sadi, both fell sick with the disease. Tiyol died in the clinic. The doctor depended on test kits for his diagnosis. The test kits were expired and yielded false negatives. As with the other children he treated, the doctor believed he was dealing with malaria and so treated Sadi's oldest son with chloroquin tablets, instead of the necessary antibiotic.

After Tiyol died, a devastated and desperate Sadi had to make a choice. Lili lay in the hut, on a mattress of used Goodwill cloths, delirious and sweating. If the doctor could not save her son, Sadi reasoned, then it must not be a "hospital disease." It must be a "leaf disease," meaning that it required herbal and spiritual treatment. At that point, she recounted to me, Ram became useless: "I don't know what happened with him," she told me, "It was like his hands were bound."

Apparently, according to Ram, he had tried very hard to make treatments for Tiyol and Lili. But they were ineffective and so Sadi had turned to the clinic doctor. But Tiyol died and afterward Ram felt defeated. He stopped coming home and slept instead in homes of his other wives. "The whole load fell on my head," Sadi said. "I put Lili on a donkey and I led her up the mountain to a *bokor* known for treating this particular disease."

Lili survived, and to this day in a corner of the house, tied up in the rafters, hangs a cola bottle with the herbs and medicines that had driven away the demon that devoured her brother and almost consumed her as well. The bottle hangs there to make sure the demon does not return.

I had moved into the *bokor*'s house for several reasons, to escape the begging, pestering, and teasing as well as the mosquitoes. But there was another reason as well

Before moving in with Ram and his family, my first residence in the Hamlet was in the house of my friend the conch diver, Givme, a name that—although I was unaware at the time— was derived from English ("give me") and reflected the half century of charity and influence from evangelical missionaries and foreign aid experts that I mentioned earlier.

Medium height, a lean 150 pounds, coal black with fine chiseled features; Givme was the best swimmer I've ever known and undisputedly the best in the Hamlet and surrounding area. He could go down one hundred feet under the sea and stay there hunting for conch, lobster, and fish for three to four minutes. As much out of the need for a friend and guide as a common interest in diving, I befriended Givme. Every morning during my first several months in the Hamlet, before the trade winds were sucked in and began to howl across the bay and the water became cloudy with stirred-up sand, Givme and I would go spear fishing. So, to make fishing easier, I moved into his house with him and his family.

I liked Givme, I liked diving with him, I liked his three young daughters, his three-year-old son, and his wife, Lorna. But things did not work out between us. Indeed, it was a disaster.

The problem was that I made the mistake that so many *blan*

make in Haiti: I started giving. Givme wanted to buy a big sailboat so that he could transport dried fish and charcoal some thirty to forty miles up the coast from the Hamlet to the city of Baie-de-Sol. He thought he could then haul mattresses, bicycles, and other imported goods back to the Hamlet and sell them to people in the nearby Village and to farmers in the mountains. So with me playing the role as financier, we purchased an old thirty-foot, handmade wooden sail boat that needed to be repaired. To patch the boat we bought a living oak tree, cut it down, and paid two professional sawyers to hand-cut the tree into boards (the only way it is done in Far-West Haiti). For caulk we bought *bré*, a sap derived from a nut of a local tree that is black and tar-like when heated over a fire but turns to a hard glass-like substance when cooled. And we bought locally wrought nails. I also bought extra diving fins, masks, two large nets, six fish traps, and two pigs to fatten and sell so that we could earn money to pay for any craftsmen we needed to do special repairs.

For reasons that still mystify me, Givme did nothing. He did not make the smallest effort to repair the boat. And worse still, he did things that would have been unthinkable were he dealing with any one else in the Hamlet. He never once gave me my 50 percent of the catch due as the owner of the nets and traps. In a year, Givme gave me two fish. Even when I pulled in the nets, Givme would make off with the catch saying things like, "My wife will sell these for us." But I never saw a single *goud*. The pigs that I paid for and Givme was supposed to feed went hungry and became a nuisance to others in the Hamlet, stealing fish off racks and raiding kitchens. Eventually a neighbor woman caught one of the pigs in the act of invading her kitchen. She heard the pig knock the pot of beans off the fire and came running, machete in hand, arriving in time to sink the blade into the animal's skull. The other pig disappeared. I suppose that Givme sold it.

Meanwhile, Givme took a second wife, a woman who lived in the Village and who had three children of her own. He acquired another rowboat, a boom box, a watch, a gold chain, new clothes and shoes, a fancy sea captain's hat. By the end of two months Givme had been transformed from a barefoot fisherman in rags to what appeared to me, and to many of the people of the Hamlet who took to criticizing him behind his back, a stylish and overdressed gigolo. His daughters got gold earrings and his first wife, Lorna, became an active market woman, not just in fish, but in produce and used clothes. God knows what his new wife was buying and selling.

But that was not all that bothered me. Givme had begun to do things that suggested he hated me. Twice while spear fishing he took off in the rowboat and abandoned me in the middle of the bay, an offense that anyone else in the Hamlet would have considered attempted murder. Indeed, people in the Hamlet became appalled. Once I had to swim a half mile to the nearest shore and then pick my way, barefoot, three miles through cacti and thorn bushes, to get back to the Hamlet.

Other people in the Hamlet saw what was happening and although no one ever advised me to break with Givme—as I now know, no one ever would, for that would have been an invitation to sorcery—people began to taunt me with pointed questions like "Timoté, friend, how many fish you find in the hands of Givme today?" and "How's the boat getting along?" (The boat having been left abandoned on the backside of the Hamlet beach).

So over the course of months I began to spend less and less time at Givme's house.

The final straw came when Givme blew up at me and in an argument over a piece of rotting plywood, threatened to split my head open with a club.

Following the argument, a group of the younger men led me off to the Village to drink rum. And that afternoon, people I had never spoken to sought me out to tell me not to pay attention to Givme, not to abandon the Hamlet.

But I did abandon the Hamlet.

Givme's tirade was the last straw in an increasing psychological burden. I was already fed up with the begging, the deceptions, the relentless pestering and teasing. So I went to live not far away on the white sands of a paradisiacal beach in a tent. There I spear fished and worked nets with other fishermen. When I returned to the Hamlet two months later, it was to the house of Ram the *bokor* that I went.

At the same time that I moved in with Ram, Sadi, the girls, and Robè, I also quit bringing gifts back from my forays to the city and to Christian missions. I began to deliberately run out of money. I would leave my vehicle and most of my cash with a family of American missionaries who lived on the mountain. Then I would put on a pair of torn swimming shorts, a T-shirt, ragged flip-flops, and I would hike the four hours down the mountain to the Hamlet, where I tried to feed myself spear fishing and gathering conch, tasks that I enjoyed but at which I was not notably skilled and so, soon hungry, I did not feel as sorry for the women and children. The men could not harangue me into buying them cigarettes and rum. I also had become more settled in Ram's house, so I did not feel an obligation to buy things for other people. I had my family.

But, as oddly as it seems, even to me, for the people of the Hamlet, and especially for Givme, the reason I had abandoned my "friend" and began sleeping at the home of the *bokor* had nothing to do with Givme taking advantage of me—something they were vociferously aware of—or with the pestering I had been forced to endure or with the mosquitoes that made nights so miserable and sleepless. Indeed, it seemed never to have occurred to anyone in the Hamlet that their incessant questions, jokes, and begging could have annoyed me and no one ever ventured inside the home of the *bokor* with the goal of verifying if what I said about the mosquitoes was true. For Givme and the rest of the people of the Hamlet, the reason I had moved out of his house and in with the *bokor*, and the reason the gifts stopped coming was something completely different: It was *maji* (sorcery). I had, they believed, fallen under the spell of Ram's magical powers.

An insidious fury roiled through the Hamlet. The people blamed Ram, his wife, and his children for the change in my behavior and they suspected that they were hoarding for themselves all the gifts and money I had previously given so freely—secondhand junk that my friends and family in Miami would load me down with whenever I returned to Haiti. I was being prevented from sharing. On several occasions conflicts broke out with other family compounds.

People would stand in their yards hollering across the Hamlet that Ram was keeping the goods the *blan* had for them. People would walk by the house loudly saying to no one in particular, "Oh they think they are going to be rich." They warned me to leave Ram's house, *ou pa ka rete a moun sa yo,* "you can't live with people like that."

Givme and his family were especially angry. Even before his tirade, Givme had quit visiting Ram's house. Both he and his wife no longer said hello to Ram and Sadi. There were fights between their children. I was sure that Givme was actively seeking help from another *bokor*. After my move into the house of the *bokor*, my new hosts several times roused me at night so that I could peek through a hole in the crumbling mud wall and see candles burning in Givme's yard, a sure sign of witchcraft. So nothing seemed clearer to me. Through the language and cultural barrier that was slowly crumbling, I understood that the people of the Hamlet believed Ram had stolen me away from Givme and that Givme and his family were out to settle the score.

I learned that Ram was to be killed by *maji* and once Sadi claimed to have surprised a strange man in the act of sprinkling powder at the door of the house. Events occurred in my presence that spooked me. The most peculiar event happened one night while we slept. An eight-inch poisonous centipede had somehow gotten into Ram's bed and bitten him. I awoke to Ram howling and jumping frantically around the room. It was something that I was unable to discover having ever happened to any other person in the Hamlet and, while I didn't know for sure how it had gotten into Ram's bed, I suspected that it was no accident.

At the same time that the *bokor* was having a hard go at it, Givme's luck also went sour, very sour. He squandered most of the money he got from me. The masks and spear guns wore out, mostly from neglect. A $150 pair of diving fins, the best pair I used to own, he put on a tin roof in the sun "so," as he told me later, "they could dry out." They shriveled up like burnt toast. The fishing weirs I had bought for us to make money to repair the boat were swept away in a storm as was one of the nets. The other net was stolen. To help support his new wife and her two children he sold his watch and gold neck chain and then, desperately trying to hold on to her he, bit by bit, borrowed all of his principal wife's market money. Not a good idea.

Growing frustration with Givme, who was not originally from the Hamlet, exploded in a row over a bicycle that belonged to his new wife. Givme's in-laws, members of largest family in the Hamlet, that of the *gran lakou*, "the Big Yard," descendants of the Hamlet's founder, gave him a brutal beating.

The problems with Givme and the Hamlet's anger at the *bokor* began to affect my research. People refused to answer my questions about their families. A rumor spread that, under the spell of the *bokor*, I had been sent to gather their names so that he could sell them to *djab* (demons).

The fear seemed ridiculous. Ram, as with all the adults of the Hamlet, knew all there was to know about virtually everyone else living there. Lives in small communities like the Hamlet are never a secret. But what seemed obvious did not change the fact the people in the Hamlet were no longer cooperating with me and that because of me Ram's family was having problems. And so after more than a year in the Hamlet, I left. I had satisfied my obligations to the National Science Foundation and to my graduate school, both of which had had funded me. I had become functional in the language and had gained insight into family life and local livelihood strategies. Not wanting to cause any more problems, I left the Hamlet and went to the nearby Village of Jean Makout, where three NGOs had hired me to conduct a demographic survey.

After I left the Hamlet, I felt obliged to help the family of the *bokor*. I sent money (about US$500) for the construction of a new house. But I could do nothing about the ostracism and the torment they suffered from others and that continued after I left. Indeed, the more I helped the worse it seemed to get for the family. The other people of the Hamlet made up derogatory songs about them. Lili quit school because of hazing.

Then Ram fell sick. Sadi came to me and told me he was feverish, coughing through the night and spitting blood. I learned from other people of the Hamlet who visited me in the Village that he was being killed for evil deeds, that he was a victim of sorcery. They said that he was being killed with a *poud*, a poisonous powder that another *bokor* had made, and that it was retribution for his killing people.

One night at 11:00 I surreptitiously borrowed a vehicle belonging to one of the NGOs who I was working for and drove over the mountain and down the washed out desert road to the Hamlet. I took the *bokor* and his family back to the Village where I put him in a hospital for tests and treatment, an ordeal that went on for nearly three months. In the meantime I supported him and the family and let the girls sleep at my house. Despite a sense of anthropological duty, an obligation to be a neutral and objective observer, I really wanted to heal Ram. I wanted to show the people of the Hamlet that their superstitions were bullshit, that *maji* and *poud* could not kill.

But there was no saving Ram the *bokor*. After his stint in the Village hospital under the care of a French doctor who was the hospital director and a friend of mine, it was conclusive that Ram had AIDS. I and Western medicine were defeated.

It was three hours after dark. I drove the borrowed Mercedes SUV over the last rocky outcroppings, down the makeshift road and then glided across the hard-packed sand of the beachhead, past rickety drift wood fences and the thatch roof huts of the Hamlet. I turned the steering wheel, and the headlights brought into view the house I had paid to build for Ram and his family. It was one of the finest in the Hamlet. The roof was made of fronds from a special and rare type of palm that lasts for as long as thirty years. The walls were solidly built of cut lime rocks Ram had scavenged from an ancient and crumbling French fort. The floor was not dirt as with most of the houses in the Hamlet but concrete.

The house had been prepared for a funeral, Ram's funeral. A long thatch awning had been added to the front. Beneath the awning, dark-skinned men sat in crude wicker chairs playing dominoes at wooden tables. Heavy set women squatted on the ground next to small tin-can oil lamps, their black, age-creased faces flickering in the light, the treats they had brought to sell spread out on the ground on clothes in front of them: Homemade hard candies, peanut and coconut brown-sugar clusters, cigarettes and rum spiced with herbs and roots. Groups of men and a few women stood conversing in the shadows. Nearby was the old house, the one where the *gombo* (*voudou* party) had been held two years before and where I had subsequently lived with Ram and his family. It was now a collapsing assortment of sticks, the mud plastered on the walls crumbling, the thatch of the roof gray and brittle. Inside, women were washing Ram's emaciated corpse.

I stopped the SUV. A girl ran from one of the groups of mourners and as I climbed from the vehicle, she kissed me. It was Lili, now fifteen years old, a disarmingly beautiful *damsel*. She wore a full-length strapless dress. Her shoulders were defined and muscular and her young cleavage full and smooth. Behind her came a small crowd. First the young girls, three snickering prepubescent *damsels*: Lili's sister, Albeit, followed by Albeit's two, always present, best friends. Then young boys, the littler ones naked. Several men sauntered away from the house to shake my hand.

The people, family and visitors, were waiting for the coffin. Sadi had ordered it from her native hamlet several miles away and some two thousand feet up the mountain. The arrival of the coffin was an important moment and the mourners were excited because they knew the coffin was close by. Suddenly there was shouting and pointing. Someone had spotted torches on the bluff above the Hamlet. We watched as they wound slowly down through the darkness, negotiating their way among the cacti and brush and down the path that descends the final rocky slope from the wilderness of the *kadas* and into the Hamlet.

The coffin emerged riding on the shoulders of four men and flanked by six others carrying torches. Each bearer had his own bottle of *kleren* (raw rum), was singing, and doing an exaggerated drunken jig. Lili was the first to go out to greet the coffin. She wailed. Long whooping wails. Albeit and two half sisters followed, making a pretentious show, sobbing and shouting, "Papa, Papa, Papaaaa." Albeit threw herself, thrashing, on the ground. Now

Lili's wail changed, "Oh Papa, oh Papa, oh Papa." Then she stopped.

I stood nearby in the shadows watching. Lili had spotted the other crowd coming from the main part of the Hamlet and now she shouted to them, excitedly, *moun-yo,* "people," she shouted for all the Hamlet to assemble, *moun-yo sanble, sekey-a rive,* "People, gather, the coffin has arrived."

The approaching group was a chaotic mob of wildly dancing men and women. They formed a train that weaved between the thatch-roofed huts. Dinel, another *bokor,* was in the lead and he blew on a bamboo pipe. Several other men with pipes followed. The sound was low and always the same, "doo doo da doo, doo doo da doo, doo doo da doo."

Lili continued to shout to them, urging them to join, cheering their appearance.

The mob trailed along behind the musicians, whooping and shouting. The men and women jigged and leapt about. Others paused to take long, exaggerated slugs from bottles of *kleren* spiced with roots, twigs, herbs, and sugar. The party danced closer to the casket. Lili shouted again, eagerly, excited, "Come, the coffin has arrived."

But something was wrong. The mob ignored her; they were not celebrating the arrival of the coffin but distracting attention from it, drowning out the noise of the wailers.

Her shouts became pleading and then cursing as she comprehended the trick they had played on her. The crowd was disrespecting her father's coffin; they were mocking it. They were not celebrating its arrival; they were celebrating Ram's death. Lili stood stupidly for a moment, looking at them. My heart sank for her.

Lili should have known better. Whether the other people of the Hamlet hated the old *bokor* before I arrived or not, for the past two years he had been a pariah and the people of the Hamlet were delighted that he was dead. For me, Ram died of AIDS. But for the people of the Hamlet, sorcery killed Ram.

Givme was angry at the *bokor* for having won me away from him. I had watched him and his family burn candles and listened as he blamed Ram for causing him to mistreat me. And sure enough, on the night of Ram's funeral Givme was conspicuously absent from the Hamlet. Indeed, nothing could have been more obvious to me than that Givme would get the credit for killing Ram. But that was not what the people of the Hamlet believed.

Everyone in the Hamlet believed that Ram had been killed in retribution for having killed a man named Dipara. They said Ram had killed Dipara and ate him as a goat in a ceremony and that people close to Ram had partaken in the feast. They said that Ram was responsible for killing many other people in the Hamlet and surrounding area. They said that it had been him who had killed the thirty-some children several years before, causing them to waste away in what appeared to be typhoid, and then consuming their souls. They said that he had sold his own son, Tiyol, to the demon who aided him in his evil machinations. But Dipara was the final straw. They had set out to take their revenge. They hired a *bokor* from the distant town of Gros Mon. The *bokor* had killed Ram and the next night after we buried him they said that the *bokor* had returned, raised him from the grave, and sent him in the form a cow to his *badji* (temple) in Gros Mon. In the ensuing weeks the rumor spread that anyone who was involved in killing Dipara or who partook in eating the meat was also to die.

The number of people differed depending on who was talking. Some said nine; some said seven. But the one thing common to all the accounts was that they named a specific group of people close to Ram. They named Sadi, and they named her bucktoothed half-sister Kwaku. They named her mother Gran Terez. They named Little Rita, a jolly little old woman, my best friend in the Hamlet during my early days there, and they named Little Rita's husband, Frankor. They also named Herod, an unpopular person who was fond of using Ram's services as a sorcerer.

As I was living in the house at the time, some people added me to the list. I tried to dismiss it as a joke. But it certainly gave the sorcery issue a new twist. When I asked people about it—in teasing tones—they always responded matter-a-factly as if I had nothing to worry about,

"Did you eat any goat or beef while you were in the house?"

"*Non, non*, of course not, it was always fish that I ate, *oui*."

But the truth was I could not remember what I had eaten. I didn't believe in sorcery. I tried to put the whole matter off. But I have to confess, no matter what bunk I thought sorcery was, the idea that I might be a target was not comforting. And my uneasiness was to grow.

Granma Terez died only two months after Ram. Her death was slow and drawn out like his. Once again, the people were delighted. They said she deserved it because she would prepare and cook the intestines of Ram's victims. They also said that Ram would have sex with her—his seventy-five year old mother-in-law—a rather ugly rumor lent some credibility by the fact that although Granma Terez was elderly, before she died she nevertheless exhibited all the symptoms of AIDS; nasty sores, persistent diarrhea, low grade colds.

Like Ram, it was said that after she died she was risen from the dead and led to the town of Gros Mon where she was given to the same *bokor* as Ram, the one who had been hired to kill him. She was led away not as a cow—as had Ram—but as a zombie.

Next came Little Rita, of whom, as I said, I was fond. Little Rita made me think of a little black hillbilly granny. She was all energy, a consummate joker, a happy woman who always made me smile. When I first moved into the Hamlet she would make me coffee in the morning. She lived on the far side of the Hamlet from us and would walk over to Givme's house, carrying the coffee and when she was only halfway there shouting for everyone to hear, "Timoté, my husband, I have coffee for you." Indeed, whenever she saw me, no matter how far off I was, she would shout, "My husband, for why is it that you will not come see me?"

The last time I visited her, she lay on a straw mat on the floor of her hut, comatose and curled up in a fetal position. The next day Little Rita was dead.

Her husband Frankor died two months later. Both, according to the people of the Hamlet, led away as zombies to the *bokor* in Gros Mon—whose house by that time must have been getting crowded.

Next was Herod. He had a severe heart attack, but survived, something the people of the Hamlet credited to his relationship to a particular demon.

Then there was Kwaku, Sadi's buck-toothed half-wit sister who had lived with her mother, Granma Terez, in the same compound with Sadi and Ram. And of course there was Sadi. Both were mortally sick. As I saw it, the battle was with AIDS. It was AIDS that had killed Ram. I knew that because my friend the French doctor who treated him had told me so. I don't know what had killed Little Rita and Frankor, but it seemed eminently logical to me that Sadi and Kwaku now had AIDS, a simple enough deduction. They had both been sexually active with Ram and both showed all the classic symptoms: Persistent low-grade colds, diarrhea, bouts of fever, sores that would not heal.

But as Sadi saw it, the battle was with sorcery. Everyone in the area knew about and understood AIDS, or at least that is what they said. When asked, anyone in the Hamlet would say that AIDS could be spread through sexual intercourse. But they virtually never attributed death to the disease—nor, for that matter, any disease. They attributed it to malicious mischief of someone else, someone using *maji*, deadly powders and sorcery.

The coincidence of so many people dying who had been associated with Ram, the fact that they died over a relatively short period of time, and that people of the Hamlet predicted their deaths was extraordinary. I am not suggesting that it was in fact demons, sorcery, or powders that killed these people. I do not believe in such things. I have to admit, though, it was one hell of a coincidence.

As for me, I was now living in the Village, where a new set of discoveries and experiences were whittling away at my spirit.

Chapter Three
The Village: Crime, Corruption, and Vigilantes

The Hamlet is part of Jean Makout County, located in the most remote reaches of what I will refer to as the Province, 168 square miles of radically varying terrain—mountains, plains, fertile fields, desert—and twenty miles of rocky ocean coastline. It is a region that, like the Hamlet itself, progress and time seem to have forgotten, a region that, although only seven hundred miles from Miami, appears to exist almost completely outside of the modern world. Most of the 130,320 men, women, and children who live there are scattered throughout the rugged countryside in little thatch-roof, dirt-floor shacks. To survive they cultivate garden plots, raise goats, sheep, pigs, a few cows, and to a much lesser extent they, as in the case of the people of the Hamlet, clamber aboard primitive homemade dories and tiny kayaks to fish the bays and the treacherous ocean shelf. The only exported products—coffee, castor beans, goatskins, and lobster—are insignificant, the total value for the entire county amounting in 1997 to just US$70,000, about the income for a typical U.S. family farm. Few of the rural households even have a radio. There are only three private vehicles. Most people get around on foot, donkey, mule, or horse.

In the middle of the county, a rugged half-hour walk from the Hamlet, in a hill-cradled valley, a trail winds down a knoll, connects with a road that fords a meandering river and then dumps the traveler in amongst the dirt streets and rusty tin roofs of the Village of Jean Makout. Radios blare, bicycles and motorbikes putter along the dusty dirt streets, past rickety wooden houses, an outdoor market bustling with buyers and sellers where women squat behind small piles of garden produce and fresh meat, past a crowd milling around an overloaded bus painted in wild tropical colors and stacked high with baggage.

The Village of Jean Makout is part of Jean Makout County, but it is different than the Hamlet and outlying countryside. It is the place where everything in the county seems to begin and end. Although only some 8,000 of the 130,320 people who live in there are located in the Village, it is there that one finds the local elites, the few large land owners, the big merchants, politicians, judges, and school superintendents. All of the doctors and the Catholic priests live in the Village, as do all of the public employees—or rather, since most public employees do no work, it is where they pick up their paychecks. It is from the Village that flow all local political decisions, where the police and administrators reside, where are located all of the county's secondary schools, the only morgue, and the only hospital. Virtually all meager government expenditures stop in the Village and it is here, in the Village, that university agronomists, nutritionists, and other specialists in development and poverty alleviation convene in the rural headquarters of foreign NGOs to plan their assaults on the ecological, epidemiological, natural, and manmade disasters that combine to make Jean Makout among the poorest communities on earth.

The people of the Village consider themselves better than the peasants who live in the countryside. They call them *dan rouj*, "red teeth," (a reference to their rotting teeth, not that the Villager's teeth are much better); *pie pete* "mangled feet" (a reference to their stubbed and scarred toes, flattened from a lifetime of walking barefooted); *pa civilize* (uncivilized), and *inorant* (ignorant). They laugh at them, tease them, and make fun of their illiteracy, their rags, and their rude way of talking. They seduce their daughters in exchange for false promises and a pittance of money. The more distinguished and learned among them preside over civil controversies, usually ruling in favor of whoever can pay more, has more power, or a daughter willing to acquiesce to sexual demands.

Nonetheless, although the Village elite, government officials, and police dispatched from the cities are haughty and arrogant in their attitudes toward the peasants in the outlying areas, they themselves are not always so slick and sophisticated.

Upon arriving in the Village I got an immediate taste of the bumbling incompetence and corruption of Village government. It was in the midst of the 1997 drought, one of the most severe in recorded history. The mayor had just returned from a United Nations training seminar in Peru and announced in a gathering of waiting Villagers and NGO directors that what was urgently needed was not emergency relief, but a multistoried administrative building and a public swimming pool—yes, a swimming pool—the latter being important to give the children of Jean Makout Village the sense of dignity that rich children in the capital city of Port-au-Prince enjoy (this idea of the magical and analogical power of swimming pools was one that then ex-President—and President-to-be-again—Jean Bertrand Aristide had latched on to and ardently espoused in a book titled *Eyes of the Heart*). No insight was offered into how to alleviate affects of the drought which anyway, the mayor assured his constituents, was in the hands of God and the international community.

It was only weeks later that money entrusted to the mayor for building drainage canals, roads, and meeting payrolls disappeared. The mayor was called in to court to account for what everyone knew were stolen government funds. He refused to show. He too then disappeared, reportedly reappearing in Miami and to this day never returning. A group of protestors closed city hall in the fall of 1998, leaving Jean Makout for the next two years with no functioning government.

That was only the beginning of learning how dysfunctional the system was.

"He beat himself to death," a young policeman is telling me.

I'm perplexed so I turn it into a question: "He beat himself to death?"

"*Oui,* it was terrible. He had huge welts on his head, he was all bloody and his nose was smashed over to one side."

It is the summer of 1997, not long after I arrived in the Village, and a man jailed for stealing had been found dead in his cell, the result, the U.S.-trained police officers assured everyone—and one was now assuring me—of having "beaten himself to death."

"Well," I ask, "how did he beat himself to death?"

"We don't know, *non*. We locked him inside the cell and left him there. Apparently he just went crazy, slamming himself into the walls and thrashing around on the floor. When we checked on him in the morning there he was, beaten to death. These people out here are just wild."

Unconvinced, the dead man's family and friends gathered in front of the police station, demanding the officer responsible be turned over to them. As the mob grew, so did the fear among the police officers. The 'guilty' policeman slipped out the back of the building and first hid out in the headquarters of one of the two German NGOs. Employees of the NGO later covered him with a sheet and sat on him as their SUV cautiously passed through road blocks of burning tires and angry, machete wielding vigilantes; they snuck the officer out of the Village. The entire Jean Makout police force subsequently evacuated the Village for the next two months.

It was not the first time the police had felt inclined to leave town—or as some say, had been run out of town. It had occurred on at least three occasions in the previous two years, two of the cases being responses to the authorities having killed someone. Because of such events, the police and the authorities in general were often considered more of a criminal problem than a solution, a problem that the people occasionally addressed by attacking them.

What had happened was that in 1994 the U.N. occupying forces disarticulated the traditional means for dealing with criminal problems and family disputes. Before that time it was a *Chef Seksyon*, a county sheriff, who meted out justice. The *Chef* was appointed from among the people who lived in the region. He knew the people and had deputies throughout the area and in the event of a crime, a land dispute, or some other type of conflict, would mediate or, if necessary, make arrests. Human rights organizations ridiculed the *Chef Seksyon* system for abuses.

But the system that replaced it was essentially no system at all: The police were typically young, from towns and cities, and if they knew how to mount a mule or a horse they certainly would not have admitted it. People with education or from the city as well as the peasants themselves consider riding animals the lowliest form of transportation, undignified for people in positions of power and respect. So what had been put in place of the *Chef Seksyon* was a police force, small, some 2,500 to control 9 million people, composed of urban high school graduates who were concentrated in towns throughout the provinces and who did very, very little policing. They had few vehicles or motorcycles and, even had they been well equipped in this respect, much of Haiti is inaccessible except on foot or donkeys and horses, the animals that no self-respecting policeman was going to be seen mounted on. So the policemen typically remained huddled close to the town or city where they were headquartered and where in their boredom they tried to seduce young women, played cards, went to cock fights, drank, sometimes got in fights and, being the only people back then with guns, sometimes shot people. In general the people, especially people in the rural areas, saw them as outsiders who caused more problems than they solved and who were totally unreliable in the case of crime, indeed, inclined to save the criminal and persecute the victims.

So, putting aside the rather bizarre and never resolved case of the thief who "beat himself to death," when serious crime occurred, the people of the Village came to understand that if the police got hold of the culprit he would in most cases buy his way free and maybe back again to steal or terrorize. They took to handling it themselves. A crowd often hacked, beat, or stoned suspects to death. Three examples will give an idea of how this worked.

In the first instance a thief, Jean-Robert, was suspected of robbing at least twelve stores and several houses—including my tent. Several men in the Village apprehended him, but a group of police saved Jean-Robert from a mob that gathered with sticks and stones to kill him. He was put in jail but the first night pried apart the ancient bars that blocked his cell window and escaped. Two months later Jean-Robert reappeared and was caught again, this time with his brother, breaking into a house in Blano, the seat of the neighboring county. Already having been the victim of Jean-Robert's depredations on four separate occasions, the people of Blano had no intention of repeating the mistake their neighbors in Jean Makout had made. A crowd hacked, beat, and stoned the two men to death. When they were done they doused the bodies in gasoline and set them afire.

The second instance began on a mid-April night in 1998 in a rural area of Jean Makout. For reasons that were never clear, a man named Little Mango used a machete to hack a woman, her husband, and their daughter to death. A son escaped to report the crime. A mob located Little Mango in the distant house of a *bokor*. They bound his hands and began marching him the six-hour trek back to the crime scene. People along the route turned out by the thousands to beat and throw stones at Little Mango. By the time he passed the house where I was living, in Tierre Bleu, some five hours into the trek, Little Mango had no idea where he was. Blinded, his blood-drenched face unrecognizable, he stumbled along, people in the crowd jeered at him, and an occasional tormentor rushed in and struck him. He never reached the scene of the crime, to where they were taking him, but died from his wounds shortly after passing my house.

There was a third event, the story of Enel, an event that illustrates the intertwining of foreign aid with local corruption, and with the self-governing traditions of Haitian peasant society. The event occurred while I was in Jean Makout and touched my life closely, for I knew Enel, his family, and many of his friends.

Enel was born on a 2,500-foot high red-clay plateau in Tierre Bleu, the place I mentioned above where I lived when Ti Mango was killed, a clustering of houses that is the last bus stop on a rocky washed-out road, the site also of a Catholic church and a major regional Tuesday market.

Enel's family was poor, but his mother managed to get to the Bahamas on an illegal boat voyage. She was able to find work and send money back so Enel and his siblings could go to school in the Village. There Enel learned the ways of town folks. Later, after high school, he went on to college in Port-au-Prince where he was able to further refine those aspects of more complex society at which he seemed most adept. He became an agronomist who worked first for CARE and then for UNOPS (United Nations Office of Project). He worked throughout Jean Makout and the Province. He was a good employee, cooperative and polite, always eager to do his job and determined to make an impact on the county. At least that is how his *blan* employers at the U.N. described him. There was another side to Enel.

Enel had also refined the criminal aspects of town life. He carried a gun and cultivated a conspicuous hate for the poor country folk from whose ranks he had emerged. There were many stories of Enel intimidating peasants, pistol whipping them, stopping his vehicle and leaping out, snarling and chasing their children for no other reason than the pleasure of seeing them panic and flee.

Enel had a job as a chauffeur with UNOPS (United Nations Office of Projects) when, in late 1998, the organization launched a project to build a road just outside Tierre Bleu, Enel's birth place. So Enel came home, back to his little Village, as a big shot with the United Nations. For several months he seemed to be the Mafia Don of the community, monopolizing access to jobs on the road and forcing anyone who worked on the project to give him a 25 percent kickback from their paychecks. Without the knowledge of his employers, he managed to bypass the local committee responsible for the road project, took control of the materials, and began selling off much of the cement and tools needed for the road work. He brokered deals with the heavy equipment operators to level home sites for building, cut private roads, and sell dirt to people who had emigrated to Miami and were sending money back for the construction of new, modern houses. He falsified land titles and sold lime rock pits to UNOPS for the construction of the road.

It was not to last.

One day several men sat playing dominoes in front of a little country store just as men played there every day for years.

There was an argument. One man, the loser in a game, refused to pay the wager. The unpaid man stormed off to find his friend Enel who, he promised, would settle the issue. Enel was sleeping at a friend's house. Roused, he got up, shoved his gun in an ankle holster and headed out to put the matter in order. Barely looking up from his game of dominoes, the offender shrugged Enel off. He was not going to pay. Enel pulled his gun. The men scuffled. Three shots were fired. All three hit an innocent bystander, a man in his fifties. One bullet in the eye, one in the throat, and one in the heart. The man never made a peep. Just fell stone dead. The fight stopped. Silence. Enel got up and walked to his truck. Stopped. Turned around. Came back to the dead man and leaning over, picked him halfway up. He made as if listening to his heart and then looking up, he announced the man was not dead. Enel then went back to his vehicle and drove to a cousin's house. There he found a young relative whom he sent to his mother's house to get his satchel, loaded with money, and two bank books.

Word spread immediately and people came in droves to the scene. Among the people who came was the dead man's son, Jean, a driver for another international aid agency. Jean had just returned from Port-au-Prince and stopped to see what all the commotion was about. There, on the ground, lying dead, was his father.

Jean tried to lift up his father's body so that he could put it in the truck, but people in the crowd stopped him. "No," they said, "not until the perpetrator is dead." Jean left without his father. He went to his house, where he dropped off all the supplies he had hauled in from Port-au-Prince and then headed down the mountain to the Village where the police were stationed. At the Village he picked up Judge Similus and five of the only six policemen present at the time. Returning along the narrow and muddy road they met another vehicle. It was Enel, the man who had shot John's father. Everyone got out of their vehicles. Enel was very sorry. He told Jean he would pay for the funeral. He offered money, pulling wads of cash from his satchel, and he said that he wanted to return to Tierre Bleu. Judge Similus and the police said no, that Enel had to go to the Village. He had to be put in jail and wait for trial. So two of the policeman took Enel, and his money, and with Jean, the son of the dead man, they went to the Village. The other three policemen and Judge Similus took Enel's vehicle and headed for Tierre Bleu. That was their first mistake.

When the three policemen and judge arrived in Tierre Bleu, a mob of angry peasants met them. Hundreds of cousins, uncles, brothers, and friends of Jean's father had gathered in front of the house of Enel's mother. The mother, a large, aging, gray-haired woman sat on the porch in her rocking chair. She had locked the house and refused to let the crowd look to see if Enel was inside. She said she would rather die with her son. Representatives of the crowd spoke with her. They told her they had no quarrel with her, but that justice had to be done. The mother refused.

Then someone shouted, *zak ap fet* (let the act begin). The crowd threw stones at the wooden shuttered windows and, while not harming the old women who rocked in her chair and stared off in the distance, they beat the doors down, stole everything, and set fire to the house. Then they burned Enel's UNOPS vehicle and they burned the depot where Enel stored cement and other materials embezzled from the road project.

That is when the judge and police arrived. Judge Similus and the policemen tried to calm the situation. They talked to the people. They explained that Enel had been arrested and that he would be dealt with. That was their second mistake.

The crowd seized Similus and his companions, put them in a house, and then threatened that if Enel was not turned over soon, very soon, they would die in his place. At some point in the night the judge relented and agreed that the mob could have Enel. He wrote and signed a message ordering the Village police to turn Enel over. Part of the crowd, note in hand, then set off for the Village. Similus and the three policemen, now on foot, slunk away in the other direction.

The Village, 4 a.m.: Awakened by the sound of banging on his gate, a pleasant, good-looking young man, a local athlete, the only policeman who was actually from the Village and who everyone affectionately knew as Ti-Sony (Little-Sony), got himself out of bed and went to see who was out there. He opened his door and there, in the street in front of his mother's house, he found eighty peasants armed with clubs and machetes. One of them was holding the note from Judge Similus.

"We need Enel and we need him fast," the leader explained, holding up the note. "We need to straighten this affair out, because the corpse will be starting to stink soon, we need to get it buried, and we can't do it until justice has been served."

While Little-Sony talked to the crowd, his little brother slipped out the back of the house, over the fence, and to the police barracks where he warned the other two policemen. Little-Sony stalled, talking and negotiating. Eventually he led the crowd to the police station, which by that point was solidly locked up with Enel inside. The policemen stood on the front steps talking to the crowd, trying to soothe them. They explained the principles of democracy, the judicial system, their jobs as law enforcement officers, agents of the state, guardians of the peace. They explained how things should work the right way, the decent way, the legal way. Eventually the crowd was convinced and they left.

1:46 p.m. same day: A low, grumbling roar came from the hilltop just above the Village. Everyone stopped what they were doing and looked. People came out of their homes. Women stopped washing clothes. Everyone was staring at the crest of the small hill when a force of five hundred Tierre Bleu peasants appeared.

They came jogging and chanting in unison, "*ma manje ou, ma devoro*" (I will eat you, I will devour you). Each of the men held a machete or club. Behind the mob came dozens of boys and several women. The mob descended the knoll leading to the village. There were to be no more negotiations. When the mob reached the police station they hurled stones and gasoline bombs. The three policemen stood on the steps dodging rocks and shooting their guns over the heads of the mob. A bottle of gasoline burst against the door. The policemen had locked themselves out of the building and now the last of their bullets finished, the door behind them in flames, they hunkered down helplessly on the steps while the mob pelted them with rocks.

The citizens of the Village, including by this point almost everyone who lived there, stood by watching. They had come to see the peasants from Tierre Bleu kill Enel. The peasants had the right. Enel was, after all, one of them and he had killed one of them. But upon seeing the assault on the policemen, Little-Sony's mother and his wife both began shrieking, "*Ti–Sony mouri, Ti-Sony mouri.*" (Little-Sony is dead! Little-Sony is dead!). Now the equation had changed. It concerned one of their own. The Village crowd exploded into action, picking up sticks and stones and charging the crowd from Tierre Bleu. The police themselves picked up stones and joined the fray. An enormous rock fight ensued. In the confusion, Little-Sony, who was not dead, snuck around to the back of the police station, unlocked the door, pulled Enel and his satchel of money from a cell and with the mayhem in front of the building serving as a distraction, they climbed over the back wall, through a crumbling eighteenth-century colonial fort, across the river, up a hill, down through a dry ravine bottom, back up and over a low desert mountain, and down to the rocky coast of the bay.

A few hundred yards before they reached the Hamlet, Little-Sony and Enel descended a seaside ledge. There, just at the waterline, was a cave, a perfect place to hide from a mob of peasants, most of who could not swim. If the people from Tierre Bleu wanted to discover Enel they had to climb down a ten-foot cliff and into the water.

Little-Sony and Enel stayed in the cave for over two hours while local fisherman misled their Tierre Bleu farming cousins, disingenuously showing them around the shore looking for Enel in different hideouts, everywhere but the cave.

That is when Enel's past came back to haunt him. It just so happens that one of the people who knew that Enel had descended down into the cave was a man from the Hamlet called Sigaret (cigarette), a man who Enel had previously pistol whipped for no other reason than being a smart ass. Eventually Sigaret could resist no longer and, tipping off several of the Tierre Bleu men, he settled the score.

Little-Sony emerged first. Hoping that the peasants were finally gone, he peered out of the cave and up at the cliff. Looking back at him was a crowd of several dozen Tierre Bleu men. Little-

Sony dove into the bay and swam for a rowboat that had been passing back and forth in deeper water in case of just such an emergency. Enel swam after him.

Still in his pants and wearing shoes, frightened, disoriented, and water-logged, Enel quickly winded. His feet found a reef. He stood up. The people from Tierre Bleu showered him with rocks. One rock to the side of the head and one to the face and there, in front of hundreds of people, a panicked and bleeding Enel fell into the water and drowned.

Chapter Four
The Survey and Chaos in the Court

As I recounted earlier on, in 1997, after fifteen months in the Hamlet, I went to live in the Village. Three NGOs had hired me—PISANO, Agro Acton Aleman (AAA), and the French Initiative Development (ID)—to conduct a survey of Jean Makout County. I reported to the Direktor of PISANO, who said the goal of the survey was to build a database of information regarding health, subsistence practices, and demographics. This was important because there were no recent or reliable census data on which the NGOs could base the solicitation of more aid.

It was a massive undertaking that would involve locating and marking more than twenty thousand houses scattered throughout 168 square miles of rugged mountains, valleys, and plains, most of which were accessible only on foot or pack animal. Of the 20,000-plus houses that the survey covered, teams of interviewers and nutritional specialists would have to visit 1,586 of them. The questionnaires would cover more than one thousand distinct items including weighing and measuring mothers and children, investigation into health and nutrition, agriculture and livestock rearing practices, land ownership, and migration.

It was a mammoth task. But I was going to run it. I felt as if my career as an anthropologist was about to take off.

"*Blan!*" the man is almost shouting in my face, "if you want this survey to be done in our part of the county, you need to come up with an *invlop.*"

It is the second week of the survey; I am sitting on my motorcycle, two burly peasants menacing me,

"What's an *invlop*?" I ask.

"An *invlop*, *blan*," one shoots back, jabbing a finger at my chest and repeating himself. "An *invlop*."

"An *invlop* full of money, *oui*." clarifies his friend. "Green money."

"Yeah, green money," the other one says, jabbing his finger at me again. "American, like you."

I tell them I won't do that, "Fellows," I am feeling a little out of my element, "we can only pay for actual work that people do."

"*Non*! No way," says the finger jabber, literally jumping up and down now. "For a *blan* to come here and do a survey and not give us money, no way, *non*!"

These guys were not just peasants. They were politicians and the incident neatly captured the attitude of nearly everyone in Jean Makout, especially the politicians.

I mentioned earlier that in 1994 the United Nation's occupation forces had dissolved the military junta that three years earlier had deposed the democratically elected Haitian president, Jean Bertrand Aristide. At that time they also disbanded the traditional Haitian police-politico-administrative system of appointed county sheriffs—the peasants' only means other than mob violence or personal vendetta to redress grievances and deal with criminals—and in their place created an ineffective police force. Well, they also did something similar regarding politico-administrative functions. For administrative functions they created the democratically elected positions of Kasek and Asek. The constitutionally defined roles of these new politicians were meant to be administrative, but there was effectively nothing to administrate. The little money they got for controlling access to markets and chicken fights was insignificant. The Aseks got no regular pay and no money from the central government for road building or other community public works. What they did more than anything else at that time was peddle their bicycles from one

NGO training seminar to the next—not even Aseks and Kaseks wanted to be seen riding animals.

It was the specific task of PISANO—the NGO in charge of the survey who was in actuality representing the German Government—to train the politicians. So technically being employed by PISANO and ordered to encourage this new democratic system, we sent the Aseks and Kaseks letters and we had meetings with them. But the politicians, still impoverished and frustrated after a year of total powerlessness, responded not by helping us, but by stopping the survey. They threw interviewers out of their districts, threatened bodily harm, and demanded negotiations. I even received letters threatening me. When I would go to talk to the politicians, to try to understand why they were doing this, the negotiations were always held in an atmosphere fraught with tension and menace. And the reason they were stopping the survey always turned out to be the same: They wanted money.

At times I felt as if I was living inside a 1950s comic book. One Asek sat me down in a chair in his backyard and, while four of his friends stood around me, he slammed his fist into his hand, *Blan, nou gen bezwenn isit.* "Blan, we got needs around here," by which he meant that he wanted some money.

Once I went to a meeting in a hamlet called Lester. It was market day. In the settlement of hundred-plus thatch-roofed houses covering some five acres, there were ten thousand peasants all engaged in a frenzy of buying and selling. On the outskirts of the Hamlet, thousands of braying donkeys were tethered in a corral. Next to the corral was an "administration" building, a stifling hot metal container, something like the type pulled behind tractor trailers, but smaller. Somehow, at some time in the past, it had been dumped there and since turned into the political headquarters for that section of the county. There were sixteen of the politicians inside, one of me. I was there for six hours.

How much money, they first wanted to know, is involved in the survey? How much were interviewers getting paid? How much was I getting paid? What would come of it all? What were the people going to get? Most of these questions seemed fair to me.

I mean, it was not taxpayers' money, at least not Haitian taxpayers' money, but what with us teaching neoliberal transparency and all, I answered most of them. But whatever I answered, the politicians didn't seem to care. What they really wanted to know was how much they were going to get.

When I told them the survey was costing $36,000, trying to add that this was about one-tenth the cost of the last major survey in the area, one hothead, to my astonishment, went completely berserk, jumping to his feet. "That money is mine," he shouted. "That money is for me."

Then there were the peasants themselves.

"I have a problem with your survey," says a small, wizened old man. I am standing in a yard before some one hundred peasants, all seated in rickety homemade wicker chairs. I am here because, like the politicians, the peasants in this particular area refuse to allow the survey to continue. The old man is the first to speak and he starts off saying he loved foreign NGOs. But then he says he has a problem.

"I heard that your people are going to make a list of all my children, their sex, and the dates they were born. Now if that is true," the old man is stern and serious, "how do I know that once you have that information you are not going to put my children in a sack and hang them up so that later you can eat them?"

This starts everybody off.

"*Oui*," shouts a woman, "and what about those damn numbers your people put on my house. I want those numbers off my house."

"No damn Villager," a middle-aged man waving a machete says, joining her, "is going to put the mark of the beast on my house, *non*!"

"Those Villagers shouldn't be here, *non*!" cries another raising his machete as well.

A young man stands up shaking his fist. "I want to tell you a story," he says, looking around and quieting the others, "a story that cuts me like a knife." As the people fall silent, he directs his attention to me. "A story about how when I was twelve years old a group of Villagers cornered me and called me mangled feet and red teeth." He lets the words sink in and then concludes with a loud, "To hell with Villagers."

"*Oui*," a woman shouts in agreement, "to hell with the Villagers. I hate them."

"And those damned NGOs," says a man standing on his chair so that everyone could hear him. "Those NGOs aren't doing anything but ruining the country, *oui*."

"Those damned trees," says another man, "those trees they've been planting are sucking the life out of us."

As it turned out, the trees distributed to the peasants to offset deforestation were resented. Many of the peasants said they were a trick to make their lives more miserable. They said they wanted fruit trees, but instead got useless, even toxic trees, like the Neem, which killed everything around it. Or the Lucina, which some peasants claimed caused the tails of goats or donkeys that ate its leaves to fall off. Or trees like the Eucalyptus, which sucked the water out of the ground, leaving plants nearby dead from thirst. Some people complained about the Germans digging irrigation pits that would then become breeding places for mosquitoes, that they would get so bad they would have to move to another house. And, making comments that would come to have serious implications for me—because I came to believe they were all too true—some people said food aid was destroying them.

"*Oui,* they're ruining the country," another man isshouting. "They're giving all that food to people who don't need it while we get nothing."

"It's the damn food that's killing us."

Food aid, they said, made it impossible to find people willing to work, that it was turning them into dependents. They said they would prefer technical help in their gardens so they could produce more of their own food.

I would become convinced as time went on that not only were right, but for more reasons than they were aware. I came to understand that food aid crashed the local agriculture markets, driving peasants off the land, and leaving them only three options: Emigrate to the neighboring Dominican Republic to work as semi-slave peons, risk the treacherous seas and shark-infested waters between Haiti and the United States, or move to the city and become cheap labor at starvation wages. Actually, unbeknownst to me at the time, some were already making a fourth choice: Enter the international trade in illicit drugs. But back then that was not an issue for me, nor was it as widespread as it would become.

At the meetings I was repeatedly drawn much farther into the lives of those particular peasants than I had intended. I was patient and listened. And I usually responded saying that the survey was a worthy cause and that the German, French and U.S. foreign aid experts who I worked for needed the information so they could change their current practices and provide the kind of aid the peasants wanted. At the time I believed it. Or at least, I believed in the spirit of what I was saying. I believed that foreign aid experts were there to help the peasants. The peasants, however, were skeptical. But, in the end, they always politely agreed to cooperate, saying they were glad to see me and that maybe I could accomplish something different.

Survey employees were also a problem. A big problem.

"*Non, Non, Non*! *Blan*! *Non*!" The woman is on her feet, her cheeks puffed out like her head might explode, her fists clenched at her side and the thought enters my mind that she might hit me. "You're not tricking me *Blan, Non*! *Non*! *Non*!" she roars and stomps her foot. "I've never told a lie in my life."

What had happened was this. To conduct the survey we hired supervisors and interviewers. The job of interviewer was to ask questions of the household heads and, most importantly, to weigh the youngest mother and her youngest child in each household. If one or both were not present, the interviewer was to return to the house later or arrange for the woman and child to meet him or her at our base camp.

Two weeks into the survey I went out to check and discovered that the interviewers, being practical peasants, had come up with their own solution to absenteeism: They asked questions of anyone they could find and weighed and measured any woman who was available—grandmothers, daughters, neighbors, visitors—and any available child, whether the child was actually related to the woman or not.

"*Non, Non, Non!*" she shouts again, "never, not one single lie in my life!"

She had visited sixteen households but when I went out into the field and checked—something none of the surveyors ever imagined that I was going to do—I found that she had only weighed the correct people in three instances.

"Look," I say, "I was out there. I visited the same households. Some of the people you weighed didn't even live in the house."

She never admitted it, but she left and didn't show up for work again. In any case, the supervisors were as problematic as the interviewers.

"I should eat shit and vomit on you *blan*, American pig!" one of the supervisors snarls at me. I am standing on the office porch while he and another supervisor pace the yard below, shouting and cursing me. "You did it, not us. You sabotaged the GPSs. Stupid *blan!*"

The job of supervisor, besides making sure the interviewers were doing their jobs correctly, was to count houses and record longitudinal and latitudinal coordinates. It was a simple task that involved jotting down the numbers from a handheld GPS (Global Positioning System device), a device that, at that time, was accurate to within thirty feet. To make sure there were no mistakes, I trained the supervisors myself and tested them repeatedly. I was certain that they could do it. There was nothing to it. You just write the numbers down. But when they gave me the coordinates for the first one thousand houses, I plotted them on a map and found them scattered all over the Caribbean. There were houses located in the ocean, a couple in Cuba, some in the Bahamas, one in the Dominican Republic. And that was not all. They had not just misplaced the houses with bogus coordinates; they had failed to count 20 percent of them.

It was a mess and the work had to be redone. But the supervisors didn't want to do it. That's why they were standing in the yard cursing me. And there were a lot of other problems in addition to the politicians, recalcitrant peasants, dishonest surveyors, and angry supervisors.

The very first week my assistant wrecked the survey's only motorcycle. He also stole $150 from my desk (we caught him). My mechanic drove our truck through the PISANO headquarters' front gate, closed at the time, taking out the metal gate and a sizeable portion of the eight-foot wall to which it was attached—thank God no one was standing on the other side. Not to be outdone, a chauffer applying for a job drove my truck into our office wall. I mean this quite literally. He arrived at the office to apply for a job. I asked him what he could do. He said that he was a chauffeur. I tossed him the keys and climbed into the passenger's side of the vehicle. He climbed in the driver's side, started the truck, put it in gear, and drove straight into the side of the house.

There were payrolls that didn't arrive for weeks, leaving me to deal with some forty-plus angry employees. The survey's official vehicle (that our employers provided) caught fire and burned up, "spontaneous combustion," the rather learned and smart ass chauffer told me. I was subsequently in a motorcycle accident that left a twelve-stitch gash in my arm and then, one week later, reduced to riding a bicycle, I had another accident that reopened the wound.

There were lots and lots of other frustrating events. But most important of all there was Alsibien, Tito, Arnaud, and Tobe. They had the biggest impact on my life during the survey and they continued, each in his or her way, to be a part of my life afterward.

Alsibien was from the Hamlet. I hired him as guard and cook because he had been one of my fishing and drinking buddies and, while I preferred not to hire my friends, I needed at least one assistant I could trust and who could perform basic tasks such as looking after the house, going to the store and running messages. Alsibien was perfect for that. He was my age (thity-five at the time), totally loyal and would do anything I asked. If I needed to get a message twenty miles over mountains in pouring rain with roads washed out, I could send Alsibien. He would get there and back, barefoot, in not much more time than a driver could do it on a pleasant day in an SUV.

The problem with Alsibien was that I had not considered the effect that having a salaried job might have on him. As survey guard and cook he was earning more money than he ever dreamed possible, about $10 (U.S.) per day. He immediately went on the greatest drinking binge of his life, staying sober just long enough each day to prepare lunch. By midafternoon the first thing a visitor to the office would encounter, and have to step over, would be Alsibien, sprawled on the concrete floor of the porch snoring.

The driver of our official NGO-provided Mercedes SUV was named Tito. In his mid-twenties, clean-cut, seemingly a gentle, amicable fellow, my first indication that I misjudged him came several weeks into the survey.

It had been raining for days. All the roads had turned to deep mud and we had been driving through a particularly bad stretch of it. The ruts we had to follow were over a foot deep. People, animals, and vehicles all had to follow along in them or slosh through thick, knee deep mud. Suddenly we came bumper to muzzle with a heavily laden donkey. The donkey stopped, its head drooping wearily, nowhere to go and not enough room in the narrow rut for the animal to turn around. The overweight market woman who owned him was waddling up from behind as fast as she could. She was almost there. But Tito couldn't wait. He edged the SUV up to the donkey, made gentle contact with it, and then hit the gas. The beast and its load tumbled over into the mud, scattering vegetables and sending the woman into howls of protest.

It was arrogant and insensitive treatment of a peasant. And it was stupid. Peasants get angry. Push the wrong donkey in the wrong place and at the wrong time and you could have serious trouble. You could end up like Enel.

But this wasn't the last time that Tito was a problem.

He subsequently would fail to show up for work and take off for God knows where in the official vehicle, leaving us stranded. Once while in the field he tried to borrow my one man tent—five minutes before I was going to bed down in it—and when I ordered him out, he would not go. As an independent contractor it was up to me to hire and fire, but with Tito it was different. The Germans had hired him as a driver and he was responsible for their vehicle. I finally got fed up with Tito and asked the Germans to fire him.

Tito believed that the fault for his being fired was not me, as I told him, but one of the supervisors, Sinneg, who had absolutely nothing to do with it. Tito threatened to kill Sinneg. With several of his companions he went to Sinneg's house and, finding only his grandmother at home, intimidated her. Then he managed to convince the French NGO (ID)—one of the survey sponsors—to hire him and at an opportune moment tried to run Sinneg over with one of their trucks. I wrote a letter of complaint. Again Tito got fired. Again Tito decided that the problem was not me but Sinneg. This time I encountered him on the road. He was headed for the office to get Sinneg. Accompanying him were five knife-bearing companions. In exchange for them not going to the office and stabbing Sinneg, I promised that we would have a meeting with all the NGO directors, myself, and Sinneg, so that Tito could give his side of what had happened. I also invited the police.

At the meeting I spoke first and explained to Tito that it was me who, both times, had caused him to be fired, I told him why, and I said that if something happened to Sinneg—as, for example, if a truck ran him over or a knife got stuck in his chest— we would hold him, Tito, accountable. Tito's face darkened and he delivered a bizarre speech that began. "Since I was ten years old and split my father's head open with a rock I have been taking care of myself." I suppose it was a threat. If so, police or no police, it worked splendidly. Tito finished the speech and the director of the French NGO immediately gave him his job back, right there at the table, under the condition, of course, that he not hurt any of us. We all went home wondering if we should feel relieved or afraid. (Two months later Tito drove ID's brand new US$50,000 Land Rover into a flooding river, losing the vehicle and barely escaping with his life.)

Then there were Arnaud and Tobe.

When I arrived in the Hamlet it was to study marriage and childrearing patterns of the people there. But I soon began to have my own problems in that regard. I became increasingly lonely and my celibacy was increasingly frustrating for me. The people of the Hamlet didn't help matters.

I felt it was a bad idea to have a romantic relationship with a local woman while I was in the field. And even if I had wanted to, it would not have been easy. To begin with, while I was living in the Hamlet, there were no eligible women over the age of about twenty. By that point in life the women were living with a man and had one or several children. So it seemed that my only choices, if I wanted to have a relationship with a local girl, were teenagers. A relationship with an impoverished semiliterate Haitian teenager struck me as exploitation, on both our parts. It would be exploitation on my part because not only did I have my own culturally prescribed norms that frown upon men of my age having sex with teenage women, but what I would have desired from such a relationship was sex and nothing more. On the other hand, it was clear that any girl and her family would permit such a relationship principally in the hope of exploiting me for my relative wealth and socioeconomic power. How could it be anything else? I was a pale, comparatively bumbling, linguistically and socially inept outsider.

So I ignored the girls. But nobody ignored the fact that I was ignoring them. As time went on, people in the Hamlet became perplexed. They could not understand why I did not want a wife. How could it be that an adult male lived alone? Older men would sit me down and explain to me the need for a woman.

"*Blan*," I was compelled to hear more than once, "it is need that a man needs a woman, *oui*. A man needs a woman to live. You can't live without one, *non*, you need one to make food, to clean the house, and of course to [laughter] *fe yon ti baga*y 'do a little thing.'" Men my age would pull me aside and with concern ask if I needed them to talk to a woman for me. To make a *rendevous*. My close friends, those who understood my ambivalence about the age of the girls, would get exasperated. I remember Givme half shouting, "*Monchè*, we don't have that here, *non*." Then, in a low, confiding voice, rubbing his index finger and thumb together, he gave me an explanation I was to hear from other men time and time again: "As soon as they have little pubic hairs you can screw them, *oui*."

Even women my age would tell me how I needed to go after the girls, "get them, corner them, don't let them escape." Partly teasing and partly sympathetic, they would tell me, "you need caresses, you need them." More than one young woman explained to me that I could get ill if I did not have sex. Others took a more upbeat approach. Once while walking alone with me back to the Hamlet, a friend's twenty-year-old wife said, "*Monchè*...it is tasty that sex is tasty, *oui*. Go get some!"

When my celibacy persisted, people became suspicious of me. They didn't know what I wanted, what I was about. Everyone likes sex. It was not long before people began to refer to me as homosexual. The Hamlet's most notorious closet homosexual propositioned me. Several people decided, to my horror, that what I wanted was to have sex with children.

The way I finally tried to resolve the problem was with Arnaud.

Three-quarters of the way up the mountain, hidden in the rock-strewn and parched desert, lay La Valie, one hundred acres of lush irrigated valley where three-foot wide chutes of sparking clean water gushed through gardens of banana trees, sugarcane, taro, rice, and melons. Trees, mangos, avocados, coconuts, breadfruit, orange, and grapefruit, shaded the borders of the gardens and the sides of the canals. It was a slice of paradise. And there in the middle of those lush irrigated gardens, living with her uncle and cousins, I met Arnaud.

Arnaud was exactly what I was looking for: Twenty-two years old, quick-witted, mature, bold, single, with no children, she lacked only one year to finish her high school education, a grand achievement in rural Haiti, and she was sure that she was as important as anyone alive, an attractive arrogance that allowed her to accompany me when I occasionally dined with visiting development experts—agronomists, nutritionists, and doctors sent to the area to help improve living conditions—without any hint she didn't belong. So with Arnaud there was none of the weighty guilt that comes with the thought of having sex with a young impoverished woman. No sense of an enormous and obvious gulf between me and the poor, semiliterate Haitian teenage peasant.

I moved her to the Village where I helped pay her tuition at an evangelical high school and continued our courtship in what I thought was a dignified manner.

It didn't work. She caught hell from everyone. Her classmates hazed her. Her male school teachers hazed her. Judge Similus hazed her. The mayor hazed her. Shopkeepers hazed her. They would tease her in school and in the streets. They would shout after her, "Timoté says you can *gouye*," which meant she could hump (something I never discussed with anyone). Even men who professed to be my good friends hazed her.

The only people she seemed to get along with, besides her cousins and an aunt, were the police who, like her, were outsiders in the Village. To make matters worse, this took place at a time when I was trying to convince everyone that I was poor. So when I was not with her I was wandering around penniless, in shorts and barefooted, performing lowly activities such as spending days spear fishing and consorting with the lowest of the peasants. This gave everyone ample ammunition to tease her even more severely. Young men chided her that she was with a *blan mizé*—white trash. They invented abundant names for me, "ripped pants," "sea scrounger," "Hamlet bum." It was not long before Arnaud wanted nothing to do with me.

So Arnaud had been my girlfriend until the hazing and kidding about hanging around with white trash became too much for her. But now that I was employed, had a chauffeur-driven Mercedes SUV, a fat payroll and forty employees, my status among the Villagers had changed. Arnaud decided that maybe she loved me after all. She came back into my life. demanding to resume her place by my side and to get her piece of the survey action. I initially resisted. Hiring her seemed like a bad idea as did her staying in the survey house where I lived with seven other employees. I lost on both counts. She came back into my life. And she soon brought Tobe with her.

About three weeks after Arnaud moved in I came home to find a little girl in the house, Tobe, Arnaud's cousin. She was six years old at the time and tiny. I was furious.

"This is an office, not a home," I told Arnaud.

"We have to eat, *oui*?" she said.

"Alsibien is the cook."

"He can't do it, *non*. Look at him. He's drunk," she said.

I looked over at Alsibien, curled up on the bare concrete floor of the porch, snoring loudly, spittle dripping from the corner of his mouth. She was right. Alsibien wasn't such a great cook.

"Well, the child can't cook."

"*Non,*" she said. "But I need help if I'm going to do it."

"Can't we just eat out?" I said.

"You're really an idiot, aren't you?" She shot back.

To my surprise, the other employees living in the house took Arnaud's side. The consensus was that we needed a child in the house to do small chores and run errands. I gave up. But it wasn't long before the beatings started.

Arnaud would whip Tobe for the smallest thing: A forgotten order, a dropped plate, not moving fast enough. She trained Tobe to sit on a little stool in the corner of the thatch roofed kitchen and wait, silently, for the next command. Tobe never smiled and you could see the fear on her face whenever Arnaud entered the room. When I spoke to Tobe in Arnaud's presence she would stare at the floor and give me one-word responses. Again I objected to Tobe being there and even more, to her being disciplined so severely. But others in the house defended Arnaud.

"A child needs discipline, *oui*."

"Children are the woman's affair, *oui*."

"Don't worry about the kid, *non*, Let Arnaud worry about her, *oui*."

In the first month Tobe was in the house she saw her mother only once. It happened while she was in the market with Arnaud. At the sight of her mother Tobe cried. When I heard about it, I waited until Tobe and I were alone and asked her if she wanted to go home.

"*Non,*" she said.

"Don't you miss your mother?"

"*Oui.*"

"Well why don't you want to go home?"

"She doesn't make me work enough."

Uh?

I went to see Tobe's mother.

"A child is supposed to work," the mother said.

"But these whippings?" I replied.

"Children are born to be whipped," an aunt with a scarf wrapped around her head chimed in. "They are like animals, *oui,*"

"Whip, whip, whip." said the mother with heightening conviction. "Children are born to be whipped. It helps them grow into proper citizens."

I began to challenge Arnaud whenever she beat Tobe. Several times I went so far as to threaten her if she didn't stop. Arnaud would back down, wait until I left the office and beat her twice as hard. The others in the house kept asking me to stay out of it, saying I was only making matters worse.

There is an anthropological version of the concept of "cultural relativism" that holds that the values of other cultures are understandable and acceptable in the context of that culture. Anthropologists generally reject it in cases of rape and murder and, as in this case, what struck me as type of slavery and child abuse. But as an anthropologist in the field who was supposed to be studying Haitians and their culture, I faced a dilemma. I wanted the abuse to stop. But it was my definition of abuse. Furthermore, Tobe was not my child. I had spoken to her mother who did not want to do anything about it. Then there was the fact that Arnaud actually was making a valuable contribution to the survey. In fact, at that point it is arguable that the survey could not have continued successfully without her. She was far and away my brightest and most productive employee. She ran the office, was also the secretary, and understood perfectly the goals of the survey. Not least of all, to be honest, she had also once again become my girlfriend and at the time I felt that I very much needed a girlfriend—I was miserable. So I backed off, again.

In the meantime I focused on the survey, which, as recounted, was becoming a disaster. The Aseks and Kaseks were threatening the interviewers and pressuring me; the nutritionists and supervisors were turning in bogus data; the peasants were panicked over the prospect that the survey was some kind of evil conspiracy to eat their children; I was having problems with people in the office stealing, problems with Alsibien's drinking, problems with the mechanic, and problems with Tito the driver. And then, as if I was not sufficiently besieged with problems, the former supervisors called me into court.

I had gone to the Village market to shop for vegetables and it was there that the papers were served, requiring me to appear in court on the matter of the supervisors' pay. The news spread fast. *Blan* Timoté was to be tried in court, an event that everyone felt would provide endless entertainment. Soon the director of PISANO found out about it and summoned me to the PISANO main headquarters in distant Baie-de-Sol.

The Direktor was in his mid-forties, six-three, lean and fit, piercing cold blue eyes. He inquired about my health and then got right to the point: He had a lawyer for me.

"He is a very excellent practitioner. I have used him myself."

"What's his name?" I asked.

"Kaylin Krapley."

"Christ," I said. "Kaylin Krapley is the owner of the firm that is suing me."

"Hmm. Very interesting. But why would that be a problem?"

"We can't hire the law firm that's suing me. That would be absurd."

"I am not sure what you are getting at."

"It's a conflict of interest." I searched for an analogy. "We would have the same captain for opposing teams. It's not competitive."

"I don't think this unusual. Not here," the Direktor mused then, leaning back in his large office chair. "It happened to me once before," he muttered to himself. "I won the case and it only cost $2,000." The Direktor was lost in thought for the moment. He waved his hand in the air, as if tabulating on an imaginary chalkboard, "Defense. Prosecution. Plaintiff. Judge." Suddenly he stopped and sat straight in his chair, "Let me call Kaylin," he announced. "He is an excellent lawyer. He will know if there is something wrong with this."

So the Direktor spun through his Rolodex, located the phone number, and called Kaylin Krapley, the very lawyer who had engineered the court case so that his law firm was representing both plaintiff and defendant.

Naturally, I only heard the Direktor's side of the conversation. It went like this:

"Kaylin, how are you my friend?…Yes, well, I have him right here in my office at this very moment…He has only one concern. The law firm that is representing the young Haitian men, it is yours, no?…And there is no problem with this?…No, of course not. Ha, ha, ha. Well, he is young. He has not much experience in these kinds of affairs...And the cost...Of course, that's quite reasonable."

The Direktor hung up the phone.

"It's okay. Solicitor Kaylin says this is not a problem. They can represent both you and the supervisors who are suing you."

"And the cost?"

"Only $2,000 (U.S.)."

"PISANO will pay?"

"Of course not."

I represented myself.

The courtroom was a one-room wooden shack; the floor was bare and cracked cement. The only furnishings were a battered wooden desk for the judge and the hard wooden chairs we were sitting on. It was stifling hot. Black faces filled the open windows, blocking out sunlight and any breeze. Someone leaned in the window behind me and snarled in my ear: "You're going to pay, *Blan*, green money, lots of it."

The judge came in and sat down at the desk. Like everybody else involved in these proceedings, Judge Similus had a bit of a reputation. His specialty was threatening women with jail to gain sexual favors. He was suave, light brown skin, in his mid thirties. He had the habit of cocking one eye when he looked at you, as if he were trying to divine your real thoughts, and he often wrinkled his forehead inquisitively. He immediately pulled out a leaf of lined notebook paper, hunched over it, and set to writing. I was seated on one side of his desk. The lawyer representing my accusers, not yet present, sat opposite me.

I already knew something about this lawyer. He was, as I mentioned, the Jean Makout representative for the law firm that belonged to Kaylin Krapley, the Direktor's pal, a notoriously obnoxious and aggressive businessman. The lawyer had his own sordid reputation for falsifying land titles and then trying to evict peasants from their garden plots.

I looked over at him. He was small, thin, coal black, fortyish, with taut skin and high cheekbones. Like some vaudeville comedian from the 1930s, he wore baggy gray flannel slacks and a black tuxedo jacket considerably too large for his wiry frame. His buttoned-up shirt was pinched tight against his pencil neck and an enormous tie hung down and formed a pile in his lap. He must be suffocating inside those clothes, I thought. But he was not sweating and in spite of his comical appearance he managed to present a serious demeanor, an act considerably enhanced by the fact he had arrived with something one seldom ever saw out in the province, a newspaper. He was making a great show of reading it. He leaned back in his chair, legs crossed, the paper opened wide and held high as he carefully reviewed each page with exaggerated interest, occasionally making loud comments to no one in particular about some outrage he had discovered therein. I turned my attention away from him. The crowd outside was growing, their peering bodies blocked the windows so that not a ray of sunlight or breath of breeze penetrated the room. It was smothering hot. I was sweating and wishing that I, too, had a newspaper to hide behind.

Judge Similus looked up from his desk, clicked his pen closed, cleared his throat and declared, *Nous commencion*! "We begin."

He looked at the little lawyer. "You may present your case first."

What followed would have been funny to me if it hadn't the potential to bear such serious consequences. If I lost the case I was finished. The Survey would have been over, the budget broken, and I humiliated. No NGO would want to hire me again. Not in Jean Makout. I would have to leave.

The little lawyer set aside his newspaper and rises to his feet. His tie falls below his belt, his hands disappear inside the sleeves of his tuxedo jacket and the bottoms of his baggy gray flannels cover his shoes. With an air of great importance he turns to address the Villagers whose gawking faces fill the windows and doors. In polite French that immediately morphs into harsh Creole, he declares:

"I am here to demand payment for the mistreatment of my Haitian clients. The *blan* has come here thinking that he can treat Haitians like dogs, like slaves."

He pauses, surveying the audience.

"But I am here to tell you *blan*." He sweeps his arms as if to present me to the onlookers. "Not here! Suddenly he moves toward me, jabbing his finger like a sword. Not in this town! *Non, Non, Blan*!," he shrieks, "*Vakabon*, you must pay!" (*Vakabon* is a Creole insult that falls somewhere between pig and bum).

I glance at Judge Similus wondering what he makes of all this. The judge is sitting there, calmly waiting for the Lawyer to finish. He notices me looking at him, straightens, clears his throat and asks the little lawyer, "What exactly did the *blan* do?"

The lawyer declares that I haven't paid the two supervisors for a month's work and adds, to my amazement, that I owe them US$5,000. It's actually more like US$300. But that's it. That's his case. No evidence. No testimony.

Now it's my turn.

I pull out contracts, letters, payroll receipts and the official Haitian labor code with highlighted passages and marked pages demonstrating my innocence.

One by one I place the documents on Judge Similus's desk. But the judge doesn't acknowledge them.

The little lawyer leaps to his feet. "*Vakabon*! you must pay! All Americans are *vakabon*! You must pay! You are not going to come here and treat us like slaves! Colonist! You cannot come to steal from the poor people of Haiti! Slavery no longer exists! *Non*! *Non*! *Non*!"

Judge Similus sits there calmly, looking at the little lawyer, waiting, apparently, to see what else he has to say.

But I've had enough. Since this is apparently the way Haitian courts operate, I decide to respond in kind.

"You're not a lawyer, you're a comedian," I shout.

The crowd at the windows explodes in laughter. Some of them are jumping up and down hugging each other. I can hear people running up to the windows outside and asking, "What did the *blan* say?"

I'm encouraged.

"Where did you learn the law, from a *bokor*?" I say.

The crowd roars again. They love it. This is what they've been waiting for. Judge Similus smirks. I think to myself, 'okay, I can do this.'

"Thief!" I am on my feet, "All lawyers are thieves!" Again the crowd roars its approval.

This sort of thing went on for two days.

At the end of the second day, Judge Similus asked for closing arguments. The lawyer requested US$5,000 for the supervisors and another US$2,000 for himself for, he explained, his services. When I got my turn and I said it was clear that the supervisors were trying to get something that they did not deserve and that they knew this. I pointed out the problems they had caused the survey, me, the other employees, and everyone in Jean Makout who might benefit from the survey. I said they wanted all of the survey money for themselves—in rural Haiti one of the most biting accusations one could make is that a person doesn't want to share. I asked that I and the survey be awarded US$10,000. I don't know if I had a right to ask for money and I certainly had not planned on it. But no one else seemed to know either. The judge pronounced that he was incompetent to make a decision. One of the supervisors, now present, a brutish young man, the same one who had promised to vomit on me earlier, jumped to his feet, and proclaimed that while the court had failed, I would now be tried by the *lwa*, spirits, by which he meant that having failed in court he was now going to come after me with sorcery.

The following morning the bailiff showed up at the survey office and wanted to know why I was not in court. Turns out that the gawking Villagers had so enjoyed the spectacle that they requested the trial continue. They had sent for the supervisors— who were still biting their nails over having lost—and demanded the judge send the bailiff after me.

I didn't go. And it was indeed over.

So I got a chance to reorganize the survey. The employees signed new contracts that made their pay contingent on the number of honest and correctly completed survey questionnaires. We all went to the field, where we stayed until the survey was complete. Whenever the Kaseks and Aseks gave us a problem, I called a meeting with the peasants and explained directly to them what we were doing and why it might be good for them. If the politicians threatened us, we threatened back, saying that we would simply pull out, omit the region from the survey, and they would have to explain why to the peasants who had voted for them. The politicians quickly found better things to do with their time. When we finished with the survey we compiled the data and I holed up in a hotel room in the city for two months, analyzed the data, and wrote the report.

Chapter Five
Gutless Wonders:
The Windmill Fiasco
and
The History of Aid in Jean Makout County

I am sitting on a tiled veranda around a polished mahogany table. It is the day of reckoning for the survey. Earlier that week I had turned in the report and now the Germans at PISANO have invited me to explain it. I am alone with them. It's a bad sign. No representative from the other NGOs has been invited. There are only four of us: Me, an agronomist, the Direktor and a tall large-boned, heavily freckled, fortyish German woman with strawberry blond hair. She is a newly arrived nutritionist and a self-styled general in the war on poverty. She has a Ph.D. in nutrition and holds a professorship at a major German University. Although she only just arrived in Haiti this week, for the first time in her life, she is ready to make an impact. Each of the Germans hold a copy of my report and now the Direktor looks at the big boned-nutritionist.

"Would you like to begin or should I?" he asks.

"Oh, please" replies The Nutritionist, "let me." And then glaring at me she snarls, "What is it with these wind generators?"

The wind generators stand like monuments atop a hill overlooking the city of Baie-de-Sol, the capital city of the province. They are the first thing one sees approaching the city, five majestic windmills, each one capable of producing fifty thousand kilowatts of energy. But they are useless, vandals having long ago ripped out their electrical guts. I had difficulty learning about them. No one could remember when they were installed. Government officials reported knowing nothing about them; the personnel working for the state electric company, Electricité de Haiti (EDH), reported knowing nothing about them. From missionaries I was able to learn that an unremembered foreign aid organization had installed the wind generators in the early 1990s, and that U.S. military personnel had tried to fix them during the occupation. That is all I got. But it was enough because it is the typical story regarding development all over Haiti: "It is broken, can't be fixed, and nobody knows anything else about it." And that was the whole point. To me the wind generators epitomized foreign aid. Their guts ripped out, never having functioned for longer than a *blan* sat watching and caring for them, they are a summary statement of international development efforts in Haiti. I snapped a photo and included it in the report. Thinking myself rather smart for it, I titled the photo, "Unsustainable Development," a pun on the fact that wind-generated electricity, clean and environmentally friendly, a classic "sustainable development," is—by virtue of the incompetent and dysfunctional government administration—economically and bureaucratically "unsustainable."

And now The Nutritionist, this high-powered development practitioner who only this very week for the first time in her life arrived in Haiti, is seething with anger. I mean she is really pissed off.

"These wind generators are not even located in Jean Makout," she growls.

I want to say that the wind generators are not in the main body of the report, which is indeed about Jean Makout. They are in the section concerning recommendations, something that the Direktor had insisted I include. I put them there to emphasize what everyone knows is a valid point: Foreign Aid in Haiti has been a miserable failure.

"Well," I begin to respond. But, with the curtness of an interrogator, the Nutritionist cuts me off in mid sentence, "You seem to be saying that development is useless."

I want to tell her I am not making that conclusion, although one might. I want to tell her that the point of the wind generators is to emphasize not that they were a bad idea, but, given the situation in Haiti, an ineffective and impractical one. But it is not a question she is posing and she again cuts me off in mid sentence.

"Why don't we just pack up and go home?" she snaps.

While the nutritionist chastises me for my criticism of development I think about the history of foreign aid in Jean Makout, something that in the previous two years I had learned much about.

International NGOs (Non Governmental Organizations) dedicated to developing the county began arriving in the 1950s. By the mid 1970s there were more than a dozen and by the 1990s there were seventeen. Included among them were the largest charities in the world, multinational corporations with headquarters in developed world centers of power, cities such as Washington DC, Paris, London, and Hamburg; organizations that in their entirety included thousands and even tens of thousands of employees and operations in 168 countries around the globe. Their corporate names conjured images of human compassion and assistance, such as British Child Care (UK), Bureau of Nutrition and Development (Dutch), InterAid (French), World Vision (USA), Compassion International (USA), CARE International (originally based in the USA). Others bore names denoting their affiliation with the Western world's major religions, Adventist Development and Relief Agency (USA), The Baptist Mission (USA), The Mission to the Greeks (USA), Unenvangelized Field Missions (USA), and Catholic Relief Services (USA). Others were affiliated with the most powerful International organizations in the world, such as UNICEF and the World Food Program, both of the United Nations. The most important and powerful were sponsored by the major developed world governments: CARE International, funded in Haiti almost entirely by the U.S. government, and the organizations that sponsored the survey; Agro Action Aleman and

PISANO, both funded by the German government, and Initiative Development, funded largely by the French government.

When the NGOs arrived in the early 1950s, the county boasted banana plantations and refrigerated ships that regularly visited the Jean Makout harbor and hauled the produce to Miami; a five thousand-acre sisal plantation; tobacco farms; a major rum distillery; and a sugar cane plantation. There were thriving export houses to which the peasants sold goat and cow hides, coffee, castor bean oil, and aloe. But by the 1980s all that was gone. There were no more private companies, no mining operations, no manufacturing industries, no plantations, indeed, no agroindustrial enterprises at all. Beyond the small peasant homesteads and their semisubsistence gardens and the few animals they tethered to bushes, there was nothing left in Jean Makout county but the NGOs and the Haitian government.

The government was the underfed runt of the two. For example, in the space of six years, 1994–2000, just two of the organizations, German PISANO and CARE International, spent more than US$36 million in Jean Makout; during the same period the Haitian government spent about US$1 million. During the 1980s and 1990s, 90 percent of all machinery and vehicles in Jean Makout County belonged to the NGOs. In 1997 the NGOs provided all of the approximately thirty thousand temporary jobs and over 400 of the 650 full-time salaried jobs; the paltry remainder were government or teaching jobs in tiny primary schools.

But what I had learned in the past two years of interviewing people living in the county and from poring over clinic and development reports was a paradox: Despite all the money dedicated to aiding and developing Jean Makout, conditions had gotten steadily worse. *Real income* in the region had fallen from per capita US$54 in 1977 to a mid-1990s level of US$22. Malnutrition among children zero to seventy-two months increased from 30 to 46 percent. Life expectancy had dropped from fifty-two to forty-five years; more than one infant in ten was dying before their first birthday; 20 percent of children did not survive to the age of five. Each year 6 to 10 percent of women suffered from sexually transmitted diseases such as chlamydia, HIV/AIDS, and syphilis; and each year another 10 percent of the population experienced debilitating diseases such as malaria, typhoid, and hepatitis.

As if the picture was not gloomy enough, if Jean Makout were a country it would have been among the ten most densely populated on earth (775 people per square mile), and it was growing at a terrifying and seemingly unstoppable rate. Even with great numbers of people fleeing on boats or migrating to the cities, the number of people living there doubled from 67,925 in 1982 to 130,320 in 1997. There was no relief in sight. Attempts to reduce population growth had been a fiasco. Contraceptives provided free of cost at the clinics were all but completely ignored. Women continued bearing an average of 7.1 children per woman, equivalent to the second highest country birth rate in the world, a rate that promised to double the population again in the next twenty years.

So in the face of what was skyrocketing population growth, rapidly deteriorating health status, and collapsing income, the first and only line of defense for the people of Jean Makout County, beside their own efforts, were the NGOs responsible for distributing foreign aid. But the aid appeared to be having no effect at all. Indeed, what I discovered and what I try to show in this book is that it was precisely the aid that was sabotaging the capacity of the Jean Makout economy, the social and medical systems, and the people living there to overcome the growing crisis that confronted them.

On the surface, it appeared quite different. To anyone dropping in for a short stay it appeared that aid organizations were frantically scrambling to keep up with an expanding disaster. In the village itself there were a half dozen charity headquarters equipped with the latest technologies, computers and Internet, dozens of motorcycles, four-wheel-drive vehicles, and a steady stream of highly educated foreign and Haitian consultants. In the rural areas there were dozens of reforestation and erosion projects, roads were constantly under construction or being repaired, and there were potable water projects, irrigation projects, clinics, nutritional programs, agricultural projects, and livestock breeding programs.

But beneath the surface it was a fiasco. Massive reforestation projects had consumed millions of dollars, but when I investigated they turned out to be decades-long failures. Irrigation projects meant for the poor turned out, when I investigated, to be owned by congressman and senators, doctors and nurses, engineers, and lawyers, some of whom were living in the United States. I could tell about a dike that became a dam and caused flooding and about a dam built at the cost of hundreds of thousands of dollars but that with the first heavy torrent snapped like a stick. I could tell about roads the NGOs built that became massive gullies. About twenty years and hundreds of thousands of dollars spent on BIGs (Bio Intensive Gardens that are small, highly productive vegetable gardens) that the peasants never paid the slightest bit of attention to but into which CARE International went right on pumping hundreds of thousands of dollars of aid. I could tell about a massive seed project in which, despite the fact that the Jean Makout rainy season is only three months, the NGO agronomists distributed long season seed varieties, causing the peasants who accepted and planted the seeds to lose their harvests, to be driven deeper into poverty, and I could then tell how the project was continued for four more years, how the peasants instead of planting the seeds took to soaking them to remove the pesticides and then ate them. I could tell about hundreds of barefoot doctors trained to the tune of hundreds of thousands of dollars and two years of effort, but when we tried to hire them for the survey, we found only five of whom could accurately take a pulse. I could tell about networks of local agricultural extension agents who were even more poorly trained, about the United Nation's million dollar fishing projects that were flops as well: Smoking pits going unused, *gran neg* (political bosses) commandeering refrigerators and solar panels meant for the storage of lobster, motor-powered fiberglass boats that never went to sea for any other reason than joy riding and sightseeing when local and visiting VIPs could afford the US$2 per gallon for gasoline. I could tell about all these failed projects and most bizarre of all, I could tell the same stories several times over for they have been repeated in Jean Makout and throughout Haiti for over half a century: The same projects, often in the same places, and always with the same result, failure.

But the point is not simply the waste. The waste was bad. It was a foregone opportunity to turn back the crisis. Worse, however, was the impact of the waste, for it seemed to be causing many of the problems.

Between the 1950s and the 1970s foreign aid had become the only significant source of wealth in the county and because of the associated corruption, negligence, and near total absence of any accountability, it had become a monster. All the politicians and any industrious, entrepreneurial, and ambitious individual focused on the NGOs. Politicians, schoolteachers, craftsman, contracters, they were all feeding at the trough of foreign aid. It was the singular economic force, the pace setter, the final and only front in the war being waged against a disaster that in retrospect I try show in this book was largely the making of the NGOs themselves.

What happened was that the NGOs were collecting money from donors ostensibly because they were able to show that Jean Makout—as well as elsewhere in Haiti—was in a state of dire emergency. The donors, governments, and individuals were responding, sending money and food in vast quantities. By the early 1990s 10 percent of *all* German overseas emergency food relief was being sent to that one tiny spot on the globe, Jean Makout County. The U.S. and French governments were also sending massive quantities of food. The money and food were sent to urban centers and then passed on to technicians, engineers, and doctors, all of whom were being paid handsome salaries to help defeat the massive crisis confronting the county. But the aid was being squandered on shoddy, poorly thought out, and even damaging projects in which no one was held accountable; the food was being indiscriminately distributed during harvest seasons when it was not needed, crashing crop prices for Jean Makout peasant farmers whom the NGOs were supposed to be helping, and in an ironic twist of good intentions, the food was, as will be seen shortly, increasing malnutrition. Indeed, food aid was perhaps the single greatest factor in destroying the peasant economy and creating the disaster that currently confronts not just Jean Makout

County but all of Haiti. And not least of all, both the food and the money were also being embezzled in terrific quantities and no one, absolutely no one, had ever, nor has anyone since, been indicted in Jean Makout for embezzling aid—and probably not in all of Haiti.

The only good that was being done was in the area of medicine. Vaccinations provided through NGOs were saving thousands of lives. But in Jean Makout only the French NGO was involved in medicine and they would soon abandon their medical projects, turn them back over to the Haitian state, whereupon medicines would disappear and doctors would quit showing up for work. This left the rather ironic scenario that when one arrived at the village hospital, one was greeted only by Cuban doctors and nurses on loan from the Castro government and blustering with frustration over the fact that the Haitian doctors had made off with the medicines, leaving them nothing to treat the impoverished patients.

The peasants fought back against the obvious corruption and abuse of them as bait for aid they never saw. They fought for the aid and they fought to change the situation. The fight began earlier in 1983 when Jean Makout farmers stood by aghast as teams led by *blan*—foreigners, in this case from the United States—and accompanied by Haitian soldiers searched out and slaughtered their pigs, a USAID-led multimillion dollar solution to an African swine fever epidemic on the island. With U.S. veterinarians supervising, Haitian military units swept through the countryside—in virtually all of Haiti and the neighboring Dominican Republic—riding down on the small semisubsistence farms and slaughtering the local Creole pig, a small, black animal uniquely adapted to life in rural Haiti. The peasants were to be paid for their losses but by most accounts military attachés kept the lion's share of the reimbursements and gave the peasants little and sometimes nothing for their dead pigs.

Following the pig eradication, the OAS (Organization of American States) spearheaded a massive pig repopulation project. But rather than introduce an economical pig similar to the ones eradicated, a type of pig that abounds on other Caribbean islands, U.S. experts prevailed on the OAS to introduce a hybrid from

Iowa—one that needed vast quantities of U.S. imported corn, water, and assiduous care to survive. The peasants vilified the repopulation centers as part of a U.S. plot to bilk Haitian farmers and it became a standing joke that *blan* had exterminated the *small black Haitian* pig so that they could replace it with a *big, white American* one. In Jean Makout the effort ended when members of *tet kole*, Haiti's most powerful peasant organization, attacked a center and slit the throats of the imported pigs.

Then, in 1987, in an event that ominously presaged the future fate of Jean Bertrand Arisitide and his Lavalas movement, a movement propelled by the poor, the madness that revolved around foreign aid dollars in Jean Makout County, climaxed with the tragedy accounted at the beginning of this book, a massacre not of pigs but people. What happened was that a young Catholic priest named Jean Marie Vincent, a liberation theologist and close associate of Aristide, had gotten control of a multimillion dollar development fund and began educating farmers on the merits of land reform and social revolution. His agropolitical action groups, called *gwoupman,* pressed for access to irrigated land that a few powerful and wealthy local families controlled but sharecropped to other impoverished peasants.

In defense against land reform, organizations called *antigwoupman* were formed and it was not long before all hell broke loose. On July 23, 1987 *gwoupman* and *antigwoupman* clashed, farmer against farmer. More than one thousand *gwoupman* armed with clubs and machetes were surrounded in a valley. With machetes slicing through the air, *antigwoupman* descended upon the *gwoupman* in overwhelming numbers, sending most fleeing for home. Those who stood to fight were killed; some on the field; others were bound and led to the Village of Jean Makout, where they were slaughtered in the streets. Throats were slit. Some of the captured were decapitated. As I recounted, one survivor had both hands chopped off. Soldiers stationed in the Village, reputedly sympathetic to the big landowners and the *antigwoupman*, simply watched. The next day the leader of the *antigwoupman* claimed before a foreign news camera that he had organized the killing of

1,042 "communists." The official number of dead was 139, but no one really knows.

Since the massacre, there have been other absurd, astounding, and violent incidences surrounding aid in the county. Peasants marched on the headquarters of German Agro Action Aleman (AAA), once even threatening over public radio to kill the director for cutting back food-for-work projects. A PISANO agricultural project was once physically destroyed in favor of an AAA project that peasants feared the former was supplanting. There were fights between peasants on other projects and fights between the foreign project workers themselves, as when AAA staff accused PISANO of undermining a bean project or, much more vehemently, accusations launched at CARE for undermining the work of other organizations. In one instance, ID staff came to renegotiate contracts with staff at the Jean Makout hospital and a crowd of booing hospital employees met them at the gate, the entire affair ending with hospital employees chanting "CARE, CARE, CARE" in expression of their preference for CARE, who was reputedly paying nurses ten times the rate that the State government and other organizations paid. (In the end the hospital employees got neither CARE nor ID.)

I could go on, and any foreign aid worker in the area at the time or since could surely add his or her own stories. But the point is that, for better or worse, after the massacre, the direction, will, and political organization to resist were gone. Subsequent efforts amounted to no more than fractured and desperate attempts to get a piece of the aid. Corruption, negligence, wanton distribution of aid, and the total lack of accountability ultimately defeated these feeble efforts as well.

In short, an industry of poverty emerged, one in which the university-educated consultants in the field and the masses of foreign charity bureaucrats back in the city and overseas derived their salaries, not from curing the poverty, but from its existence. When the money, materials, and food arrived in Jean Makout, the Haitian employees, politicians, administrators, pastors, priests, and school directors embezzled it and when they had accrued enough money, most of them migrated to Miami, the only option left for many. This left the poorer peasants behind to deal with the disaster that seemingly no one and nothing could abate.

The final ironic twist in this twisted labyrinth of systemic disaster was that the collapse of the economy and the failure of the NGOs to do anything to offset it— indeed drawing off the intellectual and entrepreneurial energy that would otherwise have addressed the problem—drove the peasants back into traditional livelihood strategies in order to survive. Those who could not escape watched the foreign market disappear and the local market crash under the weight of unrestricted imports from agroindustrial countries. With less cash they could not afford to invest in intensive production, to buy fertilizers and pesticides, special crop strains, and fruit trees or to fence livestock, or invest in water pipes, irrigation pumps, tractors, or tillers. They were forced back into a semisubsistence local economy, back into dependence on the associated household mode of production and in this way they were compelled to depend on labor-intensive survival strategies: two-hour walks to retrieve water, five to ten hours per day moving and caring for livestock, hundreds of hours per year tilling garden plots, processing the harvest in the most rudimentary and labor intensive ways, six hours per day of intensive food preparation, several hours gathering firewood, and long hours hand washing clothing. They were forced to make charcoal for sale in order to survive hard times, forced to cut more trees to pay for their children's school and medical bills. In doing so, in turning back to the household means of production to survive, peasants in Jean Makout County needed children more than ever and so they despised the contraceptives clinic nurses offered to them and they ridiculed the idea of fertility reduction and instead continued bearing large numbers of children and in doing so continued feeding a population explosion.

So reflecting on all this, I think about how the appropriate response to the big-boned militant nutritionist's sarcastic remark, "Why don't we pack up and go home?" might be "yes, if we really want to help, perhaps we should never have come in the first place." But that is not what I say. I simply thank the Germans for the opportunity to work and I go back to my hotel. To hell with it, I think, I did the best I could and now the job is over.

Back at the hotel, that evening, I am just falling asleep. The survey is over, done. The report has been turned in. The pressure's off. I am finally a free man again. There is a knock at the door. I drag myself out of bed to find a Haitian girl standing outside. She tells me there is a man downstairs to see me. I lean over the balcony and there, standing below looking up at me, is The Direktor.

"Would you come down for a beer?" he asks.

The hotel restaurant is a dirty, open-air, bare-cement patio where rats scamper in the shadows. Its only redeeming quality is that it is built out over the edge of the channel of La Torti, providing a cool breeze and, during the day, a spectacular view. Across the channel some five miles away is the Island of La Torti, as the Haitians call it, where the historic seed of Haiti as an independent country first took root 370 years ago with the buccaneers and the French filibusters. I try to discern the outline of the island with its more than one hundred thousand inhabitants and three thousand-foot high mountains. But I cannot see anything. Not a single light. I cannot even tell if the island is there. It is as if it has disappeared into the blackness of night.

The waitress serves each of us a beer and then, leaning over the table in the candlelight, The Direktor begins to speak.

"Let me tell you about the wind generators," he says with a mischievous smile.

As it turns out, the wind generators, the photograph of which had so infuriated the militant nutritionist, had been installed some ten years earlier, a gift from the German embassy, or what the Direktor calls "The Ministry." Purchased in Germany, shipped to Haiti, installed by experts, all at the total cost of several million dollars, the Germans apparently forgot about them, never having been informed that they only functioned for a few days before the Haitians simply shut them off. By the end of six months they had been vandalized.

But then, in 1998, only six weeks before this day, the same day that I presented the final report for the survey, the German Minister wanted to see the wind generators. Her term as ambassador was over, she was being recalled to Germany and so before she left she wanted to see an example of lasting good that her country had done in Haiti during her tenure. She called the Direktor to arrange a special visit. The Direktor called the Baie-de-Sol manager of Haiti's State Electric Company (EDH). The manager promptly sent out a crew to make the road up the hill to the wind generators passable.

The ambassador arrived and the Direktor led a convoy of five Mercedes SUVs up the road to the scenic heights overlooking the city where sat the five majestic wind generators. The motorcade rounded the final curve for the summit and there they were, the wind generators, guts ripped out, mangled wires protruding from bashed circuit boxes. Even the relay shack had been broken to pieces and the cement blocks carted off.

"The Minister was shocked," says The Direktor with a smirk, "it was a real eye opener for her."

"To top the story off," he continues, "the Minister left and the new Minister arrived four weeks later. The new Minister came to Baie-de-Sol and called a meeting with all the German organizations working in the area. During the meeting he announced that he had a vision." The Direktor looks at me quizzically, a wry smile comes over his face. "The new minister heard that Baie-de-Sol was a very windy place and would like to investigate the possibility of installing wind generators."

The Direktor winks. "And that my idealistic American friend is how foreign aid works."

The Direktor takes a log sip of his beer.

"You must understand," he says almost apologetically, "Foreign aid development programs are never long-term. We operate on three-year budgets. You have a sum of money and you have a program and you spend that money. If you do not spend the money, you failed. No one thinks beyond that. That is how it is done. It might not be right, but that is how foreign aid works."

Chapter Six
CARE International:
Dedicated to Serving Itself

In June 1999 I rode my motorcycle out of the county of Jean Makout, through desert scrub, up into the fertile and misty heights of the Massif du Nord mountain range, down into more desert scrub, through dry, rutted roads, and down a different coast. I glided over sandy roads, along the shores of the placid Gulf of La Gonave, headed back up and over more dry and barren mountains, skirted the flat port city of Gonaives and then picked up National Highway Route One, the principal highway that bisects Haiti. I rode along the pitted and pot-holed highway through choking clouds of dust, dodging oncoming traffic, cattle, goats, boulders, and the rusting skeletons of wrecked buses and cars, through more desert, across the Artibonite flood plain, a vast green patchwork of rice paddies, through the decaying port town of St. Marc and at last, as I barreled down a coastal asphalt road beside a beautiful aqua blue sea and then rounded a bend there, in the distance, shrouded in a haze of grey smog, I could see Port-au-Prince, the capital of Haiti.

"The Port of the Prince" is the Haitian "Big Apple," where people are proud to live; where is located 60 percent of all secondary schools and virtually all universities and state technical schools; where more than 90 percent of public employees work, and 87 percent of all government expenditures are made; from whence flow all political decisions, the commandments and revolutions that have shaped modern Haitian history and where today all foreign NGOs have their headquarters.

Sunburnt and covered with dust, I ride into the bowels of the city. The streets are crammed with traffic. Roaring, smoke-spewing trucks and muffler-less, teeth-grinding motorbikes shriek past. The main thoroughfares are pot-holed and dangerous. The stoplights do not function. Policemen stand in the streets waving vehicles on, trying to enforce some order on the gnarled, honking morass. Cracked and broken sidewalks and open sewers wait to sabotage the distracted driver or careless pedestrian.

The people in the streets are black-skinned African descendants and they are everywhere, teeming. People in suits and people in satin jogging pants, people sitting on the ground and on sidewalks, poor wretches leaning back against storefronts. Sinewy men in sweat-soaked rags push wheelbarrows. Women and girls sell chewing gum and cigarettes out of washbasins or peddle their wares off painted wooden tables. Casually dressed men, each with several cases of liquor stacked in front of them, line one part of a street. Market women walk along with loaded baskets and plastic tubs balanced on their heads. Heavy-set women sit at corners and on roadsides behind huge cauldrons of rice and steaming sauce, fried bread and sizzling morsels of pork. Groups of children walk by carrying gallon jugs. They prod and shove one another and poke sticks through fences at snarling dogs. A teenage girl with a five-gallon bucket expertly perched on her head strolls past like a young fashion model. People wait on the corner to cram into a bus painted in wild tropical colors. A flood of clean, scrubbed, and uniformed black youths cascade out of a schoolyard, the girls in smartly creased skirts and the boys in trousers and buttoned-up shirts. They flow through the streets, filling taxis and buses, pouring into snack shops. A girl, a child servant whose mother gave her away to a middle class family, runs by carrying a loaf of bread. I pass a group of homeless little boys, street urchins wearing unwashed rags, their uncombed hair in a patchwork of tight knots, and their skin crusty with scabies and mosquito bites. They call out to me as I ride by, "*Blan*, givme wun dola."

To the unaccustomed foreigner, Port-au-Prince is a sprawling slum that seems to promise nothing but filth, poverty, and disease. But to the people of the provinces, the capital is a wondrous place, beautiful and bountiful, full of hope and possibilities. It is where the fortunate go and where every Haitian sends his or her children at the first opportunity.

Moments later, I am winding up the mountain, leaving the hot city behind, and soon I enter the cool mountain heights, where smooth, patched concrete and asphalt roads curve through spacious neighborhoods. Big houses with swimming pools and tree-shaded flower gardens stand behind stone walls that are crested with embedded shards of broken glass, sharpened steel spikes, and looping rolls of razor wire. Satellite dishes and amateur radio antennas poke up through the tropical canopy. Mercedes and Jaguars sit parked in cobblestone driveways. It is to these heights that the gentry long ago began retreating from the rising tide of rural immigrants below. And it is in these heights, in the elite neighborhood of Petionville, where one finds the headquarters of CARE International.

The CARE office is located behind a ten-foot stone wall in the former mansion of a wealthy Port-au-Prince family that, when their fortunes changed with the bloody overthrow of a political regime, moved to France. I pass through an entrance guarded by four armed men, down a shaded walkway, through gardens, up the steps, and into the cool air-conditioned lobby of the stone mansion. Hung from the lobby wall is a poster that grabs my attention: a seminude black child with a distended belly. Written below the child are the words,

CARE
Dedicated to serving the poorest of the poor

Soon I am standing in a meeting room before a large mahogany banquet table. Seated before me, among a dozen empty and haphazardly scattered chairs, are three CARE staff members. I take a seat and they begin telling me that CARE has been operating in Haiti since 1954; since 1959 the organization has had an uninterrupted presence in Jean Makout County, where I have been working and doing research. CARE helps the peasants with their gardens, they build roads, they have reforestation projects. and hold education seminars.

"We currently supply food lunches to 1,999 primary schools, an endeavor that CARE is proud of," says one of the directors, a sharply dressed middle class white woman from Maryland. "In addition to the primary school feeding program, we have what are called MCHN programs. That stands for *mother, child, health, and nutrition* programs, in which we feed malnourished pregnant women and nursing mothers."

"What we are interested in," says another staffer, an elegant black woman from Hawaii, "is helping the rest of the most vulnerable people out there, the orphans, elderly, handicapped and terminally ill."

"It is of paramount importance that we help these people as soon as possible," cut in an assistant director, another middle class, middle aged white woman, this one from Denver. She adds, pausing to let her words take effect and looking at me with what seems to be heartfelt sincerity: "Conditions in the provinces are rapidly deteriorating and CARE is dedicated to creating a safety net for the most vulnerable people out there."

I take all this in without comment, trying to look enthusiastic. But what I heard in the CARE office, I already knew, was a world class line of bullshit.

It was in the city of Gonaives that two hundred years before, 1804, an African-born slave, Jean Jacques Dessalines, ripped the white out of the French tricolor and declared Haiti an independent nation, the second in the western hemisphere to throw off the yoke of European colonialism, thus freeing half a million slaves. From that moment on, Haiti constitutionally decreed all of its inhabitants to be black, no matter the color of their skin. It is also in Gonaives that today, on a hot, flat, asphalt road just outside of the city, one finds CARE's Food Security Support Unit (FSSU).

It is a modern two-story building with large tinted windows. Next door are five enormous warehouses, each over a football field in length and at least fifty yards wide. That is where I am headed, to the warehouses. I climb the steps to the loading dock, walk past more than a dozen shirtless and sweating Haitian men and enter through the massive doorway. I walk down towering aisles of food stacked twenty feet high. Thousands upon thousands of boxes of cooking oil and sacks of whole dry green peas, lentils, and those special concoctions, Wheat-Soy Blend (WSB) and Soy Fortified Bulgar (SFB)—referred to throughout the country as *blè*. The fifty-kilogram sacks and the cases of cooking oil are marked: "USA not for sale or exchange."

Each year some forty million kilograms of food moves through these warehouses, off-loaded from megaton ships in the Gonaives harbor, trucked to the warehouses, and then dispatched to primary school directors, nutritional clinics, and food-for-work programs throughout CARE's activity zone (pop 860,972). Or perhaps I should say, dispatched toward these objectives because, as will be seen, much of the food never gets where it's supposed to go. Still, it is a mammoth operation. In all, there are 700 employees, 158 motorcycles, 60 cars, 25 freight trucks, 2 dump trucks, 1 back hoe, 12 generators ranging from a 6.5 kW—that could run a U.S. household—to a 150 kW that could light up Jean Makout Village. There are CARE station bases and guesthouses throughout the three thousand square kilometer area the organization serves. In most areas, the CARE guesthouses represent the most advanced administrative and communicative technology in the region with their ham radios, food depots, and dozens of beds.

My job at this point is to evaluate the CARE food distribution process and so I head out into Haiti's Province—an area I had the advantage of knowing well-- to talk to recipients, representatives at the charitable institutions that receive food aid.

"Any food would be a great help," says Harry Zamilus, a well-dressed, middle-aged Haitian man who runs La Pwent

Hospital, the largest charity run hospital in the Province. "But we have had problems getting U.S. food aid."

As it turns out, CARE used to give the hospital food. Then deliveries became sporadic. Food would arrive in the middle of the night and be unloaded onto the ground outside the gate. They had to buy the night watchman a wheelbarrow so he could retrieve the food before it got stolen. Then, without any notice, the food stopped coming altogether. Harry went to CARE food headquarters in Gonaives, where the warehouses are located, and there he spoke with Paula, a German woman who was then head of CARE food distribution. Paula said that she would send someone out to the hospital. No one ever came. Harry went to Gonaives twice more but was not able to get past the secretaries to talk to any of the directors.

"The last time I spoke with Paula," Harry says in disgust, "was when I passed her and about twenty other CARE vehicles in caravan touring the area. I flagged her down and she told me that I would have to come to Gonaives. Can you believe it? Three times I had gone to Gonaives. That was all I could take. Let them do whatever it is they do with their food."

"CARE! Hmmph," grunt s Sister Michelle, the heavyset Haitian director of the Montfort Institute for Deaf Children, the most respected school for the deaf in the Province. CARE, she tells me, gave food to the school from 1991 to 1997. Then Dutch BND took over and they gave the food. But last year they ended their program, announcing that CARE would again be responsible for delivering the food.

"They informed us of this before the distribution ended, so to be absolutely certain we were not going to be left out, I went to Port-au-Prince to talk to CARE staff."

They directed her to Gonaives. She sent a letter. No response.

"Then it came time for school and no food."

So she went in person to visit the then CARE food director John Saloman.

"But he was in the field examining damage from Hurricane George and I didn't get to see anyone."

So she sent another letter to Gonaives. Then she went to see them again and she talked to a subdirector who said they would send a monitor to see her. No one ever came. That was a year before my visit.

"Well, that's strange," I tell her, "CARE feeds some 1,999 schools, 1,200 of which are in this province. Certainly you guys qualify as an elementary school."

"No, no, that is what I am telling you. We have tried and tried. We can not even get food as a school."

As I turn to leave Sister Michelle calls after me.

"CARE is a bluff. They're liars. I just about can't stand to see them anymore. Listen, if you don't send any food, don't come by here again, you hear."

And so it went, institution after institution, I heard the same stories: at St. Louis, at Bono, back in Baie-de-Sol. Many of the Catholic schools, the most credible institutions in the province, had been lost in the bureaucratic shuffle. Time and time again they had sought to get in touch with people at CARE and had been given a run around.

I am back in Gonaives at CARE's food distribution headquarters. In my hand I am holding a list of 1,999 schools on the CARE feeding program and I am talking to Seraphin, the Haitian director of food distribution.

I am perplexed.

"Why aren't these schools getting food? They are the oldest and most established schools in the region."

"There are schools," he tells me, "that we want to give food to, or increase the food to, but the schools are not managed well."

I am thinking to myself, how could anyone in Haiti say that Catholic schools aren't managed well when a sizeable portion of Protestant schools are run by directors who are illiterate and La Pwent, the very best hospital in the Province—often the only one functioning and which has a primary school for recuperating children—is unimpeachable?

Seraphin reads my mind, saying they have more students than listed. "You give them more food and two weeks later you visit and find they are twenty sacks short. What can you do?"

"But look here, you guys have a lot of schools on these lists. How do you verify them all? I mean according to the records the monitors have only been checking a couple schools a day."

I look down at the list and see that forty-seven schools were deselected in the single month of April 1999, but none in the fifteen months from January 1998 through March 1999.

"What's going on here?" I ask, showing him the discrepancy.

"That's the way they wanted it," Seraphin replies.

"Who is 'they'?"

"The higher-ups, the directors. We were told to keep those schools on the list. But we suspended a lot of schools."

Then he tells me the story about how the process began.

In April 1997 CARE was notified that because of a drought in the Province, the school feeding program would be increased from 585 to 1,287 schools. "We didn't know what schools were out there or even if there were that many primary schools."

So Seraphin obtained a list from an organization called FONDEP.

"But the list was no good. Many schools were listed twice and many schools did not exist."

The CARE monitors began what Seraphin refers to as "a rigorous verification process," explaining that, "we checked and double-checked every school."

"A rigorous verification process? But you guys only had eight monitors and one month to do something that cannot currently be accomplished in a year with twenty monitors. See look." I hold out a data sheet. "Says here that in the previous six months, 530 schools have not been visited."

Seraphin shrugs. "Actually, we had even less time than that. We did not even have two weeks. We were under a lot of pressure."

To illustrate how much pressure, Seraphin says that the CARE directors in Port-au-Prince called and said they were on their way by helicopter to Bassin Bleu, a remote region in the Province, and they wanted every school in the area to have food when they got there.

"In the end," Serafin says, "we simply sent the food out."

"Whether the schools existed or not?" I ask.

"We didn't have time to find out."

He goes on to explain that by October the project was finished. The food was supposed to be cut and the number of schools reduced to the original quantity. But word came down from Port-au-Prince to hold all the schools on the program. Meanwhile the monitors were finding schools that did not exist. They put these schools on suspension—meaning that they were getting food for them, but not delivering it. When they were finally told to reduce some schools, they threw out those that did not exist.

"What happened to the food sent for them?"

Seraphin appears confused. I decide I will get back to that later. I ask a different question. "How did you guys decide what region should be getting food?"

"The only criteria for providing food to an area is the ability to receive the food. It has nothing to do with whether one area is worse off than another."

"This means whether or not there is an institution with a warehouse?"

"That's right. It is not based on population nor is it based on the poverty. In fact, the poorest areas are those least likely to get any food because they have no infrastructure."

Later I again meet with Seraphin but this time he is accompanied by two foreign consultants, food aid experts from India who are in Gonaives for a three month contract. This is my opportunity to get back to the question about where the surplus food goes.

"I notice here in the figures you guys have given me that there is a 30 to 40 percent absentee rate in the schools. Where goes the 30-40 percent of food that does not get eaten?"

The consultants are SK and VJ. SK is fortyish, gray hair, distinguished. VJ is younger, in his mid thirties, with chiseled features and a compact, powerful build. Their job is to improve food distribution and handling from the dock to the warehouse to the schools. They are serious men, sure of themselves, and they have many ideas and opinions. They are looking right at me.

SK begins in that flat monotone English characteristic of East Indians, "We deliver the food. It is in our warehouse."

I think about this for a moment and decide that if they deliver the food, then it cannot possibly be in their warehouse.

"You mean it is in someone else's warehouse?"

"In the delivery process, we try to keep a surplus at the schools in case there is a problem."

"Yes, but the food that the children do not eat, you know, the children who are not there to eat it. The 30-40percent of the children who are absent, where does this food go? Do you give it to school directors?"

"We try to stay one month ahead all the time. That is the policy."

"That is not what I am talking about. What about the balance at the end of the month, where is this food? Do you make the directors account for it?"

VJ cuts in and starts telling me very authoritatively, "We always try to keep at least 15 to 25 percent of food on hand. In case there is some kind of crisis."

Well that is very interesting guys, I am thinking to myself in heightening frustration, *but what about the balance, you know, the food the kids don't eat because 30-40 percent of them are not there to eat it?* I don't give up. I keep at it, trying to get an answer.

"I understand what you are saying," Seraphin takes over. "We give that food to the teachers."

"You give it to the teachers?"

"No, I mean that we leave it with the directors, but they do not give it to the teachers."

"Oh no," SK perks back up. "They must account for it. I will give you a list."

That afternoon I get the list of food that is left with the directors, but it is bizarre. I also get more absentee lists. There are wild fluctuations in the percent of children fed, fluctuations that do not coincide with the absentee lists. I go to see SK to tell him that it is crazy and he eventually tells me they just started doing this.

"Wait, you mean this is the first time you have asked the teachers to account for the balance? This is the first list?"

"Well, we haven't really started yet."

"And this list?"

"Well, that is a list that we have."

I am sitting with Dr. Gaston, the director of Gros Mon hospital, and Mari Claude, his secretary. Dr. Gaston is telling me the now familiar story that the hospital used to get help from CARE, but it was cut off. One of the catholic sisters who works at the hospital asked CARE for renewed assistance but was told that CARE had "changed its orientation and no longer gives food to the sick." Dr. Gaston says that it would be good if they began giving to hospitals again.

"*Li ta pi judicial*," he says. "It would be more just."

"But," I point out, "CARE currently tries to feed all the primary school children. What could be more just than that?"

"I am not 100 percent against the school feeding programs. But those threatened with death and disease should be the first."

"What do you mean not 100 percent against? Is there something wrong with the school feeding programs?"

Both the doctor and 1the secretary look at each other and smile uneasily. Then Dr. Gaston turns back to me, "I have some doubts," he says, "that all the children really get fed."

"We have some doubts," echoes Mari Claude.

I am stopped, sitting on my motorcycle on a stretch of sandy desert road, cacti and scorched rocks as far as one can see, and I am chatting with a CARE food monitor who was sitting on his motorcycle. I befriended him years ago, before he began working for CARE. He has always been candid with me and so I am asking him, "Someone told me no more than 50 percent of CARE food reaches the children, do you think that is true?"

My friend looks at me as if I have said something stupid: "You are an intelligent guy," he says, "You have been around here for the past eight years. You know how things work. Think about it. It isn't 50 percent. I would consider it a miracle if the children get 10 percent of the food."

I am talking to Joseph, a retired steelworker turned missionary. Joseph tells me how one of the missions he works with is next door to an elementary school. Joseph befriended the school director and helped him get this and several other of his schools on the CARE feeding program. Later, Joseph asked to visit the other schools. The director was hesitant but eventually agreed so long as they went on predetermined days.

"When we got there," Joseph tellsme, "they were all full of students. I mean like there would be 150 students in one little room."

Then one day Joseph was at the mission and he watched as next door at the elementary school several Haitian men loaded CARE food onto trucks.

"I asked them where they were going and they said to Port-au-Prince."

Joseph wondered why they would be reloading food meant for rural school children and sending it back to the city. So being an adventuresome type, Joseph found his own way back to the schools he had visited with the director.

"Before," Joseph tells me, "when I visited with the director they had some 150 students. Now they had ten and fifteen students. What is that?"

I am back in Gonaives where the CARE food headquarters is located. Gonaives is surrounded on two sides by desert, one side by sea, and one side by a lush irrigated area. But Gonaives itself is a reeking, subtropical marsh of a city. In the midst of its own small quagmire and surrounded at a respectable thirty yards by overpopulated shanty towns, sits the CARE guest house. Peculiarly, it is modeled after an alpine ski lodge. It is made of timber and inside is a huge living room, large roughhewn and stained wooden beams support high vaulted ceilings. A bar partitions an open kitchen off from the rest of the room. Off the main salon, a hallway leads to a series of comfortable cottage-like rooms. At the end of the hallway there is a short flight of steps that leads to a loft. I drop my belongings in the loft and head out to find a French priest named Olivier who has been in Haiti for more than twenty years and who runs a home for the terminally ill.

Everyone, literally everyone, in Gonaives knows Father Olivier. I simply ask directions from the first person I encountered in the street and soon I am seated in his living room. The short, balding old French man with a face that looks like it was put on earth to be nice to children is standing in front of me scowling. "Yeah, yeah, you work for CARE. Get to the point."

I tell him that I am evaluating CARE food distribution.

"CARE has never given me anything," the priest says curtly and then, as if remembering, he walks over to the window and looks outside. "Except they fixed the road in front of my house." I too have gotten out of my seat and I am standing behind Father Olivier, a full head taller than him, staring out the window at the road.

You see there." he says, nodding toward the road, "Did a nice job too. I am glad." Then, somewhat absentmindedly, as if speaking to himself, he adds, "But I am not sure why they did it."

Then the little priest turns, looks up at me, and squinting says, "*moun ki bezwenn yo pa jwenn anyen,* "people who need, they don't get anything."

We sit down and he tells me about false CARE centers and a guy he once met who checked CARE feeding centers and found that all were, as he calls them, "zombies." He shakes his head. "Every single one he checked."

"A lot of CARE centers are trucks," the little priest explains. "They drive one truck out of town and load onto another truck, which comes right back to town. Go down to the market and you will find plenty of CARE food. Oil, cracked wheat, peas. CARE, CARE, CARE, all for sale."

I did go to the market. And the wizened little priest was right, there was plenty of CARE food. Cases of cooking oil, sacks of cracked wheat and peas stacked high. Just as the priest said, "CARE, CARE, CARE, all for sale." But it wasn't really CARE.

At least it didn't say CARE on the boxes and the sacks. It said
"USA."

The next day I raised the question with the CARE
consultants and they said that the food, "could," SK clarified,
"come from other distributors."

That same night I am dining in one of the finer of
Gonaives bad restaurants when I have a chance meeting with
Seraphin, the Haitian head of food distribution. He has been filling
me in on the recent history of CARE food distribution. We are
several beers into our conversation when I ask him, "Why is it that
the CARE directors don't seem to care about the food stealing? I
mean everyone knows. All you have to do is walk down to the
market."

"They do care," says Seraphin, "but it is very difficult for
them to do anything about it." He then tells me about a trip he
recently made with CARE executive Susan Ross and several
visiting VIPs. Seraphin explains that, "Susan wanted to show the
visiting VIPs the CARE feeding program in action."

Seraphin accompanied them on a tour of the Northwest.
When they arrived at the first school the school director said they
had already fed that morning and were going to feed again in the
afternoon.

"It was only 8:30 in the morning," Seraphin muses and
takes a slug of beer.

"Did they call the guy on it?" I ask.

"No" he says, "nobody said anything. We just got out of
there as fast as we could. It was a bit embarrassing for Susan."
They visited two more schools. Both were not feeding. "They also
gave lame excuses. We didn't visit anymore schools."

Next Seraphin talks about corruption. He tells me about the
1992 firing of all CARE food staff, saying there were jealousies
and people began snitching on one another for stealing food. "They
fired everybody." He tells me he knows several of the people who
worked with CARE at that time, "They made lots of money. Some
will never have to work again."

Then Seraphin talks about himself, about how he is different than other people in CARE. He says that his high integrity is due to his father.

"There are two things my father hated to see, thieves and free riders."

Six weeks later Seraphin would get fired from CARE for being, as his American boss explained to me without elaborating, "tricky; very, very tricky."

It is night and I am in my loft room in the Alpine lodge in the midst of the CARE quagmire, I am thumbing through CARE reports written to explain their activities and goals to USAID. It is incredible how neat everything is on paper, so thought out, so successful: I come across a summary of feeding that declare: "We have successfully fed by 10:30 a.m. in 80 percent of our schools." *Now how in the hell do they know that when they cannot even visit all the schools in a year's time?* I remember Seraphin's account of the three visits Susan Ross and her VIP pals made and how none of the directors were feeding at all. *It's a bald faced lie. "Successfully fed by 10:30 in 80 percent of our schools," my ass.*

In the Long Range Strategic Planning (LRSP) report for 1990-1995, CARE announced it was getting away from food, saying unequivocally, "it does not promote development." *Ah, so they know.*

In a 1995 CARE report: "Feeding is ineffective, we are shifting our focus."

Very good. Why haven't you done it?

In the 1995-2000 LRSP report CARE acknowledges the irony that it is still distributing massive amounts of food aid, attributing it to "unforeseen crises."

What the hell is going on?

I was soon to find out.

Back in Port-au-Prince at the CARE mansion, my supervisor at CARE tells me to visit charitable institutions headquartered in the capital, to "get a feel for how the other organizations work and how the food distribution system operates at the highest levels."

So I spent the next two weeks visiting other charitable corporations and doing research. I learned much about corruption, and the failings of the systems that are meant to deliver aid in Haiti. But more than that, I learned about CARE and the politics and economics behind food aid. I learned what the hell was going on.

Kari is American, mid–thirties, straight black hair, an easygoing, academic, activist type who works for Catholic Relief Services (CRS), another major food distributor, which is responsible for a region of Haiti separate than that of CARE. She was still working on her Ph.D. at Tulane—some configuration of public health and sociology. Her dissertation concerns the impact of food-for-work programs in Ethiopia where she was employed before coming to Haiti.

"There is something disturbing about food aid," she says and explains, "CARE and CRS revenue comes from two sources: Donations from organizations and individuals are one. But here in Haiti and in many poor countries the biggest source is food. CARE and CRS and many of the other big charities get paid a fee every time they transship food for USAID. They also get large gifts from USAID in what is called monetized food aid which means that USAID gives money but they give it to them in the form of food and the requirement is that the food must be sold on the local markets. Without food distribution CRS and CARE would be nothing. If we want to do other projects [of which at that time CRS Haiti had only one that did not involve food aid], we must distribute food. And we need income. We have costs. Twenty-some percent of all revenue that we take in here goes back to the headquarters in Baltimore to pay salaries and operating expenses. For CARE it is much more."

"Do you know that it is the sale of food aid that funds much of development?" I am back at CARE talking to Niche Pierre, an assistant director at CARE. She is an American citizen, grew up in California, university-educated, pleasant, intelligent black American woman who has been with CARE for some five years. She is telling me, "Five million of CARE Haiti's $15 million annual budget is from monetized food, food that we sell directly on the market. The rest of the money comes in cash from USAID and donations."

"I have problems with CARE." I am talking to Mary Grogan, a Canadian who has been in Haiti for twenty-three years. Mary is early- to mid-fifties with slightly graying auburn hair and an interesting short hooked nose that makes her look Arabic. She has been working for CARE for ten years and has eighteen days left, at which time she will become a CARE consultant. She is an education specialist and she has a gentle and apologetic way about her, the quintessence of serene, except that she never stops talking, albeit in a very soft voice. She continues, "I do not feel comfortable talking about it. I don't think that a person should work for an organization and then turn around and stab them in the back." But, she talks about it anyway: "There is something wrong with CARE's approach," she continues. "I don't think they are really committed to development. CARE has partners that help them, to use the exact words the directors use, 'deliver their services more cost effectively.' They talk about 'competitive advantage' vis a vis other charitable organizations."

"I find it interesting that CARE is supposed to be aiding the poorest of the poor," says Helga, a fiftyish, German, Ph.D. U.S.-educated CARE survey specialist. "But CARE's new policy in Haiti restricts all infrastructural activities to irrigated areas. These guys in the irrigated areas cannot possibly be the poorest of the poor."

I tell her about a study ten years before in La Valie, where I met Anaud and where Helga has recently done a survey on behalf of CARE. As it turns out CARE had just recently renovated all the irrigation canals there, something that Helga suspects was not for impoverished people at all. I tell her that she is right, that I did my master's thesis research in La Valie and there are some poor families that own land but that most is owned by elderly men. In my research I found that these men had on average twenty children, that the children predominantly live overseas and that included among them doctors and lawyers, one ambassador, and the two most powerful leaders in the Haitian legislature. "How is that for the impoverished?" I ask and she tells me that she finds it very interesting that CARE is not only often helping people who are in fact relatively wealthy, but also that she was looking at a list of private contributors and found that many were single working-class mothers, not wealthy people. She shakes her head. "It is as if the poor in rich countries are giving charity to the rich in poor countries."

A short while later she is concluding, "It just is not what you think it is. CARE began as a charitable organization of volunteers. Now it is professionalized. They do not even accept volunteers. Whenever I go out for dinner or to a party with my coworkers, the conversation always turns to pension plans and benefit packages."

"Am I working for CARE to help people or simply trying to find a way to get rid of food?"

I am in the comfortable office of Mike Harvey—not his real name—the director of food aid for USAID. A classic Washington type, mid-forties, slight, short, spry, gray-haired Colorado native who is a devout Republican and even looks and acts like he could be a member of the Bush family. His opinions are conclusive and passionate; his mind and manner quick and emphatic.

My question about whether I am helping CARE give away more food hits a nerve with Mike. "No," he snaps, "The food does not have to come. There is no politic that says it must come. But there are people very interested in it." Mike looks right at me. "There are organizations that have a strong interest in seeing food aid continue and," Mike points his finger directly at me, "you're working for one."

"Some people," I say, "think that it is USAID who is pushing the food."

"Yeah, I know all about it." Mike is flustered. "With my own ears I heard Phil Gilman [a former director of food aid at CARE] say that USAID forced CARE to take the food. It is simply not true!" Mike reddens, his voice rises, and he almost shouting "CARE has never once said they did not want the food or that people in Haiti did not need the food. If CARE said that, I don't think anybody in Washington would agree to give Haiti food."

The tension in the room is suddenly very high. There is silence and Mike is looking hard at me. He is on the defense. I am not sure what to do, so I change the subject, slightly.

"Does USAID know how much the average farmer in Jean Makout grows?"

"I think," Mike is calm now, his voice low. For me the topic has not really changed but it seems that Mike does not yet see what I am driving at. "I think that in the 1994 baseline study we paid CARE to find that out and they reported that households were dependent on agriculture for 30 percent of their income."

"Yes, but do you know how much food they are producing?"

"It's not in the CARE report?"

"No. CARE never measured it."

"Hmmm."

"I did. Or at least I asked a large sample of Jean Makout farmers. They claimed that in four out of five years they produce surpluses, big surpluses, surpluses well beyond their nutritional needs."

Mike looks at me with astonishment, "For Christ's sake!"

The story of what should be a crushing embarrassment for any developed world food aid worker begins with the fact that the quantity of food aid sent to Jean Makout is astonishing. During the mid to late 1990s, Jean Makout, a generally fertile agricultural region where in four out of five years farmers get surpluses, was receiving 8 percent of all the German government's emergency overseas food aid; at least double that, another 3,142 metric tons of food aid per year, was coming from USAID via CARE; the French government was financing ID with some 350 metric tons of food that they were required to monetize on the Jean Makout market.

Production Figures for Jean Makout Farmers

Table 1: Yields in kilograms per hectare (FAO, 1997)

Region		Corn	Beans	Sorghum and millet	Peanuts
Jean Makout	Mountains	172	201	—	1,273
	Plain	1,116	558	372	—
	World Average	4,130	662	758	1,336
	Africa	1,621	688	756	—
	Lowest Country Average	333[1]	236[2]	210[3]	—

[1]Cape Verde [2]Ruwanda [3]Botswana

Production figures reported in this survey (n = 104) appear low at first glance. Yields on the plain of Jean Makout are about 1/5th the world average for corn, 5/6ths the world average for beans, and about 1/2 the world average for sorghum and millet. But this image of production is obscured by the fact that farmers in Jean Makout intercrop. This means that the same low-altitude hectare that yields 1,116 kilograms of corn is simultaneously planted in pigeon peas, lima beans, pumpkin, manioc, sweet potatoes, and okra (see Appendix E). Corn and beans do not grow well in the mountains and farmers there reported expecting yields lower than the lowest country average in the world. But mountain farmers only marginally depend on corn and beans. Instead peanuts are the premier income-generating crop in the mountains and farmers enjoy yields respectably close to the world average (1,273 kilograms per hectare). Furthermore, peanuts are also intercropped with a variety of other plants, including tobacco, castor beans, sorghum, melons, squash, okra, pigeon peas, sweet potatoes, and sesame. Thus, if Jean Makout farmers can be believed, it would appear their gardens are not so unproductive. Furthermore, agriculture intervention specialists—foreign agronomists working in Jean Makout—unanimously report that local farmers could increase garden crop yields, and some estimate by as much as 300 percent, if only the farmers would use fertilizers and pesticides.

Conservatively, this worked out to about half a pound of food per day for every man woman and child in Jean Makout (see Appendix C for raw data). This was to say nothing of other smaller agencies. Dutch BND was not far away, there was also the Haitian

Baptist Mission, and at least ten other major organizations were feeding in the region, among them World Vision, Child Care, and Compassion International.

If this food aid was necessary, if it were not being stolen and resold on local markets, if it was arriving during times of need, and if it went straight into the mouths of hungry people, it would surely have been a good thing. No one would ever argue with that. But if delivered to farmers when they are not in need, stolen and sold on the local markets, as it was, it could only have a catastrophic impact.

Why? Any anthropologists or social scientist worth his salt could explain. But I'll let a peasant do it.

"What happens," says my friend Dajenson as we sit under a tree in his yard, "is, one, they deliver it and sell it on the local market when we are selling our own crops; two, even when they intend to feed it to the hungry, very little gets here. Most of it is stolen or embezzled and then sold. That crashes the market." The land around us is a fertile plain that stretches two miles to where the Masiff de Nord mountain range rises some three thousand feet up. "Look, you see out there," Dajensen points to the mountains, "there used to be irrigation chutes that came out of those mountain valleys and irrigated the plain. They're gone now. Nobody was interested in fixing them. But still, every spring, when it rains, the water floods across the plain here and irrigates our crops. Yes, we are farmers. This is a farming economy. Everyone from the teachers at school to the shopkeepers in the Village depend on livestock and gardens. See that plot there," Dajensen points again, "Judge Similus owns that one. And that one there, that's for the school superintendent. Even they are farmers. And there, that one is for my mother. She also has mountain land that she plants in the fall and she's got another plot up the road. She's harvesting something almost every month of the year." Our attention is drawn to the dirt road in front of his house. A train of market women approach, They walk single file down the road. Some of the women walk in front of their little donkeys. Several larger women are perched on top of mules. Sacks and bundles of fresh grasses for fodder are piled high on the animals. They walk by, the hooves of the animals kicking up little tufts of dust with each step. The first woman walks in front of a little donkey loaded with sacks of beans and millet and she greets us as she passes, *bonswa miseu,* "good afternoon gentlemen." A line of six other women and donkeys follow. They are on their way to the distant market in Baie-de-Sol where they can fetch the best prices for their produce. I knew many women such as these. They come from little homesteads out here on the plain of Jean Makout and up in the mountains. The women set out for Baie-de-Sol in the late afternoon and walk behind their loaded animals all night, fording streams and winding their way down trails worn deep into the earth, some of which have not changed course since the Taino Indians used them five hundred years ago. On a straight, flat stretch of road flanked by lush banana trees, the women come at last to their final obstacle, *Gran Rivié* (the Big River). Normally a meandering, knee-deep stream, rainfall in the mountains can quickly turn this tranquil creek into a muddy, life-threatening torrent that woman and animal must wade across to reach the city. Once on the other side, the women find themselves on the windswept dirt streets of Baie-de-Sol. They sell their produce among decaying vegetable heaps in a bustling, seaside market. After making their sales, many turn around and head home that very day, without ever having slept and without having purchased anything to sell back home because the Baie-de-Sol market has little to offer that can not be bought more cheaply in Jean Makout from the handlers of imported food-aid or from the *gran marchanns,* who ply their trade with Port-au-Prince.

"But we aren't subsistence farmers," Dajenson continues "We need cash. And we get cash from farming. And we got no way to store crops. Never once has any one of these foreign organizations tried to help us with storage technology. So when we can't sell our crops for a good price it hurts. We have to buy soap, water vessels, brooms. We have to pay school tuition, we have to buy books, pay bus fares to the city and, more importantly than anything else, we have to pay for medicines when one of our family gets sick. And brother, we get sick."

The damage food aid has on market prices is not a secret to the agronomists, nutritionists, and doctors who oversee NGOs in

Jean Makout. All of them—and I spoke with every one of them working in the area at the time—agreed, food aid hurts the market. In 1993 the director of French ID went so far as to measure it. He tracked the impact of 225 metric tons of corn his organization sold on the local market during the spring harvest season (March to June). With the first delivery, the market price for local maize fell by 50 percent; with the second delivery it dropped another 20 percent; and with the third delivery it dropped yet another 10 percent (Table 2). The director was concerned about the impact on the local economy and there was unanimity among the agronomists and nutritionists that ID should try to avoid selling food during the harvests. But they did it anyway. And then they did it again in the spring of 1996. And they did it yet again in the spring of 1999.

Why did they do it? Because the French government gives them support in the form of surplus French corn under the condition that they sell the produce locally. Why do they sell it during harvest season? Good question. Perhaps because they have no choice. They have to meet payrolls. After all, NGO employees must eat too.

Table 2: Corn price variation by ID imported corn deliveries (in *gdes*)

Date of delivery	Comments [made by ID director]	Local price* 1993
15 Apr 1993	Before introduction of French corn	13.0
7 May 1993	First introduction of French corn	6.0
14 May 1993	Additional delivery	5.0
21 May 1993		5.0
28 May 1993		5.0
4 June 1993		5.0
11 June 1993	Two more trucks of French corn arrive.	4.5
18 June 1993		5.0

*per mamit; price in Haitian gourdes.   Unpublished ID Report, 1993

German AAA's staff also followed the impact of their food distribution on the market and became so convinced that food aid pushes market prices down, that in 1999 the director called for a halt to the food program. This was not the first time. When I talked to the director he told me that the 1998–1999 AAA project had originally been designed to turn the process on its head and buy local produce for redistribution in food for work projects. "To help the farmers and stimulate production," he explained to me, "like we do in our own countries." But these plans had never materialized. Not for ID, not for AAA, and not for any of the other foreign charities working in the region. Instead, what always seemed to happen was that little food was sent to Jean Makout when it was needed but, when it was not needed, the area was inundated with it.

During the summer drought of 1997 the United Nations World Food Program (WFP) allocated fifty tons of emergency flour to the Commune of Jean Makout. But the food did not arrive until a full year later, in the middle of the bumper crop of July 1998. Again in September 1998 the WFP issued emergency food aid, this time because of destruction from Hurricane George. But again the food arrived in May 1999, eight months after the crisis had passed and, again, right in the middle of a good harvest. PISANO distributed no food during the 1997 drought—a crisis severe enough to warrant international media attention and a visit from a team of U.S. congressmen (they landed a helicopter on the village soccer field, churning up an enormous dust cloud and blowing the roofs off of three houses). But, during the spring bumper crop of 1999, PISANO distributed 250 tons of rice and beans.

In the thirteen-month period from September 1996 through October 1997, a period that began in the midst of a good harvest but ended with the summer drought mentioned above, ID and AAA gave away enough food to meet the caloric needs of every one of the 130,320 men, women, and children in the commune for 68 days, or approximately 1 of every 6 days of the year. For at least part of this period, and for the minority of the needy who actually received any of the food, it helped stave off crisis. But in the six months from November 1998 through April 1999, a period that according to farmers included the most bountiful harvest in thirty years, ID and AAA joined PISANO to distribute an average of 15 percent more food per month than during the 1997 summer drought (see Appendix C).

Witnessing all this and then working with CARE, I decided that food aid had to be having a devastating impact. It had to. So I tried to reconstruct food deliveries and compare it to changing health status of people living in the area. It was not easy.

I asked Mike Harvey at USAID, but they didn't have any long-term data. I wrote to CARE and they didn't have any either. Nor did PISANO, nor did AAA, nor did ID have any data that went back more than six years. Nor could I get data on changes in health. All the organizations claimed to specialize in health, derived large portions of their budget specifically from nutritional programs, but none of them reported having any longitudinal nutritional data. None. Finally, I hit on something. CARE had already done exactly the type of research I was after: Indeed, as it turned out, CARE was the champion of poorly timed food deliveries and they had documented the catastrophic impact it had on child nutrition.

Here's what happened. In 1993, all of Haiti was suffering from an embargo that the international community had imposed against Haiti's military junta. The region in and around Jean Makout was experiencing the additional hardship of a prolonged drought, something the poor in Jean Makout wittily called the "second embargo"—the first one was from the United States; the second one, the drought, from God. Coming to their aid eighteen months after the drought began, CARE expanded its school and emergency feeding programs in their activity region that includes Jean Makout. The number of intended beneficiaries grew from 164,000 in May 1993 to 708,200 in June 1994 (out of a total regional population of 860,972 people).

CARE staff defined what they did as a well-intended gesture. Niche Pierre, the CARE director mentioned earlier, had told me that the aid was to offset droughts and the embargo. And it's hard to disagree with that. People in the region were suffering. But here's the catch. The drought ended in 1993. Harvests once again became bountiful. Yet CARE continued to swamp the region with food aid for the next two years. I plotted on a chart the

CARE-distributed aid over a six-year period (the only six years for which I could obtain data) and compared it to the embargo and rain cycle (indicators of drought and need). There was no relationship at all (see Chart 1). Or rather, there appeared to be a nearly perfect relationship, but in the wrong direction. CARE consistently distributed the most aid not during the embargo and droughts, when it was needed, but after the embargo had been lifted and during periods of heavy rainfall, the best harvest years, when it was not needed at all.

Chart 1

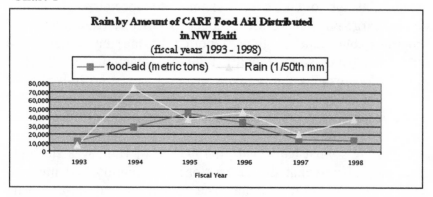

When I discovered this, I remembered two CARE health reports in which nutritionists had evaluated child nutritional status in the area—one report was for 1994 and the other for 1996. I found them. As it turns out, I subsequently discovered from the nutritionists involved in the evaluations, they had done these nutritional assessments precisely so that they could evaluate the impact of the food program. And what they found was that child nutritional status worsened during 1994–1996 feeding program. I looked the data over again. Precisely when CARE swamped the Province region with enough U.S.-subsidized surplus grain to meet more than 20 percent of the population's food needs, CARE researchers found that the number of both chronically and acutely malnourished children increased more than 20 percent. So what I was looking at was that children were better nourished at the end of the two year drought (1992–1993), before USAID and CARE came to the rescue, than they were after the subsequent two years of unprecedented "relief."

Table 3: Percentage of child population malnourished in CARE activity area
(CARE 1997; CARE et al. 1996)

Indicator of malnutrition	Year	
	1994	1996
General (WAZ)[1]	16.7	21.6
Stunting (HAZ)[2]	19.8	23.9
Wasting (WHZ)[3]	3.8	4.7
Normal	69.7	50.8

[1] Weight for age [2] Height for age [2] Weight for height

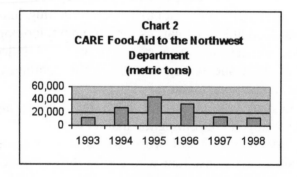

Chart 2
CARE Food-Aid to the Northwest Department
(metric tons)

Table 4: Chronic (HAZ) nutritional status by age

	Nutritional status (n= 474)	
Age in months	Malnourished (1990)	Malnourished (1997)
0 thru 72 months	29.9%	45.9%

PISANO Survey c. 1990, NHADS Survey c. 1997

"You can't be sure about that," says Niche Pierre, the assistant director who told me about monetized food aid. "There were a lot of other things going on."

"Such as?"

"There was the embargo."

"It was over."

"There was the drought."

"That's the point, it too was over. In fact, it was over six months after you guys started the feeding program, before you guys quadrupled the number of beneficiaries. And look, we're talking about the heyday of CARE food relief in the area."

"Look," Niche says, and she makes an odd change in direction, "many of the people who work for CARE, especially those of us who studied development before getting into this job, we don't like food aid." She pauses for a moment, looking at me as if to let the impact of her words sink in. And indeed, I am astonished at what she is saying. "But," she continues, "there's nothing that can be done about it."

"How can you guys ever hope to promote agricultural production when you are ruining the market with food?"

"Every consultant who works for us says the same thing."

"Wait. Every consultant who comes through here says that food aid is disruptive?"

"That's right."

"And you guys go right on delivering it?"

"I have told you, the problem is there is no money available to buy local produce and it is monetized food aid that keeps CARE alive."

Chapter Seven
The American Plan:
How to Destroy an Agricultural Economy

As it turns out, CARE had become involved in what was a very deliberate undermining of the Haitian peasant economy, the cornerstone of a plan that the World Bank and USAID had designed. This is how it happened.

Back in the 1970s, Haiti, like many countries in Central America and the Caribbean, was largely rural, its inhabitants small-scale farmers, and it had poor road, communication, educational, and health systems. It was underdeveloped.

Haiti's underdevelopment was arguably a more pressing problem than in other small countries in the region because at 168 people per square kilometer in 1970, it had a population density twice that of neighboring Cuba (76 people per square kilometer) and almost twice that of the neighboring Dominican Republic (91 people per square kilometer—see CIAT 2005). Over 95 percent of Haiti was reportedly deforested, causing erosion so severe that reputable scholars were already referring to it as the worst in the world (Lundahl 1982:7a). Erosion affected more than Haiti: the runoff that billowed from Haitian rivers into huge underwater clouds contributed to the destruction of ecologically sensitive corral reefs throughout the Caribbean. Something had to be done. The United States was the country that for almost one hundred years had taken upon itself the responsibility of policing and developing the area. It had already invaded Haiti twice before, Cuba four times, the Dominican Republic three, Honduras seven,

Nicaragua seven, Panama four, Guatemala and El Salvador once each (Grossman 2001). Moreover, there were new opportunities on the horizon. The promotion of overseas sales of U.S. corn, wheat, cotton, and rice was high on the U.S. congressional agenda. From 1986 to 2000, government subsidies for these products was 38 percent per year (Reidl 2004; Roberts and Jotzo 2002; Roberts and Jotzo 2002). There was also the EU, including France and Germany, which were also aggressive promoters of their own farm products. The EU subsidized the same grain products mentioned above at an even greater rate than the United States, 48 percent (Ibid). There was also the offshore industrial sector, particularly the one hundred billion dollar garment industry, something the U.S. government had begun to "cultivate" in Haiti as far back as 1971 when in exchange for supporting the continuation of the Duvalier dictatorship from father to son, the Haitian government agreed to create an environment hospitable to U.S. investors in the assembly sector. Custom taxes were eliminated, a low minimum wage guaranteed, labor unions suppressed, and U.S. companies given the right to repatriate profits. By 1980, there were some two hundred mostly U.S.-owned assembly plants in the country (McGowan 1997).

It is at this juncture that the U.S. government, working through USAID and the planners at the World's Major international lending institutions—the World Bank, The Inter American Development Bank (IDB), and the International Monetary Fund (IMF), all U.S. and secondarily E.U. controlled—were led by USAID in adopting policies that, with perhaps the best of intentions, would destroy the Haitian economy of small farmers.

Calling it "economic development," the growth prospects of the assembly industry meant that migrants to urban areas were economically useful as factory workers, something that justified eliminating farming as an alternative livelihood strategy. The objective conveniently articulated with those of U.S. agricultural interests and the conservationist goal of moving peasants away from destructive hillside cultivation of bean and corn crops that caused so much of the erosion mentioned earlier. The logic seemed overwhelming.

So a plan was hatched.

At that time they called it the "American Plan." For the rural areas, the policy planners envisioned neat rows of high tech agriculture, coffee, mango, and avocado plantations, and modern factory-style poultry barns. For the urban areas they envisioned burgeoning industrial parks to which the peasants could migrate and be transformed into factory workers. The new Haiti would undergo, "an historic change toward deeper market interdependence with the United States" (AID 1982, quoted in DeWind and Kinley 1988:61), a relationship that would release the "latent Haitian agro-industrial potential waiting to explode" (USAID 1982; Quoted in DeWind and Kinley 1988) and, as USAID Administrator Peter McPherson testified before the U. S. Congress, would ultimately "make the prospects for Haiti as the 'Taiwan of the Caribbean' real indeed" (quoted in DeWind and Kinley 1988:61).

The plan might not have been such a bad idea. Haiti clearly needed help. But it didn't happen like they said it would.

A good example of the impact of the policies that came about was the Haitian rice industry. Until the 1980s, Haiti was almost entirely self-sufficient in rice consumption, something made possible, in part, by protecting Haitian farmers from the heavily subsidized rice produced in the U.S. and Europe. Twenty percent of the Haitian population was directly involved in the industry. But in the political chaos of 1986—the year that the last Duvalier regime was ousted from power—USAID used the promise of continued political and financial support to negotiate a lowering of tariffs on rice from 35 to 3 percent. U.S. rice—subsidized at a rate that varied during the 1980s and 1990s from 35 percent to 100 percent—flooded into the country. By 1996, 2,100 metric tons of U.S. rice arrived in Haiti every week, an annual loss to impoverished Haitian cultivators of about 23 million dollars per year (Webster 2006; U.S. Department of Commerce 2006; Georges 2004). Haitians were not even left the luxury of controlling the importation process. About half of the imported rice came in under a monopoly held by RCH (The Rice Corporation of Haiti), a U.S.

corporate subsidiary with lobbyists in Washington D.C. (WHO 1995; Tayler 2006; Georges 2004).

To justify their actions, USAID funded reports that Haitian farmers could not feed the nation. The reports came from experts like Haitian-born, Harvard graduate, Tulane professor, private consultant Augustin Antoine Agustin MD, PhD, MPH (1993, 1997) who also happened to be one of the largest owners of private clinics in Haiti, owner of a major NGO that depended on charitable donations, and owner of Xaragua Resort, a for-profit enterprise that CARE contracted for lavish banquet dinners and seminars. Agustin and other consultants for USAID and the organizations that were paid to distribute food made detailed calculations of massive food production deficits predicting increasing malnutrition and famine if something was not done (see also USAID 1977; UPAN 1982). In a more recent report Agustin (1999) cited thirty-two sources going back to the 1950s, sources that justified the argument that Haitian farmers could no longer feed themselves, much less the Haitian urban population.

But where the production figures come from is a mystery. As seen in Jean Makout, no one was monitoring food production. No one, that is, except for one group of consultants I forgot to mention. In 1993 CARE hired a group of researchers from Auburn University. The researchers reported that farmers in the region were producing 800 kilograms of corn per hectare, translating to a calorific quantity considerably in excess of nutritional needs of the average family in the area. The report was ignored (SCID 1993).

The irony of what I am describing was captured at the national level in a report written by Food for the Hungry International. Funded by USAID, consultants working for Food for the Hungry International (FHI) went into Haiti to "improve" the food security program. Just like Antoine and others who had a vested interest in showing the need for more food aid, FHI consultants began their report with an impressive summation of statistics and indicators showing that Haiti was indeed suffering a frightening food production deficit. But, tongue in cheek, the authors then wrote,

In our visit to Haiti, we were also hoping to gather regional level data on agricultural production. Unfortunately, we were told that no such data exists. In a visit to the Ministry of Agriculture, we found out that agricultural data collection leaves a lot to be desired and as a result, there is a paucity of regional information. To remedy that, in 1994, USAID and the Title II Cooperating Sponsors established the Interim Food Security Information System (IFSIS) to "collect, analyze and monitor food security indicators." It is hoped that this initiative will begin to address this critical area of agricultural data collection. (FHI 1999:5. All punctuation in original report)

So, twenty years after the supposed rush to save Haiti from underproduction and five years after USAID launched a Food Security Information System to measure production, the reality was that no one knew what production was.

Moreover, the tip off that the prevailing U.S. political interests had little if any sympathy for impoverished Haitians was that it was decided that Haiti's farmers needed, not to produce more food or adopt better techniques, but rather, as seen, to import food from the United States and Western Europe. To help get the process started they began selling grains and beans at below market prices and, indeed, giving them away.

Food assistance to Haiti during the 1980s tripled reaching a yearly average of over $50 million in gratuitous U.S. surplus beans, corn, rice, and cracked wheat. Put in simpler terms, that was enough food to meet the calorific needs of over 15 percent of the Haitian population. As seen in Jean Makout, this food was not only given away free as a type of welfare, but granting the politicians foreign aid in the form of grain brought the Haitian government into the act. There was one stipulation, however: they could have the food; and they could sell the food for money; but they had to sell it on the Haitian domestic market.

Multinational charitable corporations working in the country also received grants in the form of food. In the 1990s, for example, $5 million of CARE Haiti's $15 million annual budget came from USAID in the form of grain and beans that it was obligated to monetize on the Haitian market.   And the United States was not the only supplier of food destined to be monetized. The German and French governments, also interested in the assembly sector, joined the fray and gave food to "NGOs" from their respective countries with the stipulation that the food be monetized in Haiti. The tiny agricultural country was so thoroughly inundated with surplus food from the United States and Western Europe that Port-au-Prince merchants were soon re-exporting cracked wheat to Miami retailers (DeWind and Kinley 1988:69–70).

The consequence throughout Haiti was the same as in Jean Makout: the near total destruction of the agricultural economy. Ships left Haitian ports empty and returned with their holds packed with hundreds of thousands of tons of United States, German, and French surplus and subsidized wheat, rice, corn, and beans. Meanwhile, throughout Haiti one could find avocadoes, oranges and even mangoes rotting on the ground or being fed to pigs. Or rather, they were being fed to pigs until 1981. Up until then, foreign agronomists considered the small and hearty Haitian pig a mainstay of the peasant's survival strategy. But as seen in Jean Makout, during the early 1980s the U.S. veterinarians led Haitian soldiers on a wholesale search and destroy mission after the endemic Haitian pig, the USAID-led multimillion dollar solution to an African swine fever epidemic on the island. Many observers say the peasants never recuperated from the eradication program. But whatever the case, there were plenty of other problems down on the Haitian farm.

While the rice industry was crumbling, the U.S. government also removed Haiti's sugar quota. By 1988, sugar exports had dropped to zero and by 1995, Haiti, once counted among the greatest sugar producers in the world, was importing twenty-five thousand tons of U.S. sugar per year (Hallward 2004). Increasingly stringent and protectionist U.S. sanitary and phytosanitary regulations—restrictions on pests and bacteria— meant that most other agricultural exports from Haiti were also eliminated. Condemning the produce as inferior quality or contaminated, USDA inspectors forbade or severely limited the importation of Haitian cacao, sisal, essential oils, and cotton exports, all of which subsequently shrank or disappeared entirely as Haitian export crops. Coffee, which still comprised 70 to 80 percent of Haiti's agricultural exports in 1990, fell from eighteen thousand metric tons in 1987 to six thousand tons in 1995 (Alphonse 1996). By the 1990s, domestic agriculture sector was shattered. Accounting for 52 percent of Haitian exports in 1980, agriculture comprised 24 percent in 1987; 21 percent in 1990; and by the mid 1990s the only produce coming out of Haiti were a few mangos and a trickle of coffee, something for which USAID, in a bid to shore up its image, was claiming as a consequence of its own efforts (Lenaghan 2005; USAID 2006). But for the vast majority of the 70 percent of the Haitian population that farmed, already among the poorest people in the Western hemisphere, life got much harder.

The Haitian government, while perhaps never of much assistance in helping its farmers, was now brought into full cooperation in *destroying* their livelihoods and trying to push them into becoming urban factory workers. In 1989 only 5 percent of the national budget went to the Ministry of Agriculture, Natural Resources, and Rural Development (Wikipedia, 2006). In hopes that small farmers would abandon the rural areas for urban factory jobs, the seven hundred thousand small plantations were left to wither. Meanwhile, customs taxes on industrial products had been eliminated, a low minimum wage guaranteed, labor unions suppressed, U.S. companies given the right to repatriate profits, and, guided by USAID, whose consultants were helping Haitian politicians draw up the budget, the Government invested instead in the construction of two of Port-au-Prince's four major industrial parks (McGowan 1997; Library of Congress and CIA World Fact Book 2006).

There was something else going on as well. The economic destruction and deliberate drive to keep the Haitian masses poor by focusing on holding wages low and avoiding investments in alternative domestic production or services was having another effect: it was driving the educated and entrepreneurial classes out of the country. The Haitian "boat people" were one conspicuous aspect of this migration. But they were only a small one.

Between 1970 and 1991, a total of one hundred thousand boat people reached the U.S. mainland (Rocheleau 1984; Saint-Louis 1988; *New York Times* 1991); but in the same period, more than one million elite and middle class Haitians boarded commercial flights and emigrated to the United States, France, and Canada (Haiti had a population of about six million during the 1980s). Some 90 percent of these migrants came to the United States. Entry was achieved legally, by applying for immigrant status, and illegally, by skipping out on nonimmigrant visas. Twenty percent of the country's seven million inhabitants had left; as much as 90 percent of the elite had gone (Schwartz 1992).

Even "boat people," often referred to in U.S. newspapers as "economic refugees fleeing poverty," represented the upper echelons of the peasantry. Rocheleau (1984) found that the average boat person had at least 5.6 years of education—enough to teach primary school in rural Haiti, and seven times the .75 years of schooling attained by the average Haitian peasant they had left behind. In a South Florida study of lower-income Haitian migrants enrolled in English courses, Alex Stepick (1984:347) found that 67 percent were semi skilled; 31 percent had between one and six years of education; 45 percent had some secondary school; and 26 percent had attended commercial, short courses, or vocational training. In a country where only 23 percent of the population is literate and few are technically skilled, these represent tremendous losses in human capital (World Almanac 1990).

To anyone looking back over the decades, it was already clear at that point in time, 1990, that things were going terribly awry. In the 1950s, 60s, and 70s, before the American Plan went into full effect, Haiti was neither significantly better nor worse off than most countries in the Caribbean and Latin America. As we've seen, population density was a high 168 persons per square kilometer in 1970 and that was a problem. There was widespread deforestation, massive erosion, and high rates of illiteracy. But the argument could also be made that it did not have to be as great a problem as it was. The population density in Haiti was lower than in Puerto Rico at 302, Trinidad and Tobago at 187, El Salvador at 176, and Jamaica at 169. Per capita GDP was actually higher than most Central American countries (Chart 1); child morality was high, but it was comparable to that of Bolivia, Honduras, and Peru, countries that today have child mortality rates less than half that of Haiti (Chart 2). Moreover, from 1967 to 1980, Haiti's real GDP grew at a respectable average of 2.5 percent per year. But then, in 1980, while income for other countries in the region increased, Haiti's stagnated. From 1985 to the present it moved backward, declining at a rate of 2 percent per year (IMF 2005). Plummeting health and infrastructural conditions echoed economic ruin. And yet, despite the "American Plan" and all the other "development" efforts, birth rates and population growth did not, as in other countries of the region, decline. Not even the massive emigration seen earlier significantly offset population growth. At 295 people per square kilometer in 1999, Haiti had almost twice the 1970 population density (United Nations 2005). No relief was in sight. Despite the highest per capita expenditures on contraceptives in the western hemisphere, the birth rate in rural areas, where 65 to 70 percent of the population still lived, was six births per mother, the highest in the Western hemisphere. Contraceptive use rate was the lowest, 21 percent (UNICEF 2006). The result was a population growth rate of 2.2 percent. The population of Haiti could be expected to double in the next thirty years.

Chart 3: GDP (deflated) in Central American countries
from 1945 to 2000 (source: Globalis 2007)

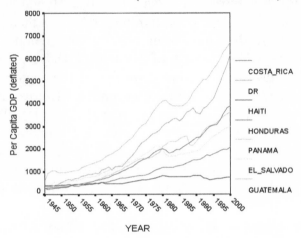

Chart 4: Child mortality for select countries, 1960–2000

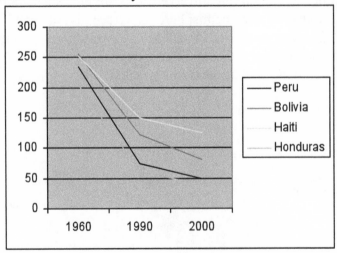

(UNICEF 2006)

Dismal as it may seem, proponents of the American Plan could still say that the plan might be working. Wealthy Haitian entrepreneurs and foreign investors could still make an argument that the economy was in a state of transformation, that the poor would enjoy long-run benefits, indeed be saved from themselves by reducing erosion and rural population pressure. The poor were, after all, moving into the cities. Rural population was declining at a rate of 2 percent per year while the urban population was growing at 4.1 percent (CELADE 1999). And there were jobs. With names like Disney, Levi's, and Nike, Haiti had one of the largest assembly sectors in the developing world. Estimates of the number of workers at the time run as high as eighty thousand to one hundred thousand people. Wages averaged less than $2 per day; no viable pension plans, nor healthcare, nor disability, nor unemployment insurance. And it was precisely during this period that the Haitian economy began to move backward, per capita GDP declining 2.5 percent per year between 1980 to 1985; and it fell in half in the years 1986 to 1991, going from $419 to $225 (UN Globalis 2006). But yes, it could still be said in 1990 that the plan to transform the economy to a vigorous industrial power might be working, might.

Then things really started to go wrong.

In applying their economic designs and sanctioning free elections to democratize Haiti and make it amenable to overseas capital investors, USAID, E.U., World Bank, IMF, and IDB planners seemed to have forgotten the very reason they had come to Haiti to promote industry in the first place: Most Haitians were desperately poor. When fair elections, another part of the development initiative, finally took place, the Haitian masses overwhelmingly voted for former priest and leftist Liberation Theologist Jean Bertrand Aristide.

Condemning capitalism as a "mortal sin," Aristide raised the minimum wage and implemented reforms that militated against privatization and the proletarization of the Haitian poor. USAID reportedly spent $26 million defeating his wage hikes; but not enough to constitutionally stop the priest and his reform movement. Seven months after being elected, a group of CIA-trained and -financed military leaders packed Aristide aboard a plane and sent him into exile—for the first time (Chomsky 2004; DeRienzo 2004; Dupuy 1999; Driver 1996; Jenson 1994: 79–81).

The Bush administration looked rather guilty. Its leaders were, of course, ardently in favor of democracy and, publicly at least, the coup appalled them. But Aristide and his reforms were apparently not what they had in mind when they said "democracy." Following a meeting between Bush and Aristide, the U.S. president's spokesman told the press, "The U.S. supports democracy in Haiti...But we don't know if President Aristide will return to power" (Heinl and Heinl 1996:700–29)

The U.S. ambassador and other diplomats were soon highlighting the atrocities of the Aristide government, atrocities that were in fact not the works of Aristide, but of mobs that supported him and that, even then, paled in comparison to the numbers of people previous administrations had killed and amounted to only a miniscule fraction of the slaughter, rape, and torture the new military junta was carrying out at that very moment (Chomsky 2004).

But whatever they had hoped for, the Bush administration now had a mess on its hands. In New York City a crowd of one hundred thousand Haitian emigrants marched through the streets in protest. In the two months after the coup, seven thousand Haitian refugees were intercepted at sea and soon a tent city of refugees swelled the U.S. Navy base at Guantanamo Bay, Cuba, to its 12,500 capacity. Journalists covering Haiti were sending pictures and video footage of the hundreds of boats being built on Haitian shores in preparation for more voyages to Guantanamo and Miami. The Coast Guard braced for an onslaught of refugees and U.S. immigration courts were overflowing with indignant lawyers. The Organization of American States and the United Nations vehemently condemned the coup and the Bush administration, said to be providing secret financing to coup members, was under heavy fire.

Plunged into renewed political instability, the years 1991– 1994 were marked by repressive military rule within Haiti and a U.S.-led international embargo from without. Assembly plants in

Port-au-Prince closed. In 1994 there were only four thousand assembly plant workers, down from a high of one hundred thousand three years before; four hundred thousand of the urban poor left the city and returned to the countryside where they had not yet severed ties, back to dependence on semisubsistence rural household livelihood strategies characterized by destructive hillside farming, intense labor demands, and high premium on child labor, practices that meant continued high fertility (Naval 1995; CPT 1998).

Meanwhile something else was happening. The embargo meant no petroleum, no imported goods, and no raw materials for industry; previous importers became smugglers of CDs, cars, fuel and, with them, narcotics. The new junta of former CIA trainees was also, according to authoritative reports, deriving great profits from the cocaine trade (DeRienzo 2004; Jenson 1994:179; see also chapter notes). But we will get back to that. For now the point is that the plan to turn Haiti into "the Taiwan of the Caribbean" had failed.

The food aid, however, did not stop coming. Haiti was, after all, poor and by this point, even if Haiti had been able to support itself ten years before, the USAID-led plan had, despite the massive return migration to rural areas, helped give way to crowded urban slums increasing the number of nonfood producers and thereby destroying that capacity. So, spurred on by humanitarian compassion, hopeful investment capitalists, and the agricultural lobbies that favored subsidies and government agricultural purchases, the plan still did not change. Still the food kept coming (see Appendix C for statistics).

In a 1994 agreement with the Aristide administration—then in exile and negotiating with the EU and UN to be returned to Haiti—the American Plan became the Paris Plan, a reaffirmation of the original version (Haiti Progres 1995). When the international community reinstalled Aristide in office on October 12, 1994, the World Bank, IDB, IMF, USAID, and the EU allies still did not change the plan. Still the food continued to come, and still, after the end of the embargo and the return of direct international aid, life for the impoverished Haitian masses continued to worsen.

There was only a fledgling resurgence of the industrial sector—to twenty thousand workers—the agricultural export economy all but completely ceased to exist, and at least 70 percent of the population was still hunkered down on small farms trying to eke out a living.

Still the plan did not change, still the food kept coming, and still life got worse.

From the year 1990 to 1999, the year that I was doing the food report for CARE, per capita GDP declined at a rate of 2.5 percent per year. This was not a simple function of the embargo, as many proponents of aid tried to dismiss it. Even after the embargo ended in 1994 and the U.S. and E.U. released massive amounts of aid, life for the Haitian masses got worse. Not only did per capita GDP continue to decline, but as in Jean Makout, severe malnutrition actually increased; on a national level it went from 3.9 percent in 1994—at the end of the embargo—to 4.1 percent in 1996—two years after the massive aid began anew (USAID 1999).

Still the food kept coming.

In the five years from 1994 to 1998, the United States, France, and Germany provided a total of 618,000 metric tons of food aid to the country, an annual average of 123,600 metric tons, enough to meet the daily nutritional needs (2,200 daily calories) of all seven million men, women, children, and infants in Haiti for twenty-seven days per year. And so still there was no market for the majority of the Haitians dependent on small farming for their livelihoods.

Most of the people in rural Haiti responded in two ways: Those who could afford it continued to emigrate overseas, most to the United States. Many of those who remained, withdrew into the local economies where an array of foods, many of which had been used since the pre-Columbian era, contributed to an amazingly adaptive survival strategy in the face of drought (see Appendix G for a description).

Still USAID, and now its fully cooperating E.U. partner, did nothing to change its plans for Haiti. The USAID, IMF, World Bank, and IDB planners responsible for providing the $2 billion

1994–1999 Haitian budgets only permitted 5.6 percent to be slated for domestic agricultural. No longer in touch with the original American Plan and its new version, the Paris Plan, USAID and World Bank consultants during the mid-1990s were left mystified and blaming Aristide and the embargo for the ongoing disaster (Richardson 1997; World Bank 1998; USAID 1998).

And that is what I witnessed in 1997 when I went to work on the Jean Makout survey and then later for CARE: A mad anarchic system of food aid, *sinistre* as the people themselves call it—a word with a double meaning, not only "disaster stricken," but sinister, ominous, and threatening—where the people didn't appreciate it, stole it with no sense of remorse, the peasants despised it and complained bitterly that they wanted to grow their own food, the NGO directors in the countryside uniformly disparaged it, and the distributors, the so-called cooperating sponsors (CARE, CRS, World Vision, ADRA), thought that everyone in the country had quit farming and were sitting around waiting for the next food shipment.

And what were the charities up to?

The designers of the plans—U.S. and E.U. government officials and employees of the IDB, the IMF, and the World Bank—provided the development funds, much of which the Haitian government had to pay back, with interest. But as was seen in Jean Makout, it was multinational corporate charities dedicated to helping the poorest of the poor that carried the plan out, delivered the aid, and executed the so-called development projects that were supposed to push the Haitian population and economy in the desired direction. For many of the high-level directors this was defensible: NGOs had budgets and operating costs and, for the largest of these interventionist organizations, the most important means of meeting costs in Haiti was far and away food aid. Donor governments gave money in the form of food; the charities sold the food on the Haitian market and then used the money to meet corporate overhead costs and to carry out programs that were supposed to alleviate suffering. But in the end, in the institutional struggle to survive and in an environment in which accountability did not exist, the world's largest multinational charities—CARE,

CRS, World Vision, and ADRA—executed the political will of institutions, governments, and lobbyists that had identified Haiti's comparative advantage as low wages, that is, poverty, and in doing so these charitable organizations dedicated to helping the poorest of the poor wound up working to make the people of Haiti even poorer. And this is what was seen in Jean Makout: unraveling economy, disappearing markets, and with nowhere to escape to, the peasants' withdrawal into near Stone Age subsistence strategies.

Did it have to happen?

It probably did not have to happen. Indeed, what I was part of in 1998 was one of the greatest and longest running foreign aid efforts that has ever occurred. For more than half a century, Haiti had arguably been the site of more religious missions and charities per square foot than any place on earth. Yet with the increase in aid, the situation had gotten worse. What is more, what I discovered and am recounting here about food aid is not a secret. Nor is it unique to Haiti. As it turns out, U.S. food aid was born in 1954 with the passage of PL 480 and the specific goal was not principally to help people but to promote overseas sales of U.S. agricultural produce. The consequences have been devastating throughout the world (see See Appendix D for extensive review and sources).

Why did nobody tell me this?

Could it be that they didn't know?

Could it be that employees at multinational charities such as CARE were unaware of what was going on with food aid?

The fact is, many of the directors must have been keenly aware of what was going on. Most, as I recounted, admitted as much over cocktails or in private conversations. Of the dozens, if not hundreds of aid workers I spoke to during the time, all agreed that food aid damaged the market.

Yet, when needed, the defense is so easy. It might be bad for the market, but the intentions must be good, why else would the United States be flooding the Haitian market? Most of us buy into it. I did. Moreover, for those profiting from the food, there is added incentive to hold on to the idea that food aid, if bad, must at least be well intended. To think, or perhaps I should say, to admit that the food is part of a plan to encourage poverty would be to recognize yourself as part of that plan. It would require guts and a good conscience to forsake the comfortable salaries, hotels, fine meals, insurance, and pension plans that came with being a professional in the service of the international charitable institutions like CARE, CRS, ADRA, and World Vision.

Getting back to the story, I got another opportunity to investigate charity. CARE wanted to expand its food distribution, so my next job was to investigate orphanages in the Province and neighboring areas and see if it was viable to distribute food to them. The experience was to turn out to be more appalling than the food investigations.

Chapter Eight
Orphans with Parents and Other Scams
That Bilk U.S. Churchgoers

After a miserable eight-hour drive from Port-au-Prince, three bumping and jostling hours from the nearest hard road, on the coast of Haiti, is Baie-de-Sol, capital city of the Province. Baie-de-Sol—the Bay of the Sun—is Haiti's fourth largest urban center, a city of more than fifty thousand men, women, and children and an unknown number of dogs, chickens, goats, and pigs. The streets are not paved, the electricity service works for less than five days per year—typically the two to three days before an election and, God bless them, Christmas—and most households have no septic system or piped water.

Just on the outskirts of the city, rising up from the Third World squalor, is a neighborhood of splendid houses. The architecture is reminiscent of the wooden gingerbread houses for which early twentieth century Haiti was once famous. But there is significant difference. These houses are made of cement, stone, and iron. The wooden sides of the gingerbread houses with their steep, shingled roofs have been replaced by elaborately formed cement and clay tiles; generous balcony space survives, but is now embellished with rows of shaped balusters and concrete turrets; fringes are adorned with embedded pebbles, cut stones, wrought iron trimming, and window bars.

Amid this modern architectural extravaganza, but quarantined from direct contact by an eight-foot cement wall, rises

The School of Jesus Christ of America, a monolithic, brightly painted, stucco, two-story, twenty-room school surrounded by equally bright and well constructed apartments and houses, workshops, and administration buildings. A brilliant yellow thirty thousand-gallon steel water tank looms above the compound like a spaceship from the heavens.

The School is a charitable operation, arguably the most successful in all of the Haiti's provinces and unarguably the top K–12 school in the Province. Tuition costs are a nominal $1.50 (U.S.) per month, low enough for even the poorest Haitian parents to afford. Every year some twenty U.S. Christians sign on as teachers. They have contracts. But instead of getting paid a salary, they pay the school. Each teacher raises $15,000 (U.S.) per year in donations and then gives money to the Missouri family that acts as administrators for the school. The money goes into the overall budget. The mission then covers the teacher's living and travel expenses and provides each teacher with an allowance.

Besides the teachers, some one hundred-plus members of U.S. churches come throughout the year to visit and help out. They come in teams of a dozen or more. Some are doctors, pediatricians, bone specialists, dentists, but most are working class people who have come to help impoverished Haitians. They stay for several weeks. They build classrooms, fix houses and vehicles, give free medical care, cap teeth, hold fairs and field days and Christmas pageants for the children, organize theatrical events and teach the children to paint, take pictures, and use computers.

Unlike so many other charities in Haiti where directors clearly embezzle most of the money meant for impoverished children—a trend that I will describe in greater detail shortly—this particular school has something to show for itself. School of Jesus Christ of America money is spent in Haiti and most of it is spent on Haitian children or on the teachers and other people who are providing the children with educations and maintaining the mission. Three 150-kilowatt power generators provide round-the-clock electricity. The monolithic school building, the administration offices, the houses, and the apartments are all air conditioned. Every classroom, house, and apartment has a television and a VCR. There is an impressive video library with all the latest children's films and a ten-thousand-book reading library. Every child in the school has a U.S. sponsor who donates $40 per month and some children have as many as four sponsors. Besides the monthly checks, the sponsors send their Haitian children gifts. Many of the children have gone on summer and Christmas vacations to visit their sponsors in the United States. Some sponsors have helped their Haitian children get into U.S. colleges, thrown graduation parties for them, helped them buy vehicles and get scholarships and given them jobs and allowances. It appears to most who have visited to be a heartwarming example of privileged U.S. citizens reaching out to underprivileged Haitians.

The secret of The School of Jesus Christ of America is the Missouri family that runs it. The leader of the flock is Reverend Richard Baxter, followed by his wife Madame Reverend Richard Baxter and four of their six children, Kirk and Sharon, who were in their mid-thirties when I knew them, and their two considerably younger siblings, Karin and Amethyst, who grew up in Haiti, speak fluent Creole and understand as perfectly as any Haitian the fine nuances of Creole culture.

The Reverend and his wife exemplify conservative American values. Married at the ages of seventeen, they are still together more than forty years later. Having grown up on a Missouri farm and worked twenty years for a U.S. electric company, Reverend Baxter can fix or, if necessary, create just about anything mechanical or electrical or that has to do with a house or building. He personally constructed and maintains the school and the faculty houses. He runs and maintains the 150-kilowatt generators and the complex electrical systems that spread energy throughout the mission compound.

Madame Reverend Baxter was the daughter of an impoverished Missouri sharecropper. Today she is the able preschool teacher and director of the family compound. She orchestrates the activities of the twenty-eight maids and cooks who she herself trained, an endeavor that is celebrated every afternoon at 2:00 when the family and some twenty to thirty American school teachers and visitors gather for a buffet lunch, typically including fresh cinnamon rolls, homemade bread, pizza and roast beef. And then, not to be forgotten, there are Madame Reverend Baxter's exquisite candlelight dinners of imported steaks or chicken, potatoes, and fresh salads.

Three of the children, Kirk, Karin, and Amethyst, teach school and are as special and talented in their own way as their parents. But more than anything else, the Baxters are compassionate people. Not only do they take special interest in educating the Haitian children, tutoring them as they need it, buying them clothes and books, but at Christmas the children are given bags of presents—bicycles, dolls, and radios. One Christmas, when it looked like the presents were not going to arrive on time, the Baxters chartered a private plane and had the presents flown directly from the United States to Baie-de-Sol.

So the Baxters are special people, all of them. But the most special of all, for me, is Sharon Baxter, the woman who made it possible for me to help the *bokor* Ram's daughter Albeit and Arnaud's cousin Tobe escape their miserable lives. Tobe from the beatings and cruelty of Arnaud and Albeit from the tragic death of her mother and father. I took both girls out of Jean Makout and brought them to Baie-de-Sol where I rented an apartment for them, and with Sharon's support they attended The School of Jesus Christ of America.

At the time I worked for CARE, Sharon was thirty-seven years old, attractive, with sandy blond hair and a body toned by rigorous daily calisthenics and ten-mile runs through the mountains above Baie-de-Sol. She was my closest friend in Haiti, my confidant, the person whom I turned to when I could no longer deal with the people of Jean Makout. She was my escape. She has devoted her entire adult life to educating Haitian children. But she does more than that. She is the school principal and she gets intimately involved in the lives of the students. When a student is having a problem, she visits the child's home, talks to the parents, and tries to find solutions. When a student is sick she takes the child to the doctor and pays the bill. When a child needs a passport or visa, Sharon gets it for them and she usually pays for it as well. When Sharon graduated her first class of high school students, she had the mission pay all the expenses to fly them to Port-au-Prince for the SAT tests. She also made sure that all got accepted to a U.S. college, that all had visas, and for those who could not get scholarships she raised the money herself. All you have to do is ride through the city with Sharon to sense the appreciation the people of Baie-de-Sol have for her. Wherever she goes someone is calling out after her, "Miss Sharon, Miss Sharon." It was Sharon, as I said, who gave me the means to rescue Albeit and Tobe, and who helped me to care for them and feed them. Indeed, had it not been for Sharon, I could never have brought them to the city where I put them in a house with a nanny and where they went to the School of Jesus Christ of America.

And it was there at Sharon's that I began my research into orphanages.

Sharon has a second-floor apartment in the compound adjoining her parent's house. It is a refreshing break from the dusty poverty outside the walls, like stepping into a suburban condominium in the States. The central air is blasting. There is a long iron-framed plate-glass dining table, an oversized refrigerator stocked full of Hershey's Kisses, Mound's Almond Bars, M&Ms, Reese's Peanut Butter Cups, packs upon packs of licorice, Goldfish crackers, goat cheese. In the freezer are prepackaged steaks, deboned chicken breasts, and gourmet sausages.

Sharon is sitting behind her desk, located in the middle of the apartment, her large-screen computer connected to the World Wide Web through satellite open in front of her. I plop down on the sofa, pick a selection of chocolates from a bowl on the coffee table in front of me, and pop one into my mouth. I tell her about how CARE wants me to investigate orphanages. "Tim," she says, her interest sparked. "You have to visit the orphanage across the street."

Across the street from The School is one of the largest orphanages in the Province. The owner is an American named Harry Wothem, who spends most of his time in the United States, collecting money for his Haitian charities. But if there is a contemporary Pied Piper of Protestant charity in Baie-de-Sol, it is Harry. Almost all the evangelical missions in the area, including the School of Jesus Christ of America, began in association with him.

Harry is a charismatic bulldog of a man, a Vietnam veteran and a terrific public speaker whose sense of humor causes frequent eruptions of laughter among his audiences. Besides the orphanage, he has a clinic and a mission. Several times a year he brings in teams of over one hundred church members from the U.S. Midwest, people who have come to see Haitian poverty and to do something about it. They build clinics and churches, hand out clothes and witness for the Lord. Each visitor pays Harry $800 for the week-long trip. Harry charters a plane, and when the teams arrive, he beds them down on the floor and in cots, feeds them rice and beans, and gives them what they have paid for: a taste of poverty. When they are not working building clinics and churches, he packs the teams into the back of a dump truck and drives them through the dusty dirt streets of greater Baie-de-Sol area to tour the squalor.

As Harry drives along with the back of his dump truck full of awestruck middle Americans, he usually disregards the small niceties of Haitian life. Harry rolls his truck through river beds, past peasant woman scrubbing the family laundry, over their drying clothes, up out of the river and over the coffee beans that peasants set out to dry on the edge of the street. In the city, with apparently no awareness of the damage he is causing, Harry crashes through private electric lines and fences. Once I just missed an episode where he drove his dump truck down the road that passes between his orphanage and the School of Jesus Christ of America, swung around a turn-around, passed a man and several of his helpers making cement blocks and, in Harry's typical way, drove right over the blocks, crushing a half dozen or so and kept right on going. The men making the blocks ran screaming after him. One man caught up to the truck, climbed up on the cab, opened the door, turned off the key, and dragged Harry down into the street.

Sharon had been watching from the window of her apartment and came running down and stopped the man, who at that point had Harry on the ground and was kicking him while the other Haitian block makers were trying to drag *blans* off the back of the truck. The next day Harry dropped by the School and tried to give Sharon a $100 bill "for heroism," he said and called it, "the Ben Franklin medal for bravery."

To her credit, Sharon refused.

In addition to Harry there is Slimette, his partner. Harry speaks little to no Creole. But back in the late 1970s he hooked up with Slimette, a thin, suave, attractive Haitian preacher. A partnership was born.

"I really don't think that Slimette is a good man," Sharon says. We are sitting in her apartment talking about the orphanage. "He locked his son in the closet all day."

"He locked his son in the closet?"

"Yeah, and the other day I was jogging down by the water and he was holding a woman by the arm and trying to spank her on the rear with a stick."

"He was trying to spank a lady on the rear with a stick?"

"He said it was for not paying her mortgage." Sharon screws her face up in a puzzled expression. "I had to wrestle the stick away from him."

The orphanage has been a smashing success and, while I never learned anything of the benefits Harry derives from the endeavor, Pastor Slimette has done quite well. Today he owns a two-story home in Baie-de-Sol, another home in Port-au-Prince, and yet another in Miami.

Besides the orphanage, Slimette has several churches in the area. He also sells swamp land on the outskirts of Baie-de-Sol. He drained the land himself and mortgages lots to poor immigrants from the countryside. His success as a pastor and orphanage manager and slum lord spawned an interest in politics. At the time I was doing the CARE survey, Slimette was the mayor of Baie-de-Sol.

I went by Slimette and Harry's orphanage. It is called the Orphanage of the Father and it is supported by Mission HW, meaning Harry Wothem. Pastor Slimette and his wife, Madame Slimette, are responsible for the orphanage, but at the time, Heith and Sandy, an American missionary couple, were living with the

orphans and supervising them. The Slimettes also run a school on
the orphanage grounds and Madanm Slimette is present during the
day.

I find Madame Slimette giving a class to some older school
children. She is a rotund woman, pretty once, and, despite a double
chin, huge breasts, and an even larger stomach, not unpleasant to
look at now. She has a sharp, congenial but no-nonsense way about
her. I learned from Madame Slimette that there were eighty
children in the orphanage, thirty-five girls and forty-five boys. All
the children are sponsored by U.S. churches.

Madame Slimette tells me, "all the children are from rural
areas" and smiling, explains how they like the young children
"because they can better benefit from what the orphanage has to
offer. The big children however," her smile fades, "they are a
problem." She tells me, "something has got to happen. They just
cannot stay." She goes on to tell me that the day before my arrival,
Pastor Slimette and the orphanage staff had a meeting about the
older children and they are going to have another meeting today.
"Something has got to happen," she repeats.

Later that day I visit Madame Slimette again. This time I
goto her home. She lives behind an eight-foot wall in a two-story
cement house as large as the orphanage itself. I tap on the big
metal gates. Tap tap. A guard opens the gates and I am allowed
into the driveway where an SUV is parked beneath an awning. Her
oldest son's 250 Kawasaki motorcycle is propped against the
house. Bicycles lay strewn about. It's a much different sight than
the orphanage.

I ask if other Haitian families ever adopted any of the
orphans.

"Only the parents can come get the child."

I am a little confused. "The orphans have parents?" I ask.

Madame Slimette's demeanor suddenly changes to
indignation. "Look," she says and then, in a comment that
surprises and puzzles me, "Our orphanage has been here for twenty
years and we do not give people's children away. *Non!*"

Her indignation causes me to back off. I am not here to offend her. So I let the obvious question go and decide to clarify the matter on my own.

I stop back by the orphanage and ask the cook if I could see the kitchen and depot. As I walk through the compound, curious children begin tagging along with me. I profit from the occasion to ask several children, "hey, where do your parents live?" I ask five orphans. The responses: "St. Angle," "St. Angle," "La Fonn," "Baie-de-Sol," "Baie-de-Sol." All cities.

All the children I interviewed not only had parents, they also were not, as Madame Slimette had told me, from rural areas. They were from urban areas. I left the orphanage wondering why they call the children orphans and why Madame Slimette misled me about them being mostly from the rural areas. What difference would that make? Unless, since in Haiti rural is synonymous with poor, it was to suggest that they took in only impoverished children, the kind that appeals to sponsors.

That evening I am back at Sharon's apartment savoring a sirloin steak dinner and the air conditioning, when there is a knock at the door. Sharon answers and in come the American couple who live at Slimette and Harry's orphanage. Heith and Sandy, a pear-shaped couple, are plain rural middle Americans from Ohio, with country common sense. Heith is semiliterate but a crack mechanic and handy at building things. Sandy is almost completely deaf. She wears a hearing aid that does little more than warn her of the approach of very loud things, like trucks or crowds of Haitian children. She is a good homemaker—Christian, faithful wife, devoted mother to two children. It is not clear to me if they know that I am researching orphanages, but they immediately begin complaining.

"Harry Wothem is here," Heith tells us with a country twang, "and this very day he and Slimette kicked out twenty-one orphans [of seventy-six, not eighty as Madame Slimette had said]." Heith explained that they kicked out all orphans over fourteen years of age, some of whom were eighteen or nineteen.

"Well, where did the expelled orphans go?" Sharon asked.

Heith, apparently oblivious to the irony, says matter-of-factly, "Most are back with their parents." Then looking, befuddled, he says, "Did you know that Madame Slimette has a niece, a nephew, and some cousins there?"

"Did they kick them out?" I ask.

Heith smirks at me as if I am teasing him.

"I did not realize it," he goes on, "but some of those kids are from wealthy families. Several are from Port-au-Prince."

Heith clucks his tongue and tells us about two brothers who were kicked out and have already rented the house across the street, one of the more expensive houses in the neighborhood, the most opulent neighborhood in a city of one hundred thousand. Their parents, who live in Miami, are paying the rent.

"Some of the orphans have two and three sponsors," Heith continues, and then, shaking his head: "You know what Harry said when I asked him why he was kicking the orphans out? He said that he couldn't sell them anymore. They are too old, people don't want to sponsor them. Can you believe that, 'he can't sell them anymore.'"

As I was to learn in the coming days, what Madame Slimette and Heith had done was inadvertently peel back the first layer of a system that benefited almost everyone involved except the poor, destitute, and parentless children foreign sponsors intended to help when they licked the stamps and put their checks in envelopes and mailed them off to the orphan foundations. The operators of orphanages and nearby or affiliated schools were, in every case I came across, spending only a fraction of the money they raised for the children and pocketing the rest. Orphanages in the area were a business.

In any case, jumping ahead for a moment, Slimette's political career ended in 2002 when he was accused of ordering the murder of a tenant who would not pay for a piece of his swamp land. According to popular belief, the land really belonged to the State. A mob ransacked Slimette's house, the big one described above, and ran him and his family out of town. His wife and her children moved to Port-au-Prince and later to Miami. Slimette has reportedly been supporting them with several surviving 'businesses' in Haiti.

The next morning I headed for Jean Makout. My first stop is my American missionary friends Goliath, a man built like a professional linebacker, and his wife Rose Ann, a woman who looks and behaves like a pioneer on the American west and has the heart of Florence Nightingale. They live near Tierre Bleu, on the high plateau above the Hamlet where they run a clinic and have twenty adopted children. Over the years we have become close. During that first year in the Hamlet I often went there in search of temporary refuge from the pestering and taunting I had to endure.

Sitting in their kitchen the next morning, Goliath and I are talking about a man named Henry Humperdickel who supports hundreds of children in the area.

Goliath says he knows that Humperdickel gets $20 per child from U.S. sponsors and he knows for a fact that at a school across the street there are eight children sponsored through Humperdickel.

He adds that the money is donated in U.S. dollars, but spent in Haitian dollars.

"But Goliath," I say, "Haitian dollars are worth only one-third of U.S. dollars."

"I know that, Tim," Goliath says a little impatient with me. "I asked Henry about it one time. He said he was using the difference for travel expenses. He said there was always so much to spend it on."

"Ah, Goliath," I say.

"I know. I know," Goliath says. "But look, I have to worry about my own relationship with the Lord."

Henry Humperdickel is a large U.S. Southerner with an amicable baby face and a sharp mind. He is always moving, always doing something. He likes to talk and he likes to shake hands, firmly. When he is done squeezing your hand, he looks you straight in the eyes, "Remember," he says, and then crisply clucking his tongue, "Cluck," he points his finger straight at you and adds, "Jesus loves you," as if he were the anointed carrier of the message. He might do this to the same person several times a day, as he did with me in the hour or so that I was last with him.

Henry has a story much like that of Harry Wothem. He supports an orphanage in Blano, a rural village in the far northwest of the Province. The orphanage was founded in 1976 by Jean-Baptist. Like Harry's partner Slimette, Jean-Baptist was a poor struggling Haitian pastor when Humperdickel came along. He claimed to have twelve orphans in his care. Humperdickel, who at that time was looking for people he could help, started giving $20 per month per orphan. Then he began bringing in teams of U.S. Christians. They built dormitories, a cafeteria, a church, a school, a house for Jean-Baptist, a guesthouse for the teams. Once again a partnership was born.

And once again, Henry and Jean-Baptist have been very successful. The number of orphans has increased from twelve to eighty-nine. And, like Slimette, Jean-Baptist has improved his own socioeconomic status. In addition to his home in Blano, he owns one in Port-au-Prince and one in Miami—where he moved his five children and wife. He splits his time between his various homes and the orphanage. And, also like Slimette, Jean-Baptist at the time of the CARE survey was the mayor of Blano, the town where his orphanage was located. Jean Baptist had come a long way.

I am at Humperdickel's and Jean-Baptist's orphanage in Blano talking to a U.S. missionary named Susana, a former drug addict with a candid and street-smart way about her. She is living behind the orphanage, alone, in Humperdickel's gymnasium-sized guesthouse, larger than the orphanage itself. She isnot supported by Humperdickel, but by her own church. However, in exchange for staying at the guesthouse she helps out with the orphans. I have been recounting to her that many of the children in the orphanages I visit have parents and she is explaining to me that a child can have a father and a mother and be worse off than a child who does not. I'll buy that. When I ask if children in Jean-Baptist and Humperdickel's orphanage ever go back to their parents, she says:

"We have children who probably could go home. Their parents are doing better. But how do we tell the sponsor? Sponsors don't like it when you write and tell them there child has left. We usually lose the sponsor. And when we lose a sponsor, we lose not just $20 that goes to feeding that one child, we lose $20 that goes into the overall budget."

Before I leave we are standing on the porch, and Susana is saying, "The poor don't get the help. You should see the kids at the local hospital."

Next I talk to Jean-Baptist, the Haitian orphanage director and mayor of Blano. He is a cool, attractive, and powerfully built man in his early fifties. I have known him since my first trip to Haiti in 1990 and I am comfortable talking to him.

He tells me, "We have a lot of orphans who return to their parent's home when they are grown."

"Yeah, but what happens when they are grown?"

"I just told you, most go back to their parents."

Before leaving, I ask if supplying more food would increase the number of orphans.

Jean-Baptist smiles. "Yes, the orphans will increase," and then he adds that he hopes to double the number in the near future, from 89 to 160.

When I leave Blano I stop back at Rose Ann and Goliath's homestead. Seated at the linoleum table in their kitchen, Goliath launches into a monologue about how Jean-Baptist is a liar. Then he asks: "Did Susana tell you about catching him fondling the girls?"

"No, we didn't get that far."

"Well, she is leaving the orphanage. Says she has caught him several times with orphan girls."

I tell him that Jean-Baptist wants to increase the number of orphans to 160, double what it is, and ask: "Why do you think that he wants to do that?"

"Because Humperdickel can find the money."

Eight years later, in 2007, Jean-Baptist would lose his support when an orphan reported to missionaries—those that run the hospital mentioned above—that he had been sodomized. A Haitian doctor confirmed and signed a statement that the child's rectum had been physically traumatized. No one accused the pastor/mayor but he took it on himself to launch a defamation suit against the missionaries. The proverbial walls subsequently came tumbling down. A landslide of testaments against him came forth, including among other bizarre accounts, regular beatings and rape of adolescent female "orphans"; four boys who "escaped" and reported to their families that the pastor had strung them from a tree branch, beaten them, and repeatedly put a nine millimeter pistol to their heads. Humperdickel's visiting granddaughter reported having walked in on the pastor and found him lying in his underwear while being caressed and fanned by a dozen naked prepubescent "orphan" girls. As the story goes, her grandfather Humperdickel was furious, not with Pastor Jean-Baptist, but with her; he disowned her and cut off her college tuition. The mystery of why grandpa cut her off was, as the story was told to me by missionaries, answered with the discovery that Humperdickel had a Haitian mistress and illegitimate child living in his Port-au-Prince church compound. In other words, he had his own secret to hide and allowing his partner to be exposed was a threat to him as well.

The next morning I head for an orphanage in Anse Wouj. I take an early morning detour over the mountains, down little paths and through streambeds, riding the CARE motorcycle past peasant shacks and garden plots. It's a route I enjoy and have traveled hundreds of times. I used to make the trip almost every day during the Jean Makout survey. The course takes me by my favorite spot in all of Haiti, a little white-washed, thatch-roofed peasant shack perched atop a four-thousand-foot mountain peak and shaded by three ancient mango trees. From the shade of the flat, hard-packed dirt yard, one can stand and look to the northeast and see beyond the lesser mountain peaks and out into the Atlantic Ocean. The water seems to stretch into infinity. To the northwest is the violent Windward Passage between Cuba and Haiti, an area that has claimed the lives of thousands of Haitian boatpeople fleeing poverty, heading for the wealthy shores of the Bahamas and the United States. To the south is the Sea of La Gonave, placid and calm, shielded from the trade winds by the mountains among which I am standing.

I drop down into first gear and gun the motorcycle up the last steep incline. When I arrive on the road above a small group is waiting for me. They could hear my motorcycle coming. I stop. The group is composed mostly of people I know; among them, however, is a pastor whom I know only vaguely.

The pastor claps me warmly on the back and asks, "How are you doing Timotè? Where have you been? We missed you."

Then, not letting anyone else speak, the pastor asks in a heavily feigned by-the-way manner, "Are you, ah, you still doing that thing, that ah, that job for ah ah...?"

"For CARE," I help him.

"*Oui,* for CARE.

"No," I lie. I have seen this act many times before. So trying to avoid what might become a long conversation I tell him, "I sent in the report yesterday."

"Ah, Timoté, we talked to our president. He said you were coming by. You never showed up. How could you do this to us? We are trying to develop up here and you left us out."

The "president" the pastor is referring to had eagerly sought me out when I was in Baie-de-Sol. He stood before me, his arms brimming over with dossiers and certificates of experience, success, and merit. I asked the president what I could do for him and he explained how his organization was very interested in Mother/Child Health and Nutrition (MCHN) programs, which just happened to be the hot new CARE agenda. I told him I was not there for that and asked about poor houses and orphanages. He muttered that they were thinking about just such a program.

Remembering all this, I explain to the pastor that while their organization was very important to the Province population, it was not oriented toward orphanages and poor houses, which was what I was investigating.

The pastor looks at me with disbelief, his mouth agape, "Timoté, you don't know about my orphanage?" He points off toward the valley I have just come from. "I have an orphanage right there. Don't you remember? You visited it during the survey in the year of, ah, ah..."

"1997."

"*Oui,* 1997. Don't you remember?"

"Get out of here. That was an orphanage?"

"*Oui*! That was my orphanage! I got fifty kids there!"

"Fifty kids?"

"Fifty kids! *oui*!" the pastor beams.

"Yeah?"

"*Oui, Oui,* fifty kids!"

"I didn't know. I didn't know!"

"*Oui! Oui! Oui*!" The pastor's large frame heaves with excitement.

I decide to see how far he is going to take this. "I'd like to see."

"But it's too late, *non,*" the pastor is discouraged, the smile gone. "Timoté, you left us out." His face draws shut. "The poor kids," he says softly.

"No, no, pastor, I can talk to the CARE directors."

The pastor perks back up and is soon insisting I come right over. So later in the day I stop by the pastor's complex.

There are three small thatch roofed two-room houses. There are five children milling about, all of whom the Pastor identifies as his own. He then hands me papers. They are lists of children. I look through them and see that we are no longer dealing with a single orphanage of fifty children, as the pastor had told me that morning. No, the Pastor has just handed me a list of eleven orphanages with a total of 1,002 orphans. Most surprising is not that this is a bald-faced lie, but that he is lying to me. I know this area. Everyone knows I know this area. I even have the survey-census for this area. I did the census! And there are not more than three hundred children in the entire area. And now the good pastor is handing me a list of eleven orphanages and 1,002 children.

As I am flipping through the lists in disbelief, I ask about a depot for the food and a kitchen. "Where do you cook?" The pastor leaps up and leads me to a small stick and thatch outbuilding in which is housed the family kitchen. Inside, a single earthen hearth is built against a back wall, two family-sized caste iron cooking pots and a large metal spoon hang on the wall. We go back outside. I ask where the children sleep and the pastor motion s to a tiny two room peasant house that is closed up. He does not offer to show me inside. I calculate to myself that maybe ten children laid side by side could sleep within each room. I ask about beds.

"Not yet, *non"* he says, "but we are going to make some, *oui.*"

"And the orphans, where are they?"

"They're around."

If you ride due south from Tierre Bleu in about one hour, providing, of course, there is no rain—in which case the mud may mean you never get there at all—you arrive in Anse Wouj.

It is a dusty, windswept town on the Gulf of La Gonave. There are some six hundred to seven hundred houses and perhaps ten churches. The houses are shabby, stick and mud, rock, thatch, a few tin roofs, and a few elaborate cement houses. Most of the streets are dirt and lime rock, but some are living marbled limestone. Wooden sailboats are pulled up on a stony beach and nets and fish hang from simple wooden racks. I pass shabby little wooden stores with hand-painted signs hanging from porch rafters. I turn up one of the dusty streets and stop the motorcycle at a dilapidated little shack with a crude wooden sign hanging from the porch: "Orphanage."

I am greeted by a gaggle of children. They swarm around me. Before I reach the house we are talking. The children are excited to see a visiting *blan* and I am asking them where their parents live. One child points to a mountain, "up there, *oui.*" I ask them how many orphans sleep here and several respond in unison,

"Fourteen."

A middle-aged woman, very black and humble, greets me on the porch. She tells me that she is the cook and "mother." I ask her how many children are in the orphanage, and she tells me, "Fourteen."

Pastor Jules Popilus is the owner of the orphanage and he arrived almost immediately, walking down the street, a short man, forty-nine years old, graying, and with a grin on his face that reveals a large gap in browning teeth. He is wearing a purple felt hat that makes him look more like a pimp than a pastor. He talks in a monotone, carefully, clearly, slowly and simply, giving him an air of humility. I introduce myself and explain that I am working for CARE. Pastor Popilus is happy I have come. We sit down by the porch. The children sit down on the porch in a long line, listening respectfully. My notebook is out.

"So, Pastor, how many children sleep here?"

"Twenty-three."

"Ahh, twenty-three?"

"*Oui*, Twenty-three. But we are growing."

I ask about the orphanage and the orphans. Pastor Popilus tells me it is the only orphanage in the Anse Wouj area. He started it three years ago,

"What was the month?" I ask, pen poised and ready.

"I don't remember, *non*," Popilus says.

"Well," I look up from the notepad, "was it the beginning of the year, the end of the year, or the middle of the year?"

The pastor stares at the ground and shakes his head, "Just can't remember, *non*."

"You can't remember whether it was closer to January or closer to June?"

"*Non,* it was three years ago. That's all I remember. Would you like something to drink? Perhaps some juice?"

I ask about sponsors. It is a question I phrase and rephrase half a dozen times.

"Who supports you?" The response is always the same. "No one."

Soon I am climbing on my motorcycle and Popilus hands me a long list of needs for the children of the orphanage.

After I leave I swing by the nearby Mennonite compound, where I have known different missionaries for some five years. I ask Anna, a Mennonite woman from Pennsylvania, about Popilus.

"I don't like him," she tells me in candid Mennonite fashion. "He is a beggar. He shows up with these lists of things he needs."

"Do you guys help him?"

"We give him $300 each month for the orphans. We also drop off boxes of clothes for them and give them other things, like shoes and sandals."

So Popilus had a supporter.

He also was illiterate and I learned when I arrived back in Gonaives that he had thirteen rural schools, receiving food from CARE for a total of exactly two thousand students and claiming sixty-five teachers. All but one of the schools was in areas inaccessible by road and none had ever been visited by a CARE monitor. None.

In Gonaives I finally encounter true orphans. There I meet Pastor Revenel Benoit, thirty-five years old, tall, robust and chubby, dark chocolate skin, impeccably dressed in a business suit complete with vest and jacket, and I am wondering why the heavily cologned, clean, cool, and reserved pastor is not pouring sweat.

Pastor Revenel Benoit may be the ultimate evangelical businessman. He has a computer school, an English school, a typing school, an accounting school, a large bakery, a food import business, a pharmacy, a clinic, and a radio and a television station. He was also, at the time of my visit, a candidate for senator. And oh, he has a church as well, and, the reason for my visit, an orphanage, both of which he includes in his list of "businesses."

The Pastor tells me how terrible it is for street kids, how people beat them and mistreat them.

"That is why I started the orphanage, *oui*. We wanted to help so we went downtown and rounded up eighteen street kids, asked if they wanted to live in the orphanage. They agreed, and so we brought them back."

Then, as if to himself, the pastor add s quizzically: "But only nine stayed for more than a few weeks."

The Pastor is soon telling me: "The problem with the orphanage is finding orphans. The street kids don't want to stay, *non*. They are wild. They love liberty. A truck goes by and they jump on it and go to Port-au-Prince." The pastor laughs, his black face shining, eyes glittering. "Tomorrow they're somewhere else. They hit the big festivals. You can find the same kids at festivals all over the country, *oui*."

I find this fascinating. I didn't know.

The pastor says he quit trying to recruit children and now takes only those who come and ask to live in the orphanage. "Preferably smaller children," says the Pastor. "They are easier to control."

Next I visit Natividad Benoit, a nurse—an auxiliary in hygiene—who works with street children. She is forty years old, a tall woman with a strong physique and a face like a lion, broad-boned nose, pock-marked cheeks where a lion's whiskers would be, her "mane" is pulled back in a ponytail. She is composed and articulate. As we stroll together through the hospital grounds she tells me that with support from Forgotten Children (an organization sponsored by a Madame Remington of Richmond, Virginia) she has rented a house for thirty-two street children. I ask if the children sleep in the house and she tells me, "Yes but they do not have beds yet. I bought them a carpet and they sleep on that."

We finish our stroll at her office which looks more like a chapel. It is big room with long benches. Her desk is in a far corner. Several other woman, nurses, chat just inside the open double-door entrance. We are seated by her desk and she repeats herself while I take notes. She got the idea to start an orphanage in January 1998. She tells me the street children sleep out in the open and there is much suffering among them, so she went out and rounded up street children and talked to them about going to school. She had them come and meet her at the hospital and she rented the house.

I mention that Pastor Benoit said it is hard to keep street children and, as she is obviously working with such children, is this a problem?

"I don't try to stifle the children," she says. "The only thing is that they have their time they are supposed to come to school – 4:00 in the afternoon – and they have to be in the house by 8:00 to sleep."

I ask her about the sex of the children.

"They are all boys," she tells me. But she has a list of thirteen girls (*restavek*, child servants who live with a family not their own) whom she does not yet know what to do with because she cannot let them sleep in the same house with the boys.

I tell her I would like to see the house and I get a surprise.

"Well, we haven't actually opened the house yet, *non*. It is still being repaired."

"You mean none of the children are sleeping in the house?"

"Not yet, but soon, *oui*."

"Well, where do they sleep?"

"In the street."

"I thought you said the kids were sleeping in the house?"

"Not yet, *non*."

"Well, when?"

"When I finish getting the house ready. I don't have a carpet yet. They are going to sleep on a carpet, *oui*."

While I am thinking to myself, *used carpet in Haiti costs a couple dollars, at best, and the pseudo orphanage has been funded for eighteen months,* Natividad begins to speculate, half to me and half to herself, about how she could assemble the children for me to see them. I decide to help her.

"You are feeding the children aren't you?" I ask.

"Every day they go to the kitchen, *oui*. They eat at 7:00 in the morning and then at 4:00 in the afternoon."

"Then I could just stop by at mealtime."

"Well," she says hesitantly, "I am not feeding them in the afternoon anymore. Just the morning. I don't have the money to feed in the afternoon, *non*."

"Why don't I stop by at 7:00 tomorrow morning?"

"Tomorrow's a bad day."

I ask who gives her the funds and she reminds me, "Forgotten Children."

Yes, *forgotten children*, I think to myself.

About that time I am looking down at my notes. I look at her name. She wrote it for me on my note pad. "Benoit Natividad." It occurs to me that she has the same first name as the last name of Pastor Revenel Benoit, the businessman.

She smiles, "No we are not family, *non*."

"It's just kind of interesting," I say, not really thinking that it is anything more than a coincidence, "that you have the same names."

"Just cousins," she says and immediately asks: "So what are you going to do for me? This is the project that I have right now, but as soon as I have some real money, I am going to open a big orphanage. If you want to start one, I will run it for you, *oui*."

And then, with no urging from me, the barriers come completely down and Natividad Benoit is making a joke even of herself, shouting over to the women by the doorway, "Wherever Timoté goes in Haiti I'm going with him."

The women laugh and then they too are asking me questions.

"Where did you learn to speak Creole like that?" "Where is your wife?"

I am soon beating tracks for the door and on my way out Natividad Benoit is shouting after me, "we need milk for my child nutrition center."

Two hours down a dirt highway, in a vast green valley filled with mango and avocado trees, fields of sugarcane, melons, and golden corn is Gros Mon.

After I get there I am accompanied by a short, attractive twenty-seven-year-old French woman, Isabelle Keisler, of SOS (Enfants Without Frontiers). Her auburn hair is a wild tangle. Her hazel eyes, clear and intelligent, seem constantly to be searching for something. Soon she is on the back of my motorcycle guiding me with pointed finger through the dirt streets of Gros Mon to visit a Haitian organization, Pawol et Aksyon, "Word and Action," funded by the Dutch government. It is an organization, I was told by one of their supporters in Port-au-Prince, engaged in rural health programs and orphanages.

The director meets us at the gate. He is a fat-cheeked Haitian man about thirty-five years old and he look s tired, as if he has been sleeping. I ask what Word and Action does and he says something about putting water systems in. Perplexed, because the

Port-au-Prince supporter had told me differently, I follow up by asking if they have any health programs.

"*Wi, boko*," (Yes, lots of them) says the director.

Isa cuts in, "Your organization doesn't work in health."

"*Oui,* well," the fat-cheeked man says with a tone of resignation, "we are not doing much of that right now, *non.*" Then with renewed vigor: "But we are preparing to do extensive programs in credit."

I ask him about children and orphanages and he says that Word and Action had a school for the deaf, but that it has been moved to St. Mark.

I ask him specifically about orphanages and he cites a woman named Nurse Matt who has recently died.

"She was a great woman who cared dearly for the orphans," he says.

Isa cuts in again: "Didn't Nurse Matt take children and then they were never heard from again?"

The director ignores her, looks around the yard as if searching for something he forgot and then, "I am very busy," he tells us, and adds that he wishes he could help more, but, well, he must get back to work.

As we are walking back to the motorcycle Isa tells me about Nurse Matt.

Nurse Matt was working for a French adoption agency. She would approach poor families and offer to adopt one of their children, usually in the five to six year age range. Promised the child would be educated and well cared for, the family would be given a sum of money and the child supposedly sent to live with a French family. Thirty to forty children left in this way. Not one had been heard from since.

Isa explains that, "Not one of the families ever received a single letter from the agency or from any of the adoptive parents."

An SOS employee obtained the address of the parent organization in Paris but, when they called, the person who answered the phone said that the agency had moved and left no forwarding address.

"I don't know what to think about it," Isa concludes. "Miss Matt died last year and it has never been resolved."

I am back in Baie-de-Sol sitting in Sharon's plush apartment. The air conditioner is blasting. Albeit and Tobe are here with us. Perhaps ironically, we have been watching the new version of Cinderella, the one where everyone is black. Whoopie Goldberg is the fairy Godmother and she turns a miserable Cinderella's orphan world into an underprivileged girl's dream come true. But I am barely paying attention. I can't shake the irony of the orphanages and the problem that is facing me: *What am I going to tell my employers at CARE?*

"Sharon," I say, "I have been to every single orphanage in the Province as well as Gonaives. They all look like scams to me. I don't think I should write a report that says the orphanages are all scams."

Sharon turns her attention away from the fairy godmother and toward me. "You have to do what you think is right," she says.

"Look at this," I say and get up and walk to where my book bag is hanging on a dining room chair. Sharon follows and we both sit down at the table. From the book bag I pull lists I got from a friend in the States.

"This thing is a lot bigger than just the orphanages I visited. Even if the orphanage directors are ripping off a lot of money, at least we know those orphanages really exist. But there is much more to this."

I show her the lists.

"World Vision and Compassion International have 58,500 sponsored children in Haiti, a large portion of these are in the Province. CAM (Christian Aid Missions) sponsors 10,000 children in Haiti, some 2,000 of them are out here. The Haiti Baptist Mission has 57,800 sponsored children, many of them out here. And these are the only ones I could get the figures for. They are only a fraction of it. In the Province you have Blue Ridge Mountain Homes, Plan International, Child Care, Tear Fund, and God knows who else. Then there are the small operations."

"Look at Pastor Sinner," I say, referring to the major evangelical school in the Village. "He gets $70,000 (U.S.) per year to help some 190 children. There are small sponsorship programs all over the place. There is Henry Humperdickel who may have hundreds of children on sponsorship. There is Harry Wothem. All throughout the mountains there are little Harry Wothem and Henry Humperdickel operations that we know nothing about. This is to say nothing of the Catholic Church which must have its own programs. For Christ's sake, there might be more children on sponsorship out here than there are children. And the corruption? At best, most of the money pays institutional expenses to educate kids who don't really need help. Okay, we could say that it is lifting crooked Haitian pastors and their families out of poverty. But now, now think about all the money that must be collected and never even gets here."

"It looks pretty bad," Sharon agrees.

"I am sure there are at least some needy children in these institutions," I say. "But I can't help feel disturbed by it all. So many people at these orphanages are outright lying. Most of the children are not orphans. That's a misnomer. The least they could do is call them 'children's homes.'"

"That's weird, huh," Sharon muses.

"Ah, Sharon, it is beginning to look like you guys are the only honest charity in the Province."

"It wasn't easy," Sharon says, and begins to tell me how difficult it was for her and her family to establish a respectable school. "At first everyone laughed at us. They said our school was no good and they sent their children to the Catholic school."

As Sharon talks I notice a pile of photos sitting on the table. In my frustration, I pick them up and start flipping through them. Americans, plain ordinary working class Americans. Husband and wife. Husband, wife, and kids. Husband, wife, and dog. Husband, wife, dog, kids, and Christmas tree. Husband, wife, kids, dog, house and yard. Husband wife and kids on stage in photo studio. I ask Sharon about them. She tells me they are sponsors. I ask her about their occupations. This one is a plumber and his wife is a secretary. Here is a single working mother. Next is a social worker. This one is a school janitor, his wife a homemaker. Here's a farmer. It goes on and on like this, plain ordinary working class American folks doing good things for underprivileged Haitian children.

I ask Sharon about her sponsorship and she proudly says, "Harry Wothem is not the only one who knows how to raise money. All of our children are on sponsorship."

She tells me that the sponsorship for The School is $40 per child per month.

"Many of our children have three and four sponsors," she says beaming and then, clarifying, she says: "But it's not like one child gets more than another. We don't just give the child the money. The money is spent in the interest of the child and that can be interpreted a lot of ways."

Sharon goes on talking and I lean back in my chair and begin to reflect on something that in all the years I have been acquainted with Sharon, her family, and The School, I have never really thought much about: *The School is full of rich children.*

The story of The School began in the mid 1980s when Sharon and her brother Kirk came down with one of Harry Wothem's whirlwind Christian tours of Haiti's poverty. They returned home and told their parents about it. The father, Richard Baxter, promptly retired from the Electric Company, went to Bible school, earned a degree and then Sharon, Kirk, their mother, father, and their two younger sisters all moved to Haiti to work with Harry Wothem. It did not take them long to become disenchanted with Harry's business style approach to charity and so they struck out on their own. As I recounted earlier, they have enjoyed dazzling success.

"It was so tough at first," Sharon is saying again, "everyone laughed at us. They said our school was no good."

The catch is, I am realizing as I sit here listening to her, that what she means by "everyone" is "everyone with money."

Sharon refers to the parents of the School's children as her parents' and as one drives through Baie-de-Sol with her she is likely to wave at anyone in an SUV, with a large stomach, and with gold jewelry dangling from his or her body and as she waves, she smiles and exclaims, "that's one of my parents."

And "her parents" are easy to spot because most of the people of Baie-de-Sol are scrawny pedestrians in ragged clothes.

There is no doubt about it: The pupils of The School are overwhelmingly not impoverished Haitian kids as it says on The School's website. They are almost entirely composed of offspring from the ranks of the Baie-de-Sol elite. The plumber in the photo I was looking at sponsors the child of a Baie-de-Sol ship owner who also owns the largest regional bakery. The single working mother sponsors the owner of a radio station, an ice plant, a hardware store, an import-export business, and the largest funeral parlor in the city. The janitor sponsors the son of a Port-au-Prince surgeon who works as resident surgeon for the private hospital at La Pwent.

"Sharon," I say, "you're giving charity to the rich. The School is the most elite school in Baie-de-Sol. There are parents in the school who have more money than the people in these photos. Much more money."

"That's not true," she snaps.

"Well let's see, virtually every major ship owner in the harbor and most the doctors I know in Baie-de-Sol have children in your school. Most of the higher-level politicians and political administrators, the mayor, the customs inspector, the chief of police, they all have children here. The owner of the Shell gas stations has children in your school. No wait, he has two families in your school because both his wife and his mistress have children here. And, Sousou, who owns the Texaco stations, his wife and mistress have children here, too. The owner of the television station, he has children here. That half-French guy from Miami, the one who is making cement blocks for the government, what's-his-name, he has a child here. And what about the Bennettes? They have seven children in your school. For Christ sake, 2 percent of the children in your school are Benette children."

"But I love her. Madanme Benette is so elegant."

"That's not the point, Sharon. The point is that the Benettes are among the largest landowners in the Province. Their family has monopolized exports in Baie-de-Sol since before the Marines arrived in 1915. They vacation in France, for crying out loud. And you're giving their children cost-free educations. You're giving them school lunches, Christmas presents, free medical care. And it's not yours to give, Sharon. The people who give you that money expect it to go to impoverished children. Not to rich people. You are no better than the people who are stealing the money."

"We have poor children, too," she says indignantly. And then, pulling out a list of students to prove it she says: "Let me show you." We go over the list: More than half the children in that particular class had at least one parent who is a medical doctor.

At that point I had visited every single orphanage in the Province and some half dozen in the neighboring Artibonite province. The ones I have not described were just as bad and the directors lied just as egregiously—and transparently—as those I have described. I had zero doubt that orphanages for Haitians and for many of the Americans who were helping them procure funds were businesses. Some orphanages, especially those in the cities, help some Haitian parents and their children, even if they do so in unadvertised ways and do not reach the poorest of the poor. By putting kids, at least some of whom are needy, in an orphanage, they are giving them an opportunity to get an education with free books, meals, and other benefits, not the least of which would be the chance to meet a *blan* who might, as they sometimes do, provide visas to the United States and a chance to further their schooling or get jobs there. But there is nevertheless something deeply disturbing about what I encountered. That something may, as in the case of the children in Gros Mon who were never heard from again, be far more sinister and dark than simply ripping off well-intended contributors and snatching charity from the mouths of the needy. Indeed, one of the reasons that I wrote this book is inthe hope that it will bring attention to such cases and lead to further investigation and clarification. But at the same time I want to make it clear that I am not against charity and certainly not charity for orphans. What I am against is false charity. I believe it is tantamount to robbing from impoverished children themselves.

The money is theirs and they are not, in the overwhelming majority of cases I encountered, getting it.

In any case, my dismay with charity and development was growing. But the job wasn't over. In pursuit of my CARE employers' desire to expand food distribution, my next job was to investigate the Haitian medical system in the Province. I was in for another alarming series of discoveries, findings that would shatter any remaining faith I had in foreign aid to Haiti.

A family in the Hamlet

Meeting Tree in the Hamlet

A local *bokor* in his *badji*

Getting water at the nearest spigot

The Village on a quiet day

The Village on a market day

The UN Road to Nowhere

The wind generators

Gully erosion

One of 100s of "grassroots" NGOs hoping for a sponsor

"Orphans" who have parents

U.S. Christian visitors loading up for a tour of the poverty

One of the five CARE food warehouses in Gonaives

Wrecked CARE truck on which four free riders died

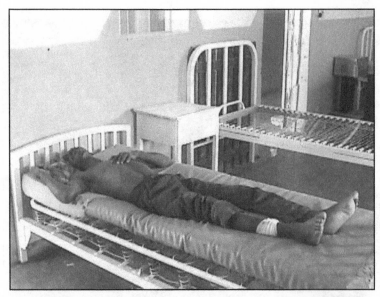

One of the two patients in the "Baie-de-Sol" hospital
when I visited the year before the Cubans arrived

Market woman returning home

Me on the abandoned and vandalized plane that
carried the cocaine shipment

Remnants of a time when Haiti had a functioning State.

Haitian King Henri Christophe built this fort--La Ferriere or, more commonly, the Citadelle--in the early 1800s to defend against the possible return of the French. Under him a Haitian State enjoyed 15 years of sovereignty and prosperity. Upon his death he had a budget surplus of 11.5 million pounds, an impressive sum at the time. Among the reasons for the success were State investments in plantations and infrastructure, and Haitian agricultural produce having access to the British market.

Chapter Nine
Medical Treatments:
Greed, Rudeness, and Renegades

In the heart of Baie-de-Sol, along a dirt street in a middle class neighborhood where there is no piped water or sewage system, is the Province's departmental headquarters of MSPP, the Haitian Department of Health. It is a pleasant looking two-story cement house. Inside, an attractive, well-dressed, and perfumed young woman sits behind the receptionist desk while an attractive, well-dressed, and perfumed young man sits on the edge of the desk and flirts with her. Excusing the interruption, I ask where I might find data on illnesses and treatments in the Province. I am directed to DSNO (Statistic Services).

The door to Statistic Services is open. Inside I find two slim, dark, well-dressed young Haitian men busily working at their desks. I introduce myself and they offer me a seat. I sit and the two well-dressed men roll their swivel chairs out into the middle of the room to face me. They are statisticians and they are responsible for archiving health information from clinics and hospitals throughout the Province, ostensibly what they were busily doing when I arrived.

"We are totally at your disposal, *oui*," says The One Statistician.

"*Oui*, totally at you disposal," echoes The Other Statistician.

"Great. What I'm looking for is a breakdown of the incidences of disease for all the clinics in the Province."

"We do not have the data, *non*," The One Statistician responds

"*Non*," says The Other Statistician, "only some clinics turn in reports."

"Could I see whatever data you have?"

"The person in charge," the One Statistician forthrightly explains, "is away on an emergency."

"Her husband," the Other clarifies, "lives in Miami and was in a car wreck. She had to go to Miami to care for him." Before I can respond The Other Statistician says, "But the data is here. It is in the computer."

I look around. There are two computers in the room. Both are covered with plastic and neither of the statisticians is moving to disrobe either of them. Trying to encourage them I ask: "In what program format is the data? Maybe I can help you get it out of the computer."

"The computers don't work, *non,*" says The Other Statistician.

Then completing his earlier explanation, the One Statistician pipes up again: "All the data is in our boss's briefcase and, as I told you, she is in Miami tending to a family emergency."

The Other Statistician has turned his back to me, rolled his office chair back to his desk and appears to have resumed whatever it was that he was doing when I arrived. But now he stops, swings back around in his chair, and rolling towards me in the chair. "Look, this is the way it is." He brings the office chair to a abrupt stop, leans forward, and karate chopping the air with both hands says, "All the data are still on lists. They are not in the computer yet."

"Okay," I say, stand up to go. I am not offended. By this point, I am used to this.

I step toward the door. "I appreciate your time." Then, remembering that I need all the names of people interviewed —I will have to turn a list in to CARE with the final report, proof that I did my job—I stop. "Oh, by the way, may I have your names?"

"*Non!*" says The One Statistician.

"*Non,* definitely not, *non,*" says The Other Statistician.

I go upstairs to see Jean-Luc L'homme, the assistant departmental director. At first glance he appears a quintessentially stupid man: Short, chubby with coke-bottle thick glasses, a fat jaw, big teeth, and his lower lip typically dangling loose. But Jean-Luc is not stupid. Thirty seconds of conversation with him and you realize that you are talking to a dynamic, charismatic, quick thinking, and profoundly insightful person. But I already knew that.

Jean Luc has been one of my most intimate friends for years. We worked together in Jean Makout. Just before we met, he and his wife were in Belgium where, to complement their Haitian medical degrees, they both picked up master's degrees in public health. Upon their return, Jean Luc spent several years supervising French ID's Jean Makout County contraceptive program. Today he is one of the most powerful officials in the Province's Department of Health.

I tell Jean-Luc what happened downstairs in the statistics office.

He laughs. "They can't be blamed. It's the system."

He pulls a report from a desk drawer and tosses it to me. "Our most recent summation of the data."

I open the report. It is from March 1998, a year prior. I flip to the section dealing with tuberculosis treatment, one of my target issues to investigate. The MSPP director is quoted as saying, "Poor functioning of Tuberculosis system in the Province." And then on the next page, after much gibberish, "There are a couple clinics, but nothing substantial." And then summarizing: "System not yet functioning."

I look up at Jean-Luc who has been watching me read, "What the hell is going on?" I ask, "Haiti is getting millions for TB and HIV treatment."

"You already know it is a mess," Jean-Luc smiles pleasantly. "In our most recent five-year plan, a top priority after vaccinations and malnutrition is HIV treatment. Like everything else, we made this plan with the financial support and guidance of USAID."

Jean-Luc stands and begins to pace: "Now what does HIV mean? It means tuberculosis asylums. [AIDS sufferers frequently come down with TB and so health officials consider it as a first stage in dealing with the spread of the other disease]. More tuberculosis asylums have been closed in the past twelve months than were opened in the five years before. That's the first year of our new five-year plan." Jean-Luc concludes, sitting back down in his swivel office chair. "So much for priorities."

"Yeah, but you are here," I say, "Why can't you do anything about it?"

"I am trying." Jean Luc leans back and the springs in his office chair moan. "But I have to work inside a system. I didn't invent all this."

Next he begins to talk about the Province's main hospital and after filling me in on the recent political history surrounding the institution, he is saying, "Go check it out. After your visit we'll talk again."

Hospital Imaccualae, the main hospital of the Province, is impressive. It sits on a hill in the middle of Baie-de-Sol. Huge double gates give way to a complex of old stone buildings with fresh white and blue paint thoroughly slopped on all the walls. The grounds are poorly kept . But the place is alive. The yards are bustling with people. Patients and visitors flow in and out of buildings. A long line of peasants and slum dwellers stand outside the pharmacy. Dozens of white Cuban doctors and nurses walk about the grounds. It is a far cry from the hospital I visited the year before. The place was not at all like this. I found no doctors. No nurses. No administrators. I could not even find a watchman. Wandering from one hollow and empty building to another I found only two patients in the entire hospital: One lay in a room full of empty beds while two family members sat nearby; the other patient was in a room full of empty beds, alone, and I could only conclude by his apparent condition that he had been abandoned there to die.

Jean-Luc had explained to me that the problem had been the director, a former member of the fallen regime of Baby Doc Duvalier. He was responsible for the hospital. Every month a check was sent to him to run the hospital and he would simply pocket the money. Then Fidel Castro decided to send doctors to Haiti. In an expression of independence from the United States, then-Haitian President Rene Preval accepted, but before the Cuban doctors arrived, there was a shake up. Not wanting to look bad in front of their Cuban neighbors, with whom they have a traditional spirit of competition, the old Duvalierist was removed—rumor had it he was furious about his removal and was actively trying to get himself reinstated—and replaced him with a vibrant young doctor named Fony.

I look for Fony and find myself being directed to the top of the hill where in the middle of the hospital grounds there is a large administration building. When I arrive I pass a group of several Cuban doctors. Each grips a clipboard. They stand in the doorway engaged in a serious and intense discussion about something urgent. Inside I find the information desk, a window with a counter through which one can see into an office. I lean through the window and can see that inside the office two Haitian women are at a desk in the far corner chatting intently. One of the women laughs and holds onto the arm of the other woman. At another desk is a Haitian man on the telephone. I cannot get anyone's attention. Then from a door on the far side of the office a middle-aged Cuban woman enters and looks at me. She then looks around the room at the Haitians and, shaking her head, asks me if I need help. I tell her that I am working for CARE and would like to see Dr. Fony.

"He is at his private clinic. But wait, I will call him."

Before long Fony arrives and I am invited into a huge office with twenty-foot ceilings where Fony is seated behind a large desk. He is in his mid-thirties, smooth light skin, short, fit, pleasant looking. He invites me to sit. He tells me that he has a clinic downtown and that he got pushed into the hospital job by a team of young doctors, friends of his, who wanted to develop the hospital. He is soon telling me that now he is building a new private clinic, his own, bigger and better equipped than the one he runs at present. If my friends or I ever need medical care, I should come visit him there.

We talk about CARE giving food to the hospital. As I am preparing to leave he tells me that food would be good. "We have our own system here," he assures me, shaking my hand and leading me to the door, "and we can make it work."

That night I am talking to Doctor Rob. He is a classic old country doctor from Missouri who reminds one of Doc on the

1960s television series *Gunsmoke,* only taller and cockier. I once spent several days on a sailboat with Doctor Rob and I learned that he got his start during the Korean War. A high school dropout shipped off to the war at the tender age of seventeen, he was a hellraiser who kept getting into brawls, a vice that eventually landed him "punishment" as a doctor's assistant. He loved it. Rob was soon an unofficial medic, stitching up war wounds and doing basic surgery. When he got out of the military, he went back to school and eventually became a real medical doctor.

He has been coming to Haiti for the past decade and has half a dozen of his own projects going. Rob also helps other missions and doctors in the area. He tells me about a sonograph machine that he gave to Fony.

"That son of a bitch, he took it straight to his own clinic. When I found out about it and asked him what he thought he was doing, he said that he was just taking it there to learn about it and was going to bring it back. He thinks I'm stupid. And you know what he does now. The bastard bombards me with e-mails. He wants me to send someone to show him how to make the sonograph work. Ha!"

Then calm and reflective again, Rob says, "I feel kind of bad that I haven't done it. I mean, at least someone would be getting some good out of it."

"Yeah, I know all about it. Look, we are all thieves," Jean-Luc tells me in late afternoon as we sit on a wall near the beach drinking beer. I have been telling him about Fony and the sonograph machine. As we talk, we watch people stroll up and down the sandy road in front of us: older women returning from market with their wares balanced on their heads. Groups of children carrying gallon jugs of water. Several finely toned young female bodies stroll gracefully by chatting as they elegantly balance five-gallon buckets of water on their heads.

"The doctors, or rather 'we,'" Jean-Luc confesses "are the biggest crooks in the country."

I notice a scrawny dog limping warily down the street toward us.

"The doctors in Haiti, my colleagues, me, we think that we are entitled to steal."

On the far side of the street the pathetic dog stops and lies down.

"Last year," continues Jean-Luc, "the director of the health department had to buy five hundred hospital beds. The funds came from an aid project. I can't remember. I think it was USAID. The director billed the project for $600 beds. Ha! They really cost less than $100 each. He pocketed the difference. "

We admire two laughing teenage girls running down the street toward us.

Jean-Luc sighs. "Look, we are all thieves. The doctors in the hospital, you know how it works. They go into the hospital in the morning and pass through the line of people who are waiting to see them. Those who look like they may have money, well, they tell them, 'Look, it would be much better for you to go down the street to my private clinic.'"

The laughing teenage girls are almost upon us and I can see that they are attractive. Their pert breasts barely bounce. Their long, lean legs stretch out in front of them as their lithe bodies glide toward us. They are both laughing and talking back and forth to each other as they run. I think *how fine it is to be young and healthy.*

"And if they don't go to the doctor's private clinic," Jean-Luc is saying, "what kind of care do you think the patient gets? They will be lucky to get any care at all. The doctors might see one or two patients at the hospital and then it is straight to their own clinic."

Just as the girls are about to reach us one of them breaks from her course, takes three athletic bounds toward the sleeping dog and lands a full kick in the animal's emaciated ribs. The dog bowls over howling in pain. The girls shriek with laughter and continue running down the road.

Jean-Luc sighs.

"Even me, whenever I buy something that my job pays for, I don't haggle. I pay full price and then talk to the guy about my rebate. And I get it."

Jean Luc is quiet and reflective for a moment. Then he continues talking, "I remember orientation day at medical school in Port-au-Prince," he goes on. "The professor who was giving us the orientation speech said, 'You are here for money and you better have your own money. You need a car, you need money for books, for your office and for your clothes. And when you take care of a patient the first thing you ask is for his address. Not because you want to check on him. *Non.* Because he is going to owe you money and you will need to know where he lives so that you can collect it.' That's what he said. Not that we should care about patients and be honest or that we are helping. *Non.* He said that medicine was a business and it was all about money."

On my way back from a second visit to Hospital Imacculae, I run into Dr. Rob again. He gives me a ride in the ten-wheel army truck that was donated to him by the United Nations' forces when they left Haiti the year before. As we ride along Rob is explaining to me that with support from their church back in Missouri he and his wife Billi — who was once his nurse — are in the process of opening a clinic in a remote mountain community in the highlands above Baie-de-Sol. I tell him about my buddy Jean-Luc, how he is the assistant director of the health department and might be able to help him.

"I already told you about my experiences with the director and the sonograph machine. We are trying to stay away from those guys, they're so darn corrupt."

"I know what you mean, but Jean-Luc isn't like that. He would really help."

"We would rather not get their attention."

We arrive at a house that Dr. Rob has rented here in the city. He and Billi have brought in a team of three nurses and a shipment of donated medicines. Rob pushes the screen door open and we enter a kitchen, where three U.S. nurses, a Haitian nurse who is going to be responsible for the new clinic, a Haitian man who owns the property on which the clinic will be located, and Billi, Dr. Rob's wife, are all gathered around a table piled high with medicines. There are thousands upon thousands of pills in hundreds of plastic bags, vials, and cardboard sample containers. Lined up against a wall are barrels full of more unsorted medicines. I can't help myself. "Wow. That is a lot of medicine." I say, "Do you guys realize the value it has here on the black market?"

Nobody pays attention to me. But later that night I am at another missionary's house using their internet service when in come the three visiting U.S. nurses. As they wait for the computer they talk about the Haitian nurse who was in the headquarters earlier that day, the one who is going to be responsible for the clinic.

"We are so lucky to have her," says one of the nurses.

"Yeah, she was so fast today," says another.

"Wasn't she though," says the third nurse, "Why it took us eight hours to sort two barrels of medicine."

"Yeah, and we left her for what, two hours," says the first nurse, "and she sorted an entire barrel all by herself."

"That girl is a hard worker," chimes the second nurse.

Two days later Rob takes inventory of the medicine and discovers that some $10,000 worth of it is missing. They were not able to resolve the crime—to my ire, Dr Rob covertly explored the hunch that Jean Luc and me might be behind it--nor could they go to the police for help as they had no license from the health department and were therefore engaged in the illegal distribution of controlled substances. Using their nurse and their Haitian liaison, Dr. Rob and Nurse Billi opened their clinic, but closed it again within the year because the Haitian man who was supposed to be responsible for the property and overseeing the clinic refused to account for his expenditures. When Dr. Rob objected the man pointed out that he and not Dr. Rob was the owner of the clinic and administrative building. They were on his property. Dr. Rob and Nurse Billi pulled out. (I could recount dozens more stories similar to this one. I can think of only one mission I know in Haiti that did not at one or several points in time have the Haitian staff, a staff member, or the owner of the property try to take over and throw them out.)

During my research into the medical system in Baie-de-Sol, I was relearning what I already knew, that the Haitian health care system is a failure.

Here's how the system works: The Haitian state has a medical school and, in exchange for providing free education, the state requires public service from all graduates. The students are supposed to spend two years working in clinics located in remote provincial areas or urban slums. But each year about half the new Haitian medical graduates legally emigrate directly to the United States, without repaying the State for their education or doing resident community service. The others take their residencies at clinics throughout the country, typically spending no more than a few weeks in the field. During their short stay, those who have any sense of commitment are able to confirm what they too already knew, there are insufficient medicines, bandages, and clinic aides for them to perform their job. In despair, most subsequently make the problem worse by taking whatever equipment and medicine there is and carrying it back to Port-au-Prince or some other urban area to set up in their own private clinic. Most also stay all their lives on the government dole as doctors on the rosters of a public hospital where they show up for work long enough and often enough to take any new medicines and equipment and lure away those patients who can pay. They spend the rest of their time in their private clinics, sometimes right down the street from the public hospitals (where they are supposed to work and from which they collect monthly government checks).

Meanwhile, people of the rural areas and the slums continue to die in appalling numbers from curable diseases that are all but completely absent in developed countries.

In 1993, a rat drowned in the Hamlet's nearest water reservoir, causing an outbreak of typhoid in which some thirty children, including Tiyol, the stepson of Ram the *bokor*, died. The government's resident doctor in the local clinic just happened to be there and his office was full of sick children. But as a local aid worker present at the time recounted, the typhoid tests the doctor was equipped with had expired and were no longer any good. The doctor kept getting negative results for typhoid. Believing the tests reliable and unable to determine that it was any other disease, he continued to treat for malaria—the symptoms of which are notably different than typhoid.

In another case, I helped Denice, a young Hamlet woman, take her four-year-old son to the city to get treatment. The boy, Ti Chapo, had been sick for several months. Denice had taken him to three different local clinics, two of which were more than a four-hour walk away. Denice had also taken him to the hospital in the nearby Village of Jean Makout. Nothing helped. Ti Chapo had lost a frightening amount of weight and his skin had become a pale, almost transparent ash color. He was weak, ate little, and began to spend most of his time sleeping. The old people in the Hamlet were predicting death. So, using a Ham radio I managed to reach Sharon in Baie-de-Sol. I gave Denice 500 *goud* and she and Ti Chapo made the twelve-hour trip on donkey. They stayed with relatives and visited doctors and clinics by day. Sharon helped them—she was good friends with many doctors who had children in her school and she would call the doctors before sending Ti Chapo and Denice, explain to them that she would pay the costs, "just figure out what the boy is suffering from, and cure him." After one week, four doctors, and $140 (U.S.)—about what the average Hamlet family would earn in a year—we had no definitive test results. Eventually Denice got frustrated by what she said were constant demands for money from the doctor's assistants— demands in addition to what Sharon was paying. Denice arrived in the Hamlet with no results and no medicine. Ti Chapo died two weeks later.

Sharon herself once felt anemic so she went in for a blood test and a fecal exam. Mind you, she lives in one of the four largest cities in Haiti and she went to a clinic owned and managed by Fony, the hospital director I mentioned earlier, director no less of the largest state hospital in the entire Province. When she came back for the test results, the technicians reported her positive for malaria and for worms. In disbelief, Sharon recounted the conversation to me.

"I asked the woman, 'worms?'"

"*Oui*, Madame, that is why your stomach hurts."

"But my stomach does not hurt."

"Oh well, it will."

The following week Sharon went to Miami, where she underwent the same tests again. She had neither malaria nor worms.

The care that people from the Hamlet and impoverished people elsewhere in Haiti get when they go to see the practitioners of modern medicine is not simply bad care. It is almost always delivered with insults and humiliation.

My very first experience with the local medical system came about two months after I had arrived in the Hamlet, before I knew everyone's name or understood much of what was going on. I passed a young girl of about thirteen, Janice, who was sweeping her mother's yard. She was holding one arm up as if it were injured. I stopped and asked her about it. She showed me an infected forearm-length third-degree burn and explained that two nights before, while laying in bed, a kerosene lamp had spilled and caught the sheet on fire. I asked her what she was doing to treat the burn and she told me that her father was applying gasoline—a common burn remedy in rural Haiti.

The next day I brought her a tube of antibacterial ointment but, clearly, what she needed was a doctor. I found her father and we took her to the local clinic.

No one was there. The doctor, we were told, was away in Port-au-Prince "on business." (That particular doctor spent perhaps one month of his entire one-year residency at the clinic). We found the two clinic nurses at the beach with their boyfriends and after much haggling, we convinced them it was an emergency.

An hour later, they arrived at the clinic, where we were waiting. Upon seeing the girl, both nurses launched into tirades, calling the father "stupid," "ignorant," "savage," and explaining over and over in loud and chastising voices that had I not brought the girl to the clinic, she might very well have died or at least lost her arm, which would have been entirely the fault of this "stupid man."

The humiliated father, old enough to have also been the father of the nurses, only looked at the floor and repeated "yes, miss" over and over.

Alone with him, I asked the father why he hadn't taken his daughter to the clinic.

"I don't have any money," he replied.

I didn't either, but I could not imagine that the clinic staff would refuse to give her treatment. Or would they?

When the nurses finished dressing the girl's wound, they handed me antibiotics and explained that if she did not take them she might die. They also handed me a bill for 100 *goud* (US$7). When I told them that I had no money, one of the nurses reached over the counter and plucked the antibiotics out of my hand. "No money, no medicine."

"But I will pay. I just can't pay right now."

"No money, no medicine."

"But nurse, you said that this girl could die."

"*Oui.* You will find the money."

The abuse and disrespectful treatment of impoverished patients in Haiti is not something unique to the Hamlet. It has inspired at least two doctoral dissertations in anthropology. One of the researchers, Catherine Maternowska, actually sat in a Port-au-Prince family planning clinic and recorded interactions between doctors, nurses, and indigent patients. The medical practitioners were so accustomed to being rude that they apparently didn't think there was anything wrong with it. The following is a direct excerpt from Maternowska:

> Yvonne enters, with some hesitancy. She is 24 years old, unemployed, and the reproductive history scribbled on her chart indicates she has four children. She has come to the clinic for more birth control pills. She stands, nervously clutching her big vinyl purse.

> Doctor (D): Enter! Have you seen your period?

> Yvonne (Y): Yes.

D: When did it come?

Y: It comes every twenty-eight days.

D: It came today?

Y: No it hasn't come yet.

D: Because—you were supposed to come on the 16th and you didn't come.

Before long the doctor is arguing with Yvonne over whether he gave her two packets of pills or one.

Y: I took them. It was two packets of pills that you gave me.

D: It wasn't two packets, it was only one, *madame*.

Y: Well, maybe you didn't mark it, I took two. I still had pills, that's why I didn't come earlier.

D: [Mumbling to himself] She took one packet in January, one packet in February, I marked it.

Y: I took two packets in January.

D: But if you took two packets—I'll tell you a little thing. If you took two packets in January, you should have come in early March. So where do you fall now? On your head or what?

Y: I haven't fallen. It seems like you didn't mark it because you gave me two packets.

D: [Throwing the chart at her] Where do you see that? Where do you see that?

When this convoluted and deprecating interchange is over and Yvonne has left, the doctor turns to Maternowska, the researcher, and, referring to the mentality of slaves in Haiti two hundred years ago, says, "Their mentality hasn't changed. It's the same thing with this woman. She's so stupid that she says she took two packets of pills but she didn't. Oh! It's all the same, they're still stupid. They still lie and they're still slaves! That woman, she can't read, she's nothing."

Maternowska subsequently checked the records to see how many packets of pills the doctor had really prescribed. Yvonne was right, he had prescribed two packets.

About a year before I was conducting the hospital and clinic research for CARE, I was at Sharon's apartment chatting with her, telling her about AIDS sufferers in Jean Makout and she tells me,

"Oh Tim, we have this terrible problem. You know Salvation?"

"Yes. He practically lives in my house."

"Seriously, you promise you won't say anything?"

"About what?"

"You have to promise first."

"Okay, I promise. Now, tell me?"

"Well, he has been sick and Mom has taken him to the doctor twice to have him tested for AIDS. Both times the tests came back positive."

In Baie-de-Sol, there was a guy named Salvation. He was twenty-two years old and had worked for the Baxters since he was sixteen. He had participated in the construction of The School of Jesus Christ of America and was the mission's most important employee. Reverend Baxter had taught Salvation to maintain the systems that kept The School functioning. He knew every branch of water pipes that coursed through the compound, bringing water down from the yellow spaceship-like reservoir that loomed above the school. He knew every tentacle of the complex electric system whose wires spread throughout the mission, delivering power from the 150-kilowatt generators to every recess, every light, television set, and computer. He knew the maze of air conditioning ducts that cooled halls, classrooms, and offices. He knew the Internet and television cables that connected the school and its administration to the outside world through satellite dishes and antennas. He knew where the telephone lines were hidden and how to operate the ham radios. He knew the maze of sewage and drainage pipes that expelled the school's waste to a massive underground drainage field. The Reverend taught Salvation to weld, repair plumbing, analyze electric circuits, and detect faults and broken lines. You would have thought that Salvation was indispensable to the operation of the School. But even more than his value as an attendant to the systems that kept The School of Jesus Christ of America alive, Salvation was like family to the Baxters.

It was not long after I had moved the girls Albeit and Tobe to Baie-de-Sol that Salvation discovered their nanny—Tobe's aunt—and became enamored with her. Salvation would come by the house with candy and flowers, follow her around the yard and the kitchen. After several weeks his overtures appeared to be having an impact. The Nanny would smile back and flirt with Salvation. And what the hell, he was a good guy. I didn't interfere. But then this night while I was at Sharon's apartment chatting with her, she tells me about Salvation being HIV positive. I am shocked.

"Sharon, you know that Salvation is interested in our Nanny?"

"No."

"Well now you do. I am going to tell her."

"You can't. You promised"

"What do you mean 'I can't, I promised'?"

"We haven't told him yet."

"Why haven't you told him?"

"Doctor Evason says that it is not a good idea to tell Haitians they have AIDS. They go out and spread it intentionally."

"They spread it intentionally?"

"That's what Doctor Evason said"

And that is exactly what doctors in Haiti did at the time, they refused to tell people when test results yielded positive for HIV because they believed they would go out and spread it maliciously. And so, at the advice of Doctor Evason, Sharon and I and everyone else kept silent about Salvation's disease. We did not tell him, a friend of ours, someone trusted to maintain the mission and trusted with the keys to all of our houses, that he was HIV positive. I did tell the Nanny in sworn secrecy to stay away from him, that he had a disease. But I did not tell her what it was. In the ensuing year, the time it took for him to developed full-blown AIDS, Salvation went on to promise marriage to a fourteen-year-old girl and became sexually active with her. She left him when he became emaciated and it was clear that he was dying from some horrible illness—she and the other Haitians who lived in the neighborhood believed witchcraft. I don't know if the girl subsequently died of AIDS. It seems unlikely that she could have avoided contracting the disease. But I don't want to know. The idea deeply bothers my conscience. It is one of those experiences that I hope this book, if anyone ever reads it, will serve in however small a manner, as redemption for my own shortcomings and failures while living and working in Haiti. In any case, getting on with the story.

The Haitian medical system and people who staff it do not just tend to be incompetent, rude, and extreme in their disrespect of the poor...they are sometimes lethal.

The French doctor who was running the hospital in the Village of Jean Makout, a hospital that before his arrival the peasants cynically nicknamed "the morgue," used to recount to me stories of incompetence at the hospital, such as the time he discovered that a nurse had prescribed a medicine that, in the patient's condition, would have killed the man within days. Before he left the area, after six years in the country, my friend told me that he thought it was much safer for peasants *not* to go to Haitian doctors and nurses.

"It is better if they go to the *bokor*," he told me, "because the *bokor* uses mostly harmless leaves and herbs and there is a 95 percent or better chance that the typical patient will recuperate on his own so long as nothing deadly is given to him. But medicines and surgery incompetently administered, now that's dangerous. The patient might never get over the treatment."

But the problem is not always confined to Haitian practitioners. There are occasionally foreign health care workers in Jean Makout who, in an attempt to fill the Haitian health care vacuum, strike out on their own. My favorite is a priest named Father Joe who worked in the Village. By the time I arrived, he had been literally run out of town and, indeed, out of the country. I heard many stories about Father Joe and met him once and so was able to delicately verify the more interesting antics.

Father Joe, sixtyish, tall, white, stately Montfort missionary priest from the United States, had no formal medical training. For more than a decade he lived in and ran the local parish that included the Hamlet. His self-proclaimed forte, in addition to intermediating for God, was treating tuberculosis. He founded his own sanatorium near a beach—the same one where, several years later, I would pitch my tent. People came from far and wide to be treated by the respected priest. Father Joe did not follow accepted modern treatment; he employed a traditional medical strategy. Instead of giving Rifampin, considered by virtually all the Western medical world to be the most effective treatment for TB, Father Joe treated his patients with the centuries-old, prepenicillin method of drinking special herbal tea and daily walks on the beach where the fresh sea air, he believed, could work medicinal miracles.

He claimed remarkable rates of success and at some point became so confident that he opened the pages of a how-to-do-surgery textbook and began doing operations such as lumpectomies on women with breast cancer. But at some point his medical practice came to the attention of local authorities who began to scrutinize it closely. His welcome wore out when he took a four-day trip to Port-au-Prince, sending his patients home for the week. As he locked the clinic doors, he overlooked one patient, one who had died inside. Three days later, the stench of the putrefying body attracted the attention of the neighbors. The police were summoned. They kicked the door down, found the rotting body, and Father Joe found himself banned from Haiti.

Back in Baie-de-Sol I am talking with Jean-Luc.

"It is such a fucking mess," I say.

"Yeah, well," Jean-Luc says, "it's not entirely our fault. There are weird things going on here. I mean yes, we are a mess, that's true. This is the Third World. But you should understand that we are under the thumb of the Western medical system and the missionaries. We can't move." Jean-Luc then begins to talk about what he calls "medical imperialism."

"Haiti is different than the U.S. We have our own medical system, an indigenous medical system unrivaled anywhere in the world. We have leaf doctors, shaman, indigenous masseuses. They are everywhere. They are earnestly interested in treating people. The peasants trust them and use their services. But we, the Haitian Department of Health, cannot use them. USAID won't let us. We cannot train them and we cannot distribute antibiotics, rehydration salts, or any other lifesaving medicines through them. Just last month, a Haitian organization tried to use *bokor* to distribute condoms. Some American missionary picked up the telephone and called his congressman and the funds to that organization were cut off the next day."

"Why?" I ask.

"Why? The missionaries don't want what they see as satanic witch doctors getting any credibility, that's why. On the one hand there is money in medicine. Almost every mission out there has a clinic. Medicines are the great white magic. It gives the distributor power. Makes people believers. And that is all that has to happen. Some missionary hears that an NGO is using a *bokor* or a leaf doctor, a phone call to their congressman and the money stops."

In Gonaives once again, I go by to see Father Olivier, the French priest who told be about the CARE "zombie" feeding centers. The little priest leads me across his back yard and toward a center for old people and AIDS sufferers. As we go, he tells me matter-of-factly that he has been in Haiti for twenty-two years. Before that, he spent twenty-two years in Laos. "Yeah, yeah," the Priest says as if he were talking about something trivial. "Left in 1975 when they dropped a bomb on my compound.

"Next they tried to execute me. Yeah, yeah." He repeats the phrase. "Figured it was time to leave."

We arrive at the Center, a square, stone building with rooms built facing inward toward a large courtyard. On one side of the building are the men's rooms and on the other side, across the courtyard, are those for women. There are twenty rooms in all. Each has five beds. In almost every room there is at least one very sick person. Many of the patients are young, some are old. First we go down the side with the men. I follow the priest into each room and stand by the door as he goes over and greets the sick with a curt "*kouman ou ye*." (How are you?)

He does not bother waiting for a response, in every case he immediately turns and walks out the door, saying in a loud voice as he goes, "yeah, yeah." In one instance he leaves the side of an emaciated AIDS sufferer. I am standing inside the room, by the door, watching. Walking past me he pauses, puts his face close to mine as if he is going to tell me a secret, but instead of whispering shouts, "AIDS. HE'S DYING."

Next we go down the women's side of the building. Passing a closed door, the priest pushe it open and pops his head throughFollowing suit, I lean over him and pop my head in too. It is the woman's bathroom and a woman is inside squatting on the top of a platform, shitting into a hole. The Priest smiles and waves. "How are you?" he shouts and then, "Yeah, yeah," and we move on.

Shortly after that, I leave. And as I go I am wondering if the Priest is simply a comic or if he is loosing his grip on reality.

The next morning, before leaving Gonaives, I went by to visit Father Olivier again, but he was not home. I ask someone in front of his house where I might find him and soon I am walking across the Gonaives hospital grounds where I am told, "he works." I am not sure where I am going. I stop a nurse. She directs me to the back of the sprawling complex. As I go the people are fewer and I pass smaller neglected out buildings. At the very back of the sprawling hospital compound, I find an old wooden house-like structure on the porch of which is a crowd of waiting women and children. I say, *bon jou,* "good day" to the crowd and the crowd responds in unison, *bon jou.* Then I ask if anyone knows where Father Olivier is. The crowd parts, giving me a path to the door.

Inside is what looks like a 19th century hospital ward, rows of neat single beds, all made up, bed pans by the side. But no Father Olivier. I am getting confused. I ask a nurse, "Is there a Father Olivier here?" She point s to a door at the back of the room. I open the door and there in a tiny office, sitting in a chair, slouched up against the wall, wearing a green hospital shirt and a stethoscope hanging around his neck, Father Olivier is looking up at me mischievously and grinning from ear to ear.

It turns out the priest is also a nurse. He specializes in skin diseases, and when he arrived in Haiti in 1978 he was "especially interested in the plight of lepers." He recalls that local health officials told him there were no lepers in Haiti. "We will see about that," he said and managed to get the back of the hospital grounds donated for his skin disease clinic. The Priest planted shade trees and erected simple wooden single-story buildings to receive patients. In the next twenty-one years, he treated 1,190 lepers.

Father Olivier led me out through the waiting patients, through another room full of beds and out back where big trees shaded a secret courtyard. A girl about seven years old is sitting at a table with a boy her age. From a distance she looks as if she has patches of smooth scar tissue on her face and arms, which I assume are scars from burns. When we get closer they look too smooth for burns. Olivier looks at me. *Lep,* he says.

He points to the boy, *li gen lep tou*, "He has leprosy too." The priest tells me the girl can heal in about two years, "but she must take her medication."

When I leave the little Priest, walking out the door of the wooden clinic, down the steps and out through the hospital grounds, I can't help but think to myself, *maybe there is some hope after all.*

Five years later, in September 2004, Father Olivier would die in the first of the Gonaives floods, one that took the lives of over two thousand people. He was caught in his home and drowned. The people of Gonaives modified the story and reported him as being swept away while trying to save people, which would have been a fitting end for a man who dedicated his life to helping the most desperate, diseased, and neglected of the poor.

Chapter Ten
Disconnected Directors and
the Arrogant Haitian Elite

I returned to Port-au-Prince. The next day I am due to present my findings to a group of CARE directors. On my way to the CARE mansion I stop my motorcycle on a hill overlooking the city and think about my experiences over the previous four years and now my experiences doing research for CARE. I no longer harbor any illusions about being involved in helping the impoverished people of Haiti, but I still have to think of myself. I have invested years of my life studying and working in the field so that I can have a career in development. If I can not save Haiti, then maybe I can at least save a few Haitians. I think about the girls, Albeit and Tobe. And maybe I can save myself. I still hope to do research and work in development, and I hope to do it for a reasonable salary.

I sit on the motorcycle looking out at the city. A splendid vista of shanty towns and open air markets spills down the Caribbean mountainside across a plain to sea's edge and then along the shore, out to the smoggy fringes of the city where more sprawling shanty towns takeover. A light haze of exhaust and smoke from cooking fires rises gently from the squalor. The sea in the distance stretches blue and vast toward an endless horizon. I think about my future here in Haiti, about this first big consultancy job with the world's largest multinational charitable corporation. If I can't help poor Haitians through development, at least I can make some money and change the lives of those close to me. Yes, and my own life. I think about the promise that should accrue from my years of effort at the university, endless hours studying Haitian culture and history, the lonely days and nights living on dirt floors, estranged from my own culture, a stranger, always an outsider, and surrounded by poverty. I take a deep breath and the scent of sewage and rotting produce fills my senses. For a moment my world seems limitless and promising, after all, I got a pay check coming.

I head for CARE to pick up my check, But first I have to get authorization so I go to the office of CARE's Chief Financial Officer (CFO) and de facto director of affairs in the CARE mansion. She is an American, late thirties, mother of four, shoulder-length blond hair, bright, commanding, holder of an MBA. I am standing in the office talking to her. The phone rings. She answers it. The conversation went something like this: "Chief Financial Officer may I help you? ... Yes, yes, everything has been arranged... Okay, Okay... I am going to have the money sent out on the next vehicle..."

As it happened, the previous week on the road that UNOPs built in Tierre Bleu, the same road that Enel was working on when he was killed, there was an accident. A produce truck went barreling down the new lime rock road Joy riders, local guys, had jumped on the back. They were hanging on and hollering as peasants in Jean Makout so love to do, *gas kolé* "pedal to the metal." Encouraged, the driver let her rip. On the first sharp turn of the new road, the truck toppled over and rolled down a steep embankment. I just happened to show up in Tierre Bleu the next day and everyone told me about it. Arnaud was living there at the time, she had been on the scene the day before, and together we went to see the remains of the truck. I stood there looking at the mangled wreckage as she described in gory detail the dead passengers she had seen the day before. There was absolutely no question, she insisted, there were four dead bodies. Four.

It turned out that the truck had been leased by CARE, it was CARE produce and a CARE driver, and now here I am standing in CFO's office and she is on the phone with a Haitian employee, a CARE monitor in the village of Jean Makout where the bodies have been put in the morgue. CARE is going to pay for the morgue and funeral expenses, the monitor is handling it and so she, the CFO, is asking the guy, "What is the cost of the morgue and the funeral services for each?...Yes, yes...How many bodies was that again?...OK, I gotcha, seven. I'll get a check out to you right away."

I leave the CFO's office and in the lobby encounter Seraphin, director of CARE food distributor in Gonaives, the same one who had recounted to me the 1992 firings and corruption of CARE staff. He is talking to two distinguished Haitian ladies. One is tall, very white, with short light-red hair. She is in her fifties, and has the manners and appearance of a sophisticated Parisian. Seraphin introduces her as a cultural expert who has spent much of the past twenty years in Paris. The other lady is an education specialist, also elite, but of a different type. She is medium height, light-skinned mulatto with long black hair. She spent the past eighteen years in New York City. I learn that the ladies are fulltime CARE consultants. Their names escape me almost immediately, but the conversation sinks in.

Seraphin introduces me to the ladies as "an anthropologist who has been living in the Far-West and is writing his dissertation."

"Do you think," the Cultural Expert turns to me and I find myself looking into the blue eyes of the most European featured Haitian I have ever met, "I mean do you believe that it is possible that a person who is not Haitian can ever really understand Haiti and the Haitian people?"

"Well there is a principle in anthropology" I reply, "the principle is that one should never study one's own culture because you are stuck inside of it, you can't see things clearly if you are involved, if you have preconceived ideas that you have grown up with, such as attitudes of superiority toward your own poor or toward other ethnic groups. That is why we study other cultures and not our own. It allows us a measure of objectivity."

"That may be true in other countries," says the *mullato* lady who has spent the past eighteen years in the United States, "but you are going to find as you learn about Haiti that it is much different here. A foreigner could never hope to understand the nature of Haitians. Haiti is not like other cultures."

"Tell us," the Cultural Expert says with polite interest, "what is the topic of your dissertation?"

"Well without boring you it concerns the high birth rates among rural women and the rather obvious probability that it results from the economic utility of children among peasant families. It is an old story I suppose. Farmers, children, work."

"Oh dear," the Cultural Expert laughs and then adds, almost apologetically, "it used to be like that long ago. But not now," and then looking to her colleague, the other highly paid consultant, "no, it's not like that anymore, no, not with imports and all? There is very little farming now."

What do you mean 'not like that anymore?' I think to myself. *I have just spent the past four years wondering around out there and I can't think of anyone who somehow isn't a farmer. Even the school teachers you guys train are farmers. Judges have gardens and livestock. Everyone is a farmer.*

"Oh no," the light-skinned mulatto lady responds with equal expertise, "In the old days when the peasants farmed they used children to help them. They were very important then," she looks at me as if to make sure that I am understanding, "But they do not farm anymore. There is nothing coming out of the rural areas. And with inexpensive imported food, no, no, farming is no longer necessary. Why for a few *goud* you can feed a whole family."

What in the hell are you guys talking about. Their words havemade me almost dizzy. *Didn't you read any books when you were over there in France and the United States? Haven't you read any reports since you got back? Didn't you look out the window when you rode through the countryside to your seminars? Have you ever listened to any of the people who you are supposed to be helping? Where the hell do you think the fruits and vegetables you eat come from?*

"Well, you see," says The Cultural Expert, looking sympathetically at me, "children are no longer economically important to the peasants."

"Perhaps," says the *mulatto* lady, "you should choose another topic."

The Cultural Expert and her friend are not unusual among the Haitian elite, famous for their haughty arrogance, and, most important of all, their ignorance of their own poor.

After leaving CARE, I head down into the city to visit a friend from Jean Makout. I turn off the cracked asphalt road and down a dirt entrance way, park my motorcycle, ask a boy to guard it for me and, arriving at a small slit in the façade of a row of bare cinderblock houses, I squeeze through, past the house-fronts and into the neighborhoods.

I follow a narrow footpath beside a drainage ditch where pigs wallow in the cool filth of a bubbling sludge. The smell of urine and feces saturates the air. and I sense the cloud of mosquitoes as it forms a funnel over my head. The path winds along between bare block walls and houses. Drying laundry hangs everywhere and a glimpse inside a compound, through a crumbling wall, reveals a girl sitting over a washbasin, scrubbing clothes with her hands. A skeletal dog barks, only to be sent yelping for cover as a bored boy throws a rock at it. The neighborhoods that I walk through are each dominated by people from the same rural sectors of the country, sticking together in the city, searching one another out just as do immigrants in any strange, foreign land. They band together under the protection and the comfort of familiarity. These are neighborhoods where thieves frequently meet swift and horrible deaths, stoned and beaten by a mob of cousins and friends. I arrive at a door made of deteriorating plywood and rusting scraps of tin.

"Onè," I shout, and a woman's voice shouts back, *"Respè."*

I push the plywood door open and walk in. The room is barren except for a small rickety table, two homemade wicker chairs, and a single iron bed that is pushed up next to a wall. The dirt floor is swept clean. Sheets hang on two sides of the room and partition it into private sleeping quarters. An exposed wall is covered with pictures from magazines: A white couple picnicking in a park with their white children, an advertisement for a stereo, a glamorous white cigarette girl, a new Volkswagen. Another sheet partitions the back of the house where the kitchenware is stored and where there is an unseen backdoor. The sheet lifts and from behind it Ma Poch appears.

"Oh Lord, my child, how are you?" The wrinkles on her face crease into a smile and Ma Poch, mother of my friend Dajenson, who worked with me on the Jean Makout survey, comes close, rises on her toes and presents a cheek for me to kiss.

"Why look at you, *pitit mwen*," she says, assessing me from head to foot. "You look as if you are wasting away. Has no one been taking care of you?"

"I've been exercising a lot, " I say.

"Ahh, good Lord, look at how flat your belly is. You haven't eaten a bite all day. Nati," Ma Poch calls out in a high-pitched half-shout for her daughter.

"I'm not hungry," I object , " really,"

"Oh Lord child," says Ma Poch exhorting me with a worrisome expression. "You need to conserve your strength, all that exercise is going to kill you."

"It's good for him Mom," I hear my friend Dajenson say from behind a sheet. "Tim doesn't do anything else." The sheet is pulled back and a smiling Dajenson walks out and extends his hand for me to shake.

"Tim has no garden to work in and keep him fit, *non Manman*," he says, shaking my hand.

"Yes, I do," I say. "That is why I am here. I got a job with CARE."

"So CARE is your garden," Dajenson laughs at the metaphor.

"Well, it's just temporary. I am evaluating CARE's food distribution program, see about getting aid to the orphanages and hospitals. But I'll make a little something and more importantly, it's a chance to get my career started, get involved in helping people in the countryside. "

"*Oui*, you're gonna be rich. I always knew it," Ma Poch is smiling and looking me over again, "My son," she says, lowering her voice and taking on a tone of seriousness, "could you get us a food distribution center?"

"Mom," Dajenson cautions.

"Nati," Ma Poch calls to her daughter again.

"*Platil Manman,*" Nati responds from somewhere behind the house.

"Bring me a plate of rice," shouts Ma Poch.

A moment later, Nati, Dajenson's eighteen-year-old sister, walk s into the room carrying in her outstretched hands a plate heaped with rice. She is the teenage image of her mother, tiny, fine featured, more handsome than beautiful.

"Timotè," she says greeting me and setting the plate of rice down on the rickety little table.

"Nati," Ma Poch informs her daughter, "Timotè has a job with CARE."

"*Gade non*" (look here)," says Nati, standing back from the table and putting her hands on her hip. "Get us a distribution center."

"Yes, we want a food distribution center in Jean Makout," says Ma Poch, smiling, "so we can distribute food to hungry people."

"You mean so that you can steal food," Dajenson reproaches his mother.

"It's not stealing brother, *non*," says Nati, "not if everyone does it."

After leaving Dajenson and Ma Poch, I decide to visit the sister of a Haitian friend from Miami whom I have visited many times before.

Doctor Bissou doesn't live in the slums, but in a neighborhood of embassies and luxurious homes. Her plush concrete house is sunken into the side of a hill and surrounded by spacious slate patios and gardens. She is divorced, in her late thirties, a plump, attractive woman, a former Cape Haitian homecoming queen. She lives with her light-skinned eleven-year-old daughter, Dee.

I came to know her because her brother, Jean-Claude, was a good friend of mine at the University of Florida. He and his sister are from an aristocratic Haitian family with roots that reach back to the revolution some two hundred years ago, when their great great great great grandfather was a colonel in the victorious army of Jean-Jacques Dessalines. More recently, their grandfather was the chief engineer for Haiti's largest (now defunct) U.S.-owned agro-enterprise, the twenty-five-thousand-acre Plantation Dauphin—one of the few plantations established in Haiti during the 1915–1934 U.S. military occupation. Doctor Bissou is one of the few members of her elite family who has not abandoned Haiti for the United States or France.

I originally met her in the summer of 1990 on my first trip into Haiti. I was working on my master's thesis. I had only a $1,000 grant to fly into and out of Haiti and do seven weeks of summertime research. I knew no one in the country. Jean-Claude had given me his sister's phone number and so after I got off the plane and checked into my hotel, I called her. Dr.Bissou said she was happy to hear from me. Her brother had informed her that I was coming and she wasted no time getting to the hotel to pick me up.

I was standing outside when she pulled up in a new Hyundai economy car, yanked the emergency brake, and popped out of the car. She is milk chocolate with a smooth complexion and her hair straightened and silky. She is wearing designer jeans, an expensive blouse, gold earrings, and a gold chain on the end of which dangled a gold crucifix. A pair of brown leather driving gloves hug her plump, delicate hands.

"Tim, *vous devrez etre* Tim," she says in thick and exquisite French.

Moments later she is driving me around the elite neighborhood of Petionville, showing me important land marks. We drive by her favorite place, Saint Peter's Cathedral. "I go to church seven times a week," she assures me. Next she shows me the grocery store and the local pizza parlor. Then we are in the neighborhoods. As she drives, her cherub face is intently focused on the road and her gloved hands expertly grip the steering wheel. She is screeching the tiny economy car around corners, racing through shanty towns built in ravine bottoms, past children playing on the side of the road and people walking along on errands, and then up a hill again, past mansions and embassies. She talks to me in broken English and she manages to do it so incessantly and so rapidly that I find myself wondering when she breaths. She tells me how concerned she is for me. She explains with an air of great sincerity that there are many desperately poor people in Port-au-Prince and that not being accustomed to such poverty I may over-react. I might feel sorry for *les miserables* in the street and do something as ludicrous as handing out my cash. The car is leaning into an especially long curve, the road is narrow, we are sandwiched between the high stone walls of two mansions and we can not see what is coming. My grip on the elbow rest tightens.

Intent on her driving and the gravity of her advice, she does not notice my fear. "You should conserve your money," she says. "After all, you cannot help everyone. And if you are broke you will not be able to help anyone. Just as importantly, Port-au-Prince is dangerous. Very, very dangerous." As if to emphasize her point, she momentarily takes her eyes off the road and looks at me. I resist the urge to grab the steering wheel. She looks back at the road and a wave of relief washes over me.

"There are thieves and con artists," she says. "You must be careful. Changing dollars for Haitian currency is especially risky."

She adds that money changers were untrustworthy at best and, at worst, someone could kill me and steal all my money.

"Then where would you be?" she asks.

For my security, Dr.Bissou insists that she change my money for me. I agree and, as it just so happens, she has a large quantity of *goud* (Haitian money) right there in her purse. So she changes my money, buys me a pizza, wishes me well, and drops me back at the hotel. Before driving away, she pokes her head out the car window and, smiling, says: "When you get to the province you won't need money."

Well, it wasn't true that I didn't need money in the province. But I needed considerably less in the province than in Port-au-Prince and that was fortunate for me, because several days later I learned that Dr.Bissou had given me half what my money was worth.

Later, when I got back to Miami and told my friend Jean-Claude—her brother—he clucked his tongue and said, "Yeah, they do it to me too."

On this visit, the doctor is not home. But Rose, her maid, is. She lets me in and leads me to the kitchen where she is cooking the afternoon meal for the doctor's daughter, Dee.

Rose is only twenty-eight, but she looks a weary and rundown forty. She is thin, her eyes droop, her cheeks sag, and her shoulders slump. I am sitting at the kitchen table listening to her while I eat a plate of fried eggs and boiled plantains. She is looking at me sadly, her long braids plopping off of her tired head in different directions. And then she launches into a long and puzzling litany of complaints. "Timoté," she says, "I can't take it here anymore, *non*. There used to be three of us, but now, now I am the only one working in the house."

"What happened to Evon and Lizan?" I ask, remembering the other maids.

"They left. Evon had a child that got sick and so she went back to the countryside to care for her. And Lizan, well the doctor wouldn't give her a raise. She only pays us 500 *goud* a month [$33]. Lizan found a job with an embassy on the other side of the street, they're paying her 1,500 *goud* [$100]. Can you believe that?"

"Wow."

"She even has her own room. And she and the other maids have their own bathroom, *oui*. They get one day off every week. Oh, Lord, if I could only find a job like that. But now they're gone, gone to where the water's fresher. And me, now things are worse for me, non, I have to do all the work myself."

"Why doesn't the doctor hire someone else?"

"We have tried. No one wants to work here, *non*."

"I would think that there are lots of people looking for a job as a maid."

"Have you ever been down in the basement? Have you seen the room we have to sleep in down there? And the doctor won't pay enough. The going rate for a maid here in Port-au-Prince is now 750 *goud* [$50]."

"Why doesn't the doctor get some children to work in the house?"

"I have tried to get her to do that. She says that she doesn't trust them and she says that she would have to send them to school. So she refuses. *Non.* We can't find anyone else. Now it is only me and I have to do everything. The doctor and her girl will do nothing for themselves." Rose huff. "That child will not even wash her own face. I have to do it. I can be downstairs washing clothes. Dee is sitting right here in the kitchen eating. She needs something from the refrigerator. What does she do? She calls me upstairs to get it out of the refrigerator and hand it to her."

"She calls you upstairs to get something out of the refrigerator?"

"*Oui,* the refrigerator that is right next to her! The doctor is just as bad. The doctor, she is undressing. Me, I am washing dishes or cooking. She will call me into her room so that she can have me take an article of clothes from her hand and drop it in the hamper. The hamper that is right next to her! I have to do everything. These people will do nothing for themselves. And I am exhausted. I have not had a single day off for over six months."

"That's ridiculous, why don't you take some time off?"

"I can't. The doctor says she needs me." Rose looks at the floor and shakes her head again. "I get up at five every morning. I make their lunches. I cook their breakfast. They don't get up until 7:00, and me, I don't get to sleep again until 10:00 or 11:00 at night, after the doctor has gone to bed. I just can't take it."

And then Rose talks about her two children, who she has left in the countryside with a family she knows, one that can better care for them and where the children work for their keep, sweeping, cooking, cleaning, and running errands for the owners of the house. She tells me that she has only seen her children once in the two years that she has worked for the doctor.

"With the money the doctor gives me I cannot even afford to pay for their school." Tears begin to stream down her face. "I want my children to go to school."

Just then Dee calls from some far recess of the house. Rose wipes her tears away and obediently goes to see what she needs. I push the remainder of the fried egg and plantain around my plate thinking about Doctor Bissou's aunt.

Whenever I was in Cape Haitian, Haiti's second largest city, I would visit Dr. Bissou and Vladamir's aunt, the family matriarch, an aristocratic Haitian woman who commands great respect, a retired professor at the prestigious Teacher's College. She raised the doctor and her brother, their parents having emigrated to the United States, and so I always felt obliged, out of respect for my friend Jean-Claude, to visit the Matriarch.

Once when I was visiting she gave me a lecture on the declining quality of Haitian maids. The Matriarch and I were leaning over the banister of an inner balcony in her colonial style house looking down into the courtyard at three maids who sat scrubbing clothes. The Matriarch has just finished barking a series of reprimands at them and now she turns to me and she says, "You just can't get good help anymore. The poor used to be so respectful. You would get a maid and keep her for years. Not anymore."

"That's terrible," I reply, not knowing what else to say—I never had a maid.

"Yes, it is. We used to call them *servan* (servant). Then they decided they didn't like that anymore and wanted to be called *bon* (good). Then it was *ed* (help). Now they don't want to be called that either. They don't know what they want to be called. I can't keep up with it."

I shake my head in a gesture of sympathy for the unreasonable demands that the servants have made on my friend's aunt and she rewards my sympathy with a story about her friend who was robbed by three thugs. The leader made the woman drink a glass of battery acid. "I don't know how she survived," says the Matriarch. "It almost killed her. She lost her voice."

At just that moment a twelve-year-old servant girl who lives in the house walks by and the Matriarch snaps at her, "Where do you think you are going, child?"

"To clean the bathroom, Madame."

The Matriarch reaches over, grabs a hunk of the girl's cheek, twists it violently and hangs on. "You lazy little bum, you have not finished the bedrooms." Still holding the girl by the cheek, the Matriarch walks her around in a circle and then pushes her back in the direction from which she has come.

"Where was I?" she asks. "Oh yes," and the Matriarch resumes telling me that the leader of the bandits, the one who had forced the woman to drink battery acid, turned out to be the woman's gardener. "Can you imagine, the guy had been her faithful servant for fifteen years. Oh, my, how things have changed here in Haiti."

Rose comes back into the room carrying an empty glass, "The little Madame would like crackers and *confiture*," she said, trying not to be facetious.

I stand up, kiss Rose on the forehead and hand her my dirty plate.

"I'm sorry, Rose," I say, and fumbling through my book bag I find 200 *goud*, hand it to her, gather up my belongings and prepare to head back to the CARE mansion. But before leaving I want to see Dee who, in gives me an uncanny, pinch-myself experience that neatly punctuates Rose's complaints.

The Doctor's daughter, Dee, is a beautiful light-skinned 11-year-old who attends one of Port-au-Prince's most elite French schools where she is a straight A student. I find her on the far side of the house in a drawing room with her face intently fixed on the screen of a color television. She turns off the television and politely offers me first one cheek to kiss and then the other. With the manners and gestures of a sophisticated woman she is soon explaining to me that she has a parasitic plant in her mother's garden.

"Would you like to see it?" she asks.

Enchanted, I follow her to the garden. She stops in front of a small tree and points to a crook in the branches where, sure enough, there grows a tiny parasitic fern.

"There, you see," bright little Dee exclaims triumphantly. "The one plant is living off of the other plant." Then looking at me curiously and carefully enunciating her words, she asks: "Do you know what par-a-sit-ic means?"

"No," I say, wanting to encourage her young mind, "Tell me."

"Well, it is like the poor here in Haiti," she says, "They live off the rich. They suck on you until you have nothing left, until you are finished."

Appalled, I ask her where she heard such an explanation and she tells me, "From my teacher at school."

Next I visit a fellow anthropologist who has been in Haiti off and on for years. I want to discuss the presentation that I will give the next day at CARE. I tell her of my findings and she gives me some advice:

"Don't tell them food aid is wholesale corrupt. It just doesn't matter. What matters is that you have a job. CARE wants to know how to get the food out. Tell them how to distribute it, how to make people accountable, and how to choose the institutions. They like recommendations. Pursue a strategy to make people accountable, to lower the corruption. But be positive. Don't tell them not to do anything or that food aid is rotten. And," laughing, "for God's sake don't tell them that food aid is a USAID and World Bank plot to destroy the Haitian economy."

The next day I gave the presentation to a group of CARE staffers. I had decided that my friend was right. I planned not to say anything about extreme corruption, international plots to intensify Haitian poverty, rotten medical systems, or the widespread social institution of fake orphanages. I decided to be positive, to put an upbeat spin on my findings in hopes that I could secure more work.

I begin moderately enough, telling them about the hospitals and the great need. But when I get to the orphanages I choke.

"I visited all the orphanages and I am not sure that it is a good idea to promote these institutions."

"Is there something wrong with the orphanages?"

"Well," I begin, and moments later I am telling the CARE staff about, "what strikes me a system of venality." And I don't stop there.

"Look, I feel that I have a professional obligation to tell you guys that your entire food program is rife with corruption."

I look at Seraphin, the lean muscled Haitian director of food distribution who will soon be dismissed for being "tricky." His eyes dart away.

"I don't just mean within CARE," I continue, "but throughout the entire system And what is disturbing is that I suspect everyone in this room is aware of it. You guys must know for instance that Jean Makout elementary school directors steal a great deal of the food meant for the children? Many of these schools were set up for no other reason than to steal food."

"Well yes," says one staffer.

"But to what degree," challenges another, "no one knows."

"So you are saying that you also know there is no working system of accountability?"

"Well that is not true," says the ranking director. "We've tried to do something about it. We integrate food aid into the community, make the peasants feel that it belongs to them, try to get them to govern themselves. For example, in our school feeding program each school director must pick five members of the community to serve on a committee that monitors the distribution of food."

"We have, however," say another staff member, "had a little problem with that."

"What is that?" I ask.

"Well, it's the school directors who pick the members of the committee."

"Yes," says a low-ranking director, "they pick their family and friends."

And so it went.

"You are very negative," Says ys one of the higher–level Haitian directors who was present when I delivered my report.

I am back at the CARE mansion to pick up my final pay check and he has stopped me in the hall. He asks me about foster homes in the U.S. and I tell them there are some problems, but that I don't know much about it. Then I realize that he has a point he is trying to make. "USAID does not want to hear that stuff," he continues. I never get the connection with the U.S. foster homes, but he is apparently angry that I discouraged the use of the orphanages. He tells me again that I am negative, "very, very negative."

Another director is standing nearby, overhears this and echoes the criticism. "Yes, we all agree that you are very negative. USAID does not want to hear that."

"But I am not working for USAID, I am working for you guys, for CARE."

"It is the same thing," says the one director. "The orders all come down from USAID and when they make up their mind to do a project, they hire a consultant to help them do it, not to tell them not to do it. If you cannot be more positive they will just have to hire another consultant to do the same thing."

I am unsure of myself.

"I am working for CARE," I stutter, "not USAID, and it is supposed to be CARE's decision whether they want to deliver food for USAID." Hearing myself I know what I have seen. I haven't made any of this up. I saw it over and over. "If it is not in the interest of the people, 'the poorest of the poor,' then CARE should be saying no." I am more confident now. "That is what CARE is supposed to be about, isn't it? They aren't supposed to be acting on behalf of USAID. They are supposed to be acting on behalf of the poorest of the poor. Aren't they?"

Now that I have heard myself say it, now that it's all out my doubts are erased. I know that I am right. CARE is one of the biggest charities in the world. CARE was the one U.S. charitable organization that I had heard of all my life. I had always thought of them as an example of U.S. benevolence. I remember CARE commericials on television, my mother telling me how through CARE we fed starving war ravaged Europe. And now I realize that something is very wrong with CARE's current role in this business of food aid and I just figured out what it is:

"For Christ sake, that is what the CARE charter says, 'help the poorest of the poor' and now you're telling me that we are all working for USAID, not the poor."

"That's right. It is USAID. Get with it. You want a job or you want to be an idealist?"

That afternoon I left Petionville and I ride my motorcycle back down the hill toward the city and the highway that will carry me back to the Province. I look out on that same paysage that I had stood admiring the morning before. But my mood has changed and I don't see the same promise. What I see is a chaotic gloom of shanty towns and reeking open air markets that jag down the Caribbean mountainside and crowd across a congested plain. Rising ominously from the squalor is a venomous haze of carbon monoxide, petro-chemicals half burnt by dilapidated vehicles and the smoke from charcoal fires burning the last of Haiti's disappearing trees. The sea beyond is brown and thick with human excrement, slick with a suffocating film of motor oil and floating morass of discarded bottles and plastic bags. My eyes follow along the shore, out to the dingy fringes of more sprawling shanty towns where the visitor is afraid even to breath the putrid air; where at any hour of any day, people can be seen wondering out amongst the ubiquitous garbage heaps and defecating while others walk nonchalantly past. Trash spreads out onto a cove and homes made of discarded refuse meld into one another, built in the trash and made of it with scraps of wood, cardboard and plastic bags. When it floods, these people, the wretched of one of the most wretched cities on earth, must crawl from their hovels and seek refuge on the highest mounds of garbage. Sick people, too weak to pull themselves to safety, sometimes drown while lying ill in makeshift beds of cartons and rags.

I think about the future of Haiti, about the things that I have learned in my first big consultancy job with the world's largest multinational charitable corporation. I think about the despair that has accrued in Haiti from years of social engineering by developed- world politicians, U.S. lobbyists, and bankers, decision makers who sit in board rooms, most never having laid eyes on Haiti much less the sordid slums they have helped create. Decision makers who believe that the only path to economic salvation is through industrialization and sweat shops, through slums and ten-hour work days for a sum of money that would not buy an order of toast in a developed-world restaurant. I think about the ladies at CARE, the cultural experts who seem totally out of touch with the people they are supposed to be helping. About the monitor duping CARE's CFO into paying the funeral and morgue expenses for three extra bodies. How could he? How could she not know? How could the system be so corrupt? So rife with negligence? I think about the Doctor, about her daughter Dee. How could a privileged child be taught in school that the poor are parasites? My world at this moment seems filled with despair and hopelessness.

Chapter Eleven
A Boy's Mysterious Death
Evokes Troubling Thoughts

On the evening of a major holiday, when parties were going on throughout the extravagant neighborhood surrounding The School of Jesus Christ of America, a boy fell dead just outside the compound wall. It was a busy spot, an intersection. Strangely, no one saw the boy die. But he was soon discovered lying in the dirt and it was immediately remembered that, to keep out intruders, Reverend Baxter had a live electric security wire running along the top of the compound wall. The news ricocheted from mouth to mouth, neighborhood to neighborhood, to the outskirts of the city, up into the hills and across The Big River. People gathered by the thousands. They poured out of the neighborhood parties. They came down from the mountains. They crossed the Big River and walked the two miles through the city streets. The police came. The mayor came. Lawyer Kaylin Krapley came. Electricians for the state electric company came. Tests were made to detect live wires. None was found.

The next day I arrive. I am visiting with Sharon.

"What happened after they couldn't find a live wire?"

"Nothing. People kept coming."

"What did the police do?"

"The police left. The crowd was getting excited and they said there was nothing they could do. They told us we should go in the house and then they left."

When I arrived at the School, even though it was the next day, there were still people milling about in the street grumbling. I parked my motorcycle and walked by three slum women standing together looking at the Baxter's house.

"The school is for the rich," one of them growled. "They are making money off of our backs," snarled another.

And now as I listen to Sharon I find that I am trying to suppress an ugly thought. I am secretly wishing the Baxters had been burned out. *Dechouke* the Haitians call it and it happens throughout the country. An abusive police captain, a known murderer, an excessively corrupt and cruel politician and one night a crowd shows up at the house, stones begin to break the windows and soon the mob is beating down the door, pillaging the house and then setting it afire. *Had the Baxter's been burned out it would be poetic justice for depriving the poor of what is theirs.*

I crush the thought.

"Nobody started throwing rocks?" I ask.

"Some people threw rocks at the gate," Sharon says. "And that lawyer, Kaylin Krapley, that pig showed up and started banging on the gate saying that he was going to sue my father."

"You should be damn thankful that you guys didn't get hurt, that they didn't burn the house down."

"I am not afraid of them."

"Sharon, you are not afraid of them, *pep la,* the people? Remember? Haitian mobs? Burning? People getting tires placed around their necks, doused in gasoline and set afire? You could have lost your dogs, all your possessions, the school could have been ransacked and they could have burned the houses, to say nothing of your own safety."

After talking to Sharon I head home. I ride my motorcycle through the dirt streets of Baie-de-Sol, past flickering fires where women fry hunks of pig fat and mashed plantains, past groups of men drinking rum, past sexy young women wearing skimpy skirts and waiting for a man to buy their affection. As I go, I think about my second voyage to Haiti. It was September 1991. I had a ticket to fly into the country on the very same day that the government of

Jean Bertrand Aristide was toppled by a bloody military coup, one that took the lives of over three thousand Port-au-Prince slum dwellers.

Aristide, himself the offspring of a poor family, began his career as an activist priest in one of the poorest slums of Port-au-Prince. He first came to national attention when he led a march to the infamous Fort Dimanch prison where over the years thousands of political dissidents had been tortured and killed. As they approached the prison, Aristide was being interviewed on live radio, when the prison authorities opened fire on the protestors. Hiding behind a car, Aristide continued his commentary, people dropping dead on either side of him. He seemed invincible. He continued vitriolic attacks against government repression, survived multiple assassination attempts. In one incident he and three other priests were ambushed by gunmen on a highway. They escaped. Yet another time, in the midst of Sunday mass, his church was invaded by a shooting, hacking and bludgeoning gang of paramilitary thugs who slaughtered some twelve of the parishioners and burned the church to the ground. Again, Aristide escaped.

With each new harrowing experience the mystique surrounding the young priest grew and his determination intensified. It was as if he was protected by God. The impoverished masses came to believe that he was indeed the incarnation of a divine being. In 1989 his radical political activism got him expelled from the Silesian order and he was soon running for president. He called his political movement *Lavalas*, after the flash floods that clean the mountainsides and the cities of filth and garbage. Like a *lavalas*, his party was going to cascade through Haitian society and politics, cleaning it of corruption and privilege. He spoke of radical change, fairness to the poor, jobs and justice, development, highways, and education. The impoverished masses loved him wildly.

Surviving yet another assassination attempt, a campaign-trail grenade attack that killed seven and wounded fifty-three of his followers, Aristide won the 1990 internationally monitored elections with 67 percent of the vote, three times that of his nearest contender, Marc Bazin, the U.S.-favored candidate—a man who had spent most of his adult life working outside of Haiti for—what else?—the World Bank. But then, after seven months of being blocked at every turn by the commercial elite, Aristide was ousted by the very military leaders whom he had appointed, the CIA-trained narcotraffickers described in an earlier chapter. As he was being flown off into exile, the military officers who had sent Aristide packing imposed a strict curfew, sealed off the Port-au-Prince slums, and had their soldiers spread through the streets selectively gunning down known *Lavalas* activists and showering any sign of protest with bullets.

During the three days that followed, at least three thousand people were slaughtered. But for me and and at least some other anthropologists and missionaries working in the country, the many coups and uprisings in the late 1980s and early 1990s were more an inconvenience than a threat. We were not targets and could resign ourselves to working around them. So while the military was gunning people down in the Port-au-Prince slums, I chartered a small plane in Miami and flew into the city of Cape Haitian. As I sat in the back of a battered taxi riding from the airport to a hotel, the driver pointed to the smoldering remains of a large house. "*Dechoukaj*," he said. "This is what the people have on their minds."

That night, soldiers shot two young men in the street below my hotel window. They were teenagers from the slums and they had been trying to write a slogan on the wall of the hotel. But for the most part, Cape Haitian was quiet. Within several days I boarded a Haitian sailboat and, thirty-six hours later, I sailed into Baie-de-Sol harbor. And that is where I met Sharon, sunbathing on a beach. She invited me to lunch with her parents, siblings, and the other teachers, we became friends and in the ensuing nine years Sharon did many favors for me. It was she who made it possible for the girls Albeit and Tobe to come to the school, who had helped me with my research, let me use the School's copy machines and Internet service and provided many meals and hot showers. She was my closest friend and made my life abundantly more comfortable than it otherwise would have been.

For several days after the boy was found dead outside the mission compound, none of Sharon's "parents" allowed their children to come to the School. The parents themselves refused to be seen at the School or at any of the mission's many homes. Some parents were bold enough to call on the telephone and give moral support, telling Sharon and her mother and father that they were not responsible, it was not the fault of the Baxters that the child had died. On the third day after the child was found dead, the father, with Kaylin Krapley urging him on, initiated a lawsuit for $300,000 (Haitian dollars, which translated at the time to about US$100,000).

That same night I was visiting with Sharon. She was indignant.

"I'm not going to pay $300,000 for that kid. We will close the school."

"No, you won't," I replied, without reminding her that she and her family were more dependent on the school than anyone else.

We had come into the conversation with me recounting how so many Haitian people with whom I had spoken in the previous days were defending the Baxters. One man had said, "It is so typical, impoverished Haitians see *blan* and they are after money." Another said, "there is no evidence." Another, "These uncouth people are wrong to be after missionaries who are trying to help the poor."

"Yes, I know." She looked at me with hollow eyes. "Several of my parents who are lawyers said they would represent us for free."

"That's nice of them."

"That's the way it is supposed to be," she retorted.

The people who I had been talking to, those who had spoken against the greedy opportunism of the poor were, of course, Baie-de-Sol elite, parents of the children in the school, wealthy and vastly different from the impoverished majority of people who lived in the city, such as the father of the boy who had been killed. In a moment of objectivity, even Sharon mused: "Everybody with children in the school is on my side and they don't know anything.

Everyone without children in the school are against me and they do not know anything either."

"Do you know who the child is?"

"No," she pretended.

"He's a little urchin who lives in the next neighborhood," I said. "His father sews shoes and has a little roadside booth where he sells rum and candies. The boy and him used to sleep together on the floor of the booth."

"What's the point?"

"Well, they're people. That's all. Maybe the man really doesn't believe you guys are responsible. Maybe he doesn't really want you to pay, just wants to know how his son died. Going after you guys is the only way he can force someone to find out the truth."

Sharon bit at her nails and stared hard at a piece of furniture.

I realized I was not being very supportive. *I should make a greater effort.* "Do you think that if you guys weren't involved anyone would spend more than half a second wondering about how that kid died? The police don't give a shit why he died."

Sharon stopped biting her nails and looked at me blankly.

I try harder. "Did you know that people say the kid used to drink with his father?"

"I heard that," she said, "and I don't believe it. He was a little kid."

Then getting to her feet, Sharon blurted it out again:

"I am not going to pay $300,000 for that kid."

Two weeks later the Baxters went to court. The judge, before beginning the trial, asked the man whose son had died if he really wanted to go through with it. The man stood and to the astonished dismay of lawyer Kaylin Krapley who sat next to him, he said "*non*," that he knew the Baxter's were good people and that if they would just pay the funeral expenses that would be fine for him. Case closed.

A month after the near *dechouke* of the Baxters, I walk into the School's main workshop. Salvation, the Baxters' twenty-two-year-old handyman, is there He doesn't hear me come in. I study him surreptitiously as he rummages through a tangled mass of power tools. He is pulling out electric saws and drills, a sander. He is stick-thin from AIDS. His wrists like twigs, his neck like a pencil, and he moves as if he is afraid that at any moment he might break. He holds one of the tools up by its cord and is looking it over. It is not clear to me if he knows what is happening to him. It has been a year since I learned from Sharon about Salvation's disease. I've kept my promise. But I've watched him deteriorate.

"Have you seen Reverend Baxter?"

At first, Salvation doesn't look at me. He just grunts. Then, as he examines another power tool he says, "He's in the house with his family. They're having a family reunion."

"A family reunion?"

"*Oui*, that's what I said."

"In the middle of a school day?"

Salvation, still not bothering to look at me, drops the one power tool, picks up an electric grinder from the pile, and looks over the cord.

"*Oui*," he says. "Kirk caught the good Reverend having sex with one of Madame Reverend Baxter's maids."

"One of the Madame Reverend Baxter's maids?"

"*Oui*, That's what I said. With one of Madame Reverend Baxter's maids." Salvation cocks his head and looks at me sideways, a mischievous grin comes over his face. "He was in one of the classrooms grunting and groaning." Salvation makes an obscene moan and rocks his hips back and forth. "Kirk heard him and went in. There's old Reverend, dick buried in the maid," Salvation laughs, grabs his side in pain, and then goes back to sorting through the pile of power tools.

Every Haitian in the neighborhood knew of the Reverend Baxter's philandering and as I got to know people in Baie-de-Sol and had my own lovers, I heard the rumors and learned who he was dallying with. Several times he had managed to get Madame Reverend Baxter to unwittingly hire girls he was having sex with. We would be eating dinner and there, serving the plates, would be one of his lovers. Sharon was not oblivious either. Once two maids hired to clean classrooms in the school were fighting. Sharon stopped the fight and when she asked what was going on one maid pointed at the other and shouted, "She's sleeping with your father." The other screamed back, "So is she."

Reverend Baxter had always managed to shrug off the accusations. But this time was different. This time the old preacher had been caught in the act, *in flagrante delicto,* pants down, by his only son, Kirk, who had gone straight to Sharon with the news. The two of them then went to Madame Reverend Baxter.

I walk out of the tool shed, through the gate, and across the street. Sitting in the corner against a wall, is a young woman, It'sthe maid. She is sobbing as she talks to another maid.

"Madame Reverend Baxter fired me," she sniffles. "I won't have the money to finish high school. My mother is going to beat me."

A month or so later, I open Sharon's door and walk into her apartment: "Hi Sharon, how's it going?" Sharon continues working on her computer.

I plop down on her plush couch. "What's wrong?" I asked, making myself comfortable.

"Nothing," she says without looking up.

"Well, obviously something is wrong."

"I just don't think I can continue like this."

"Like what?" I ask and pluck a piece of chocolate from a bowl on the coffee table.

"Like with you lying and deceiving me. I just can't put up with it."

"Could you be more specific?" I pluck another chocolate from the bowl.

"You know exactly what I am talking about. Arnaud and now The Nanny"

"Whoa, wait a minute. Do those women have something in common?" I savored the chocolate that was melting in my mouth.

"You lied to me about her too?"

"I am not having sex with the Nanny."

"Don't be snide. You're sleeping with The Nanny. You're disgusting."

The chocolate in my mouth didn't taste so good anymore and I was wishing I hadn't eaten it. "Sharon, I am not sleeping with The Nanny. And even if I were sleeping with her, that would be between me and her. You don't have any say in the matter. You are not my wife so it really is not your business. Unless you think that fucking the Nanny is exploitation in which case you might want to redirect your anger toward your father and his predation of your mother's maids."

"That's not fair."

"I'm sorry. But really Sharon, I am not sleeping with The Nanny. I don't appreciate these accusations. And my sex life is none of your business."

"I can't do it, I just can't do it. I want the money you owe me, the books you borrowed, and I want you to get all your stuff out of the school storage room."

This was a scene that had occurred at least a half dozen times. The conversation and accusations had re-emerged in different forms over and over. The problem was that Sharon and I had always had a relationship that tottered on the edge of romance. Indeed, we loved each other. But I was seldom in the city and then, with my involvement with Arnaud, our relationship had never fully emerged. At times Sharon felt bitter about it, as if I had let her down or misled her and the tension would erupt in jealousy. She would get angry and out it would come. She would accuse me of deceiving her and having affairs. This time it was a temporary maid I had hired. Another time it was a neighbor. She would then announce that we were no longer friends. I would pay all the money I owed her — and I always owed money for items she was having sent from Miami. Then I would return all the books I had borrowed — she had a great collection of books. But when I would come to get my belongings out of her storage room, it would stop. Suddenly everything was alright. She was nice again. Relations would be normalized. Then a couple months later it would happen all over again.

Why, I would ask myself, did I continue to go through this?

One reason was Sharon had power. When her telephone didn't work and she couldn't get it fixed, she summoned the children of the head of the state-run telephone company from their classroom and sent them home with a message, 'tell your parents that you cannot return to school until my telephone is fixed.' When the school couldn't get fuel for the generator, Sharon picked up the phone and called the parents who monopolized the regional gasoline trade and who had children in school: Gasoline arrived that evening. When she had a problem with papers for her vehicles she simply opened a spot for another child in her school – for the son of the director of the division of motor vehicles – and registration papers were no longer a problem. When she had problems getting goods through customs she did the same thing, admitting the children of the director of customs.

She also had a plush air-conditioned condominium, a video library, refrigerators and freezers the contents of which looked like a merger between a candy shop and a steak house. She had the ability to get anything imported from the United States free of charge and with the rapidity of Federal Express—which, need I say, didn't serve the region. Often I did not even have to pay for what I ordered. I had two pairs of free prescription eye glasses, half a dozen high-priced tape recorders for my research, parts for my motorcycle, free medical care.

Then Albeit and Tobe became involved. Sharon put them in her school and she took special interest in them. She tutored them and she had them over to her house in the evenings. The girls would watch videos and eat ice cream. Sharon gave them dolls and dollhouses, clothes and money, and all the things that middle class U.S. children get. She transformed their lives, made them happy, and was giving them an education that would have cost thousands of dollars a year any place else.

But while the girls were experiencing a Cinderella transition, I was sinking into a self-righteous crisis over charity. The realization that the school was a nest of elites began to eat away at my conscience. These were the same elites who looked down on and spurned the impoverished peasants, fisherman, and slum dwellers, who referred to them as ignorant and uncivilized, as subhuman, who called them *dan wouj* (red teeth) and *pye pete* (cracked feet). It infuriated me. The impoverished children in the

Hamlet could not get medical care and when they did it was bad medical care that they had to pay crushing fees for. But the children of the Haitian doctors who extorted them and the children of the other Baie-de-Sol elite were getting medical and dental care for free. They were getting Christmas presents flown in. They were getting a virtually cost-free education. It wasn't meant for them. It was meant for poor children like those in the Hamlet. The kids at The School of Jesus Christ of America didn't need it. Their parents could pay for it. If the Baxters didn't give it to them, their parents would send them to private school in Port-au-Prince or Miami. Some parents had taken their children out of school in Miami specifically to send them back to Baie-de-Sol to The School of Jesus Christ of America, specifically to take advantage of the free education, of the charity, the charity meant for children like those of the Hamlet.

On top of all this, the Baxters regarded themselves as altruistic. They thought of themselves as good Christians who made a great sacrifice by coming to Haiti to help the poor. Visiting missionaries thought of them as dedicated spreaders of biblical truth, somehow holier than ordinary Christians, closer to God, better than the rest of us.

I'm not a religious person but it had seemed to me too that the Baxters embodied charitable and family ideals that, while I myself may fall far short of fulfilling, I nevertheless had tremendous respect for. I respected them, admired their honesty, their good works, the closeness of their family. I had gone to their church services, stood with them holding an open bible in my hand as the Reverend read the words. Then it turned out to be bullshit. *Helping the poor? The hell they were!*

Now what I saw in the Baxters was a perversion of Christian idealism and I despised them for it. The country-style buffet lunches, the candlelight dinners on the patio with Haitian servants standing off to the side waiting for tea glasses to get low so they could rush in and refill them, servants who were likely as not the objects of the old man's sexual depredations, servants who had been trained by the mother, a sharecropper's daughter, using money meant for the poor to turn them into waiters and maids so that she could live out what were no doubt childhood fantasies of being a wealthy planter's wife. Those meals on the patio became a mockery of everything that The School of Jesus Christ of America was meant to stand for. It was like CARE, a perversion of American charitable ideals, with its false claims to be aiding the "poorest of the poor" when what it was really doing was throwing exquisite banquets at plush hotels while carrying out U.S. political policy in the interest of international venture capitalists and agro-industrialists. The charity and Christian morality of the Baxters was a smokescreen, a rationale like "food aid" meant for the hungry. The Baxters were living like royalty, buying their way into Baie-de-Sol elite, rubbing shoulders with the beautiful people, granting them free education in exchange for favors while they used as lords use serfs the poor who they were supposed to be helping.

Chapter Twelve
Keys to the Research Goldmine: Nepotism and Testing the Obvious

In the fall of 2000 I boarded a freighter for Miami and then returned to my University to submit and defend my dissertation. Almost a year later, after I had finished writing and been awarded a doctorate, I headed back to Miami where I stayed with a friend, Serge Boisette, and his wife, Carmelle, mailing out my curriculum vitae to the census bureau, to CARE, to consulting agencies, to NGOs. Nothing. Then one afternoon the phone rang. Serge picked it up and a moment later handed it to me. The woman on the other end of the line introduced herself as a famous university professor who I had heard of, an anthropologist who specialized in nutrition. She sounded delighted to have gotten in touch with me and explained that she was a good friend of one of my professors.

"He has given you an excellent recommendation and I think that you are perfect for a position we need filled."

The position was field director of a new project in Haiti. The project was to be funded by the World Health Organization (WHO) together with a new USAID-supported organization called FANTA. In her excitement the Professor told me that her husband was on the WHO funding committee. "A little conflict of interest," she apologized, "but never mind that. It is going to be a great project and you're perfect to run it. But it starts very soon. Could you be on the plane Monday to interview with us in Port-au-Prince?"

I arrived in Port-au-Prince Monday afternoon, caught a cab and checked into the chic Hotel Village Creole, where, at the cost of US$90 per night—about five times CARE's estimated per capita annual income in Jean Makout—my prospective employers had made me a reservation. The woman at the desk handed me a large manila envelope that my prospective employees had left for me and I retired to my room where I flopped down on the bed and opened the envelope. Inside was a twenty-page proposal for a food-aid research project put together by the Professor and a team of her colleagues, a collection of high-powered, world-renowned university nutrition professors. I read it. It was a grammatically well-written proposal with lofty research reviews and dazzling academic digressions that underneath the fluff came down to this: An evaluation of the hypothesis that feeding children food supplements before they are malnourished is a more effective health care strategy than feeding them supplements after they are already malnourished.

WHAT? We're testing the hypothesis that feeding nutrients prevents malnutrition? Well no shit! I turned to the budget. It was a two-year project funded to the tune of $836,000.

My first reaction was anger. They knew goddamn well what the data would show.

My second reaction was that maybe I was kidding myself. I was bound to be biased. I was bitter about my experiences with food aid and I realized that no one was inclined to do anything about the impact of food aid. Most the people who were outraged about the food and the crashing of the market were Haitian and many resented *blan* anyway. The only other development experts and academics who openly opposed food aid were, at that time, thought of as radicals, people such as Laura Richardson of Grass Roots International and Phil Gilman, CARE's own food director. They had spoken out against food aid and found themselves shuffled out of Haiti. I was not so sure I wanted to be associated with them. Did I want to be an unemployed troublemaker for the rest of my career or was I going to be a serious field researcher? What I needed were mentors and the university professors were perfect. They were serious players, big-time nutritionists, professors at a major university. The hell with it! If they wanted to prove that feeding children prevented malnutrition, I was their man. I would be the best damn research director they ever imagined. And I was perfect. They weren't going to find anyone had the mixture of qualifications that I had. No one who knew Haiti the way I did, who knew field surveys, who appreciated solid data, and who was hungry to prove himself the way I was. I would give them my best effort and in the process I would make these people mine. I would cinch my career. I promised myself that under no circumstances, under no circumstances whatsoever was I going to say anything negative about food aid. Not a single negative word!

"Food aid in Haiti is an absolute sham," I was concluding. "It is undermining the entire economy." It was two hours later, and I was sitting in the lobby being interviewed by my prospective employers and the idealist buffoon inside of me had burst out and was in the process of blowing any chance of getting the job. Here's what happened.

At about 5:00 in the afternoon a woman rings my room. The Professor could not make it, but her associates would like to meet with me. In the lobby I meet a woman I will call PA, the Professor's Assistant, an attractive woman in her late thirties, Ph.D. in anthropology, who is the Professor's partner in the project. Accompanying her is one of the Professor's graduate students, a pleasant East Indian woman. Present also is The Nutritionist, a professor emeritus who, unbeknownst to me at the time, is a world-famous expert and proponent of food aid. Also present is PA's husband, an agreeable man with a decade or more experience at the highest levels of the USAID food program in Haiti.

PA takes control, introduces everyone, and then gets right to the point.

"You read the project, what do you think? Might you be interested?" She is beaming. Then she seems to realize that she is moving too fast and backs up.

"Let me give you a little background," she says. "My husband, sitting next to you, is a USAID supervisor for FANTA, which is an organization created in the past year to review and revamp U.S. food aid throughout the world."

"One of FANTA's main tasks," PA continues, "is funding research projects to look into the effects of food aid. My husband is currently USAID's fulltime FANTA consultant and advisor to the project." Something that, she adds, "is a little bit of a conflict of interest, but he will be removed once the project is underway."

As I ponder the significance of PA's husband being an insider with FANTA while recalling that Professor's husband worked with the other funding institution, the World Health Organization, PA finishes her explanation, looks at me with her sharp, business-like eyes and asks that question: "Have you had any experiences with food aid?"

Squirming over the revelation of the lavish nepotistic funding process, my bitterness about my experiences with food aid, and an earnest desire to befriend these refined insiders, I try to be cool.

"Well, yes," I say, "I have had a little experience with food aid," and I tell them about working in Jean Makout where, slipping into my now familiar role as food aid critic, I tell them that, "I couldn't help but notice some problems with the food programs."

PA nods thoughtfully.

"It appears," I continue, "that the school directors who are supposed to feed the children steal much of the food."

"Really."

"But just as disturbing is the performance of the organizations that are meant to distribute it."

PA nods.

"Such as the World Food Program which delivered the relief for the 1997 summer drought a year late, in September of 1998, right in the middle of a bumper harvest."

PA looks at her husband, who might have been one of the few people outside of Jean Makout who can verify what I am talking about, "Is that true?" she asks.

"Well," he hesitates, "yes, it is true. But they had some internal problems at the time."

"And then," I continue, "there was hurricane George in 1998, when the World Food Program once again delivered the emergency food almost one year after it was needed, in May 1999, right in the middle of another bumper harvest."

PA looks at her husband again. He nods his head with resigned affirmation.

"And then I had some experiences with CARE during which I couldn't help but notice that CARE food deliveries tend to increase in directly opposite proportion to the need for food."

"Hmmm," says PA, "Is there more?"

"Yes, there is something else. CARE found the level of child malnutrition dramatically increasing precisely when they were giving away the most food."

My listeners sit quietly.

"I can't help," I go on, "but find something about this food aid business deeply disturbing. Have any of you guys read this book by DeWind and McKinley where they show how food aid was part of a World Bank and USAID plan to drive peasants off the land and into slums so they could be put to work in sweatshops?"

And so it went. After I finished we all shook hands. It was decided that we would meet for breakfast at 8:00 a.m. and we wished one another goodnight.

I headed for bed. They headed for a Port-au-Prince social gathering of high-level development executives.

When 8:35 the next morning rolled around and I was the only person sitting at the breakfast table I knew that I had destroyed any chance of getting the job.

I was shattered. I had sabotaged myself. On the one hand I was still gripped by the insidiousness of food aid in Haiti and the political policies behind it. I felt that I had discovered a moral outrage that any intelligent and compassionate person could understand and in doing so would be as outraged as I was. I had tried the argument out on hundreds of people, had written it up in my dissertation and I knew that I was not crazy, that the data was sound and that people understood the logic. I knew that with the exception of the Professors, virtually all the aid workers I had ever

talked to about the subject—Haitian, American or European—
shared a moral indignation regarding food aid. But I had also
learned long before that, professionally at least, it was best to keep
my mouth shut about my idealist arguments and moral objections.
And with the Professors I had calculated in advance. I would have
done anything for the job. I no longer gave a damn if they wanted
to shove food in Haitian mouths until it gagged them. I had already
done all I could and I had been defeated. I needed a job and I
would have helped them. I was broke. Even my Haitian friends
were telling me to leave it alone and get a job. They too had hope
that if I did, if I did find a good job, I could help them. Why had I
run my mouth? I only wanted to be a researcher. Screw the
Haitians. Let them choke on food aid. I was sorry. I wished I could
go back. I wished I could do it all differently. I wished I could redo
the meeting. I wished I could keep my big mouth shut.

I went back to the Hamlet beaten. I spear fished and sat
around in the evenings drinking *kleren* and talking with my old
companions. The second day that I was there I wake up to
shouting. "You are killing me. You are taking food out of my
mouth," hollers Dinel. He is shouting at Wonel, his youngest
brother. Wonel is protesting, his voice breaking with submission
and uncertainty. "But brother, I was only trying to do what is
right."

But whatever it was that Wonel did, Dinel doesn't think it
was right.

"Don't you ever *fout* talk to me again." Dinel shrieks. "You
are no longer my brother."

Next I hear Dinel's wife, Manmin. She is shouting for the
entire Hamlet to hear. "His own brother. Can you believe it? His
own brother. We have six children together. I have eleven total.
Eleven, mind you. How could Wonel do this? How could he do
it?" And then in the typical fashion of a Hamlet woman she
concludes, "I should go over there and split his head open with a
stick."

As it turned out, the fight was over CARE food. A CARE
monitor had come to the Hamlet two weeks earlier and announced
that CARE had a new program to help the most vulnerable people

in its activity zone—part of the same mandate for which I had been hired to do research the year before. The monitor explained that the Hamlet was slated to receive food aid for the eighteen most vulnerable households in the community. Because Wonel was the teacher and had been receiving food aid for schoolchildren, the monitor gave him the task of deciding who the eighteen people would be.

Wonel was a good man. I had known him since he was in high school, before he had a wife and children. My first experience with him was when I had just arrived in the Hamlet. He was then sixteen years old and he fixed a flat tire on my bicycle. What I thought was a favor turned out to be the most expensive tire job I ever had. It pissed me off and I didn't talk to Wonel for a long time. Months. But eventually I got over it and a year or so later as we sat in a rowboat together, Wonel told me how it was that a few months earlier he had slapped a policeman in the middle of the Village's main street but was not arrested. The reason, he was saying, is that he had magical powers.

"For example," Wonel explained, "if you were to shoot me with a gun, *oui,* the bullet would go right through me."

"Yes it would, Wonel. And then you would be a man with a bullet hole in him. Maybe even a dead man with a bullet hole in him."

"*Non, non.* You don't get it. It would not bother me at all. It would just pass right through me. I have a prayer for things like that. I just say the prayer and I am immune to bullets."

Wonel had greatly matured in the three years since he told me that he was bulletproof. He had gotten married, now had two children and, at US$5 per month, he was the director of the Hamlet primary school. He was trying. He was spending much of his time in church and he desperately wanted everyone to see him as a *neg serié*, a serious, respectable man. So when the CARE monitor gave Wonel the task of choosing the eighteen most vulnerable households in the Hamlet he could not, in my opinion, have picked a better man for the job—given, of course, the other choices.

Wonel's first choice was the Hamlet's most emaciated alcoholic, Ti Tonton, and his emaciated alcoholic wife, Ralia, who together had ten children. He also chose Mamoun, who had six children at the time and was also a drunk. He chose Nana, Mamoun's brother, another drunk. In fact most the people who Wonel chose were drunks. But that didn't mean they were not deserving. For obvious reasons the Hamlet drunks and their children were in worse shape than anyone else. Whether being drunks made them extremely impoverished or whether their extreme poverty drove them to drink was irrelevant: They were the people who had the least food and their children were the scrawniest and the hungriest in the Hamlet.

But in choosing whom he did, Wonel inadvertently brought on the wraith of his older brother and his sister-in-law. I had been exposed the previous day to various opinions about it. Now, I wipe the sleep out of my eyes, and wade into the middle of the fight. I tell Dinel I didn't think he was being fair to Wonel. "WHAT?" screams Dinel and moves toward me, eyes flashing with anger.

His wife Manmin is approaching me from the other side. "Timoté, how could you!" Manmin shrieks, "I have eleven children. He gave food to Ti Tonton and Ralia, *oui*. Does Ralia have eleven children? You know what they are going to do with that food? Do you know? Timoté, I am asking you a question. Do you know?"

"No." I say obligingly, and wish once again that I had never opened my mouth, "What are they going to do with it?"

"They are going to sell it and buy rum, *oui*. You watch. Ti Tonton and Ralia are going to be drunk tonight and his ten kids are going to be over here at my door begging for something to eat."

As I walk away Ti Tonton is suddenly standing in front of me:

"TIMOTÉ," he shouts and throws a drunken arm around me, "let's go have a shot of rum." As Ti Tonton drags me toward the *boutik,* I can hear Manmin behind us: "You see Timoté. You see. Ti Tonton, you *vakabon*."

Chapter Thirteen
Anger, Disillusionment and Despair

Often during my years in Haiti I found myself trying to remember why I had left a comfortable life in the United States to go where I was deprived of even the simplest comforts, exposed to diseases and ridiculed by the people I was trying to study. I could offer noble reasons of trying to help the world's downtrodden and repressed but, in trying to be honest, the reasons are probably more selfish.

When I was growing up we moved often. My father, in the itinerant style of his and earlier generations of newspaper reporters and editors, sought to move up the ladder in search of more money, more visible jobs, and that elusive holy grail of the news business, the Pulitzer prize that would make his career. My parents eventually divorced and my older brother and I spent our teenage years bouncing between our parents' separate homes and a multitude of schools. In five years I attended thirteen schools. I was expelled from six of them.

I despised the structure and control of school. When I was not kicked out I usually flunked more classes than I passed. The last one that I attended, I had a change of heart: I got straight As and was captain of the lacrosse team. My parents were ecstatic, believing I had turned my life around. My response: I dropped out and began hitchhiking across the United States. I was eighteen.

For the next two years I worked construction, restaurants, loading docks, I even picked fruit with Mexican illegal immigrants. At some point I ended up in central Florida, mucking stalls on a horse farm. Tired of bumming around, I took a general education equivalency test to qualify as a high school graduate and enrolled in community college. An introductory course in anthropology changed my life. This is it, I thought, this is what I want to do.

As I saw it then, anthropology offered a life of adventure. I could see the world, visit exciting places, and maybe do some good for people while working largely alone and free of the authoritarian constrictions of a regular job where, not unlike the earlier schools I loathed, I would have had to take orders. I also thought that by getting away from my own culture I could better understand it, better understand the world, why people are the way they are and, surely more than anything else, better understand myself.

Why Haiti? For one thing, Haitians are poor and black and I saw it as a place where I could challenge racist notions I had acquired as a middle-class white American, something that, with the introspection that comes with studying society, began to fascinate me. My earliest memories were associated with my first awareness of black people. When I was four years old, in August 1967, African Americans in many of the impoverished neighborhoods of Detroit exploded in a frenzy of smashing, looting, and burning. The uprising terrified the residents of the upscale suburb of Grosse Pointe where we lived at the time and from where the smoke from burning city buildings was visible. By the time I was old enough for school we were living in Washington D.C., where I attended an all-white elementary school where my contact with African Americans was restricted to watching them rob people on television or perform fantastic athletic feats.

As a teenager I went to junior high school in southern Virginia, where my few short stints in public school brought me firsthand into the racial tension of the time. To me, blacks were different than us, very different. And to me and most of my friends, they were often our adversaries, sometimes violently so. My perception was also shaped by my mother and her three brothers, rural Southern-born and raised and prejudiced to the point of believing that blacks were subhuman. In my undergraduate years at college the situation did not improve. During the 1980s, relations between white and African Americans in rural Florida were marked by subdued hostility. There were even bars where blacks and whites in the area observed a self-imposed segregation left over from the pre–civil rights era: whites inside the bar, and blacks hanging out in the parking lot and making their purchases through a window.

In summary, like anyone else, I was a product of my experiences. I didn't like blacks. I thought they were different and that they were a threat. Their very existence and the hostility that I often observed them displaying toward white males like myself stirred in me a deep animosity.

But this changed when I transferred from community college to the University of Florida at Gainesville where a Haitian, Serge Boisette, became my best friend, a friendship that began when we found ourselves on opposite sides of issues during vigorous debates in a social science class. Serge later confided to me that he had wanted to get to know a real American redneck— which is what he saw me as. On my part, this black man with grace, disarming intellectual abilities, and the gift of eloquence fascinated me. We embarked on what was at first an almost forced friendship built around a continuation of our social science class arguments and intellectual bantering. We would routinely launch into exploratory arguments about ailments of society and how to fix the world. Many of the arguments would end with him saying, "you don't know what you're talking about, man, you have to go to a poor country like Haiti to know."

Eventually I did go.

Through Serge I became interested in Haiti. I read about the country and studied its history. But soon it was more than the poverty that captured my attention. The country and its people— who, courtesy of the popular U. S. media, I had until that time viewed only as crowds of skinny disease-ridden black people— enthralled me. They had their own culture and folk beliefs, their own religion. They had a history longer and arguably richer than that of my own country. Their 1791 to 1804 revolution was a spectacular and bloody thirteen years of revolt and uprising; the

only successful slave revolt in the history of the world, at the end
of which Haiti became the first independent black nation in
modern history and the second colony in the Western hemisphere
to throw off the yoke of colonialism. They had kings and
democracies that prevailed over the third largest standing army on
earth. They conquered the neighboring Spanish colony on the other
side of the island, expelled the colonists, and declared it "Spanish
Haiti."

Haitians, I learned, did not see themselves as African. They
saw themselves as Haitian and they were as distinct and proud of
their country as Americans are of theirs. Knowing this, for the first
time in my life, never having seen more than a fleeting mention of
it in any of my school textbooks, Haitians now became noble,
exotic, and enchanting.

So I decided to challenge my prejudices and prepared to go
to Haiti. After I graduated with my bachelor's degree and began
work toward a master's degree and, eventually, I hoped, a
doctorate in anthropology, I visited and studied the country
intensely.

Much had changed since then.

When I first arrived in Haiti on a grant-supported research
trip in 1990, I was enthusiastic. My enthusiasm and belief that I
could make a contribution kept me returning despite the hardships,
the violence, the coups, and the embargoes. But ten years later I
was a different person. Perhaps I was simply burned out. After all,
I had spent much of the last half decade living in thatched huts,
sleeping on dirt floors, eating bad food, battling one intestinal
disease after another. To say nothing of a bout of typhoid, hepatitis
A, and countless colds and flu strains. Perhaps more than anything
else, by 2000, I no longer was an objective researcher. I was
deeply angry at what I perceived to be the widespread fraud,
corruption, arrogance, greed, self-interest, and apathy that afflicted
the entire development community, which was, in my opinion, a
total failure, serving only to make the poor poorer and the rich
richer.

But I also harbored a burning desire to make an impact, at
least on the people of the Hamlet with whom I had lived; people

who, while perhaps having early on made my life in Haiti miserable, now accepted me; people who, while still sometimes driving me to intense agitation, I nevertheless felt had become a part of me. I had lived with them, fished with them, celebrated and mourned with them. I was, to the people of Jean Makout, the *blan* from the Hamlet and I wanted to prove I could do something to help the people there. But, alas, there was nothing I could do.

Twice I had witnessed what should have been real aid coming to the Hamlet and twice I had watched as hope fizzled and the misery and suffering, the needless deaths of infants and children went on.

The first instance occurred while I still lived in the Hamlet. One morning I woke to find a group of wealthy Haitians milling about among the huts. They were dressed in Polo and Brooks Brothers shirts, khakis and blue jeans. Their skin was much lighter than the dark black people of the Hamlet. Several were older men. One told me he was an architect who lived in Miami. Another was a lawyer who lived in Paris. A dignified, athletic young man in his mid-twenties was with them and he set up a desk under the big oak tree in the center of the Hamlet where people lined up to give their names and the number of children they had.

The light-skinned men belonged to an organization called The Real Deal. It was made up of people who had been born in the area, but who got out, emigrated to the United States and France, earned university degrees, became professionals and joined the modern world. They wanted to help and they seemed serious.

After they left, they sent used clothes. They returned once with VHF cameras and made videos of the Hamlet, thrilling everyone by showing the videos in the school. They sent some fifty coconut-tree saplings that the people of the Hamlet planted and watered, transforming the beachhead from a dull gray to a dark, lush green. They gave soccer balls and team jerseys. To the Village they shipped two enormous power generators. No one ever figured out how to hook them up or who was going to pay for the fuel if they did, but it was a nice gesture and indicative of a serious desire to help. They gave the mayor H$16,000 (about US$5,000) for a library and pharmacy, neither of which ever became a reality. But

again, it indicated a serious desire to help. For awhile, it looked
like something good might really happen.

Then The Real Deal hooked up with a woman named
Fancy Wok and things really took off.

Fancy Wok was and may still be the closest thing to a
Haitian Geraldo Rivera that exists. She worked for Tele Éclair, one
of Haiti's two main television stations, and she would come on the
air at night showing the problems people have, looking for
solutions and exposing injustices. She had been honored frequently
at elite Port-au-Prince social clubs.

Visits by Wok had been going on while I was conducting
the Jean Makout survey so I was not around. But I visited the
Hamlet right after Wok had done her camera shoot. I stood in the
middle of the beach head under the big old oak tree while young
men regaled me with stories of her visit.

With Wok narrating into a microphone and her camera
crew following, the light-skinned members of Port-au-Prince elite
moved through the Hamlet taking pictures of the miserable
poverty, the hungry half-naked children, the saggy-breasted
mothers. The people had, of course, clustered around to see the
modern technology and the weird looking strangers. It surely made
great footage, hungry crowds of starving peasants among thatch
roofed shacks on a windswept, beachhead, nothing else to do but
stare at the strangers. Then Wok spotted Ketli, a tough, middle-
aged market woman who I remember best for having sunk a
machete into the head of a pig I owned. When Wok's eye fell on
her, Ketli was squatting in front of her hut watching the show.
Wok zeroed in. The camera zeroed followed.

Nervous at the attention, Ketli fell back on an old custom
among women in the Hamlet. She reached out, broke off a chunk
of lime plaster from the outside wall of her house, took a bite, and
began to chew. This was too much for Fancy Wok, who broke into
tears as she narrated the miserable poverty she had discovered in
the far recesses of her country, poverty so extreme that it had
driven this starving woman to eat part of her house.

The young men telling me the story roared with laughter,
holding on to each other, one of them fell on the ground howling

and sputtered, "She thought that," he could barely get the words out for laughing, "she thought that Ketli was eating dirt because she was hungry!"

Together with The Real Deal, some Port-au-Prince musicians and a Catholic sister, Wok launched benefit concerts and charity drives. There were appeals for aid on television. Tens of thousands of dollars were reportedly collected. Although I was never able to ascertain the exact financial details, one Port-au-Prince doctor told me that he had seen a television program about the campaign and over US$100,000 had been collected. The people of the Hamlet were kept informed. To make sure that there was no corruption a committee was created that included the Catholic sister and the local tax collector, a guy name Jako, a friend of mine and respected member of the Catholic church, who was made the president of the committee.

The last time the people of the Hamlet report seeing Wok she showed up in November 1997 on a yacht with a group of other "foreigners." They were surely Port-au-Prince elite, but because of their light skin and fine clothing, the people of the Hamlet were convinced that she and her friends were North Americans. The yacht anchored off the beachhead. The next day all the people of the Hamlet gathered on the beach in front of Jiji's *boutik*, a little thatch-roofed store, and waited, staring at the yacht. They waited all day. Six hours passed. At 3:00 in the afternoon, as recounted by people in the Hamlet, Madame Wok came ashore and spoke with the people of the Hamlet: "What should be done," she asked, "with the money that had been collected?"

No one knew what to say.

She suggested it be given to Rigobert—a *gran neg* in the Village who had once told me that the people of the Hamlet were animals.

Dinel, acting as Hamlet spokesman, objected. "That has happened before and we never saw a dime." He was referring to a fishing project in which Rigobert had stolen all the money and materials for a cooperative, something that actually happened, to varying degrees, on two separate occasions.

In the end no one knew what should be done with the money. Wok said that she would figure it out, got on her yacht and no one in the Hamlet has seen her since. That was ten years ago. Jako the tax collector subsequently wrote a letter to Wok insisting that they remove his name from the account. That was seven years ago. When I inquired one year ago, still no one knew what had happened to the money.

The second experience came in the fall of 2000 and summed up the futility and the disgust with which the outside world seems to see the impoverished people of the Hamlet.

Lance and his wife Mary were two average, middle-aged, middle-class Americans. I met Lance on the Internet while I was back in the States putting the final touches on my dissertation. I had done a keyword search for "Jean Makout" and one of the hits was a website for a clinic in a place called Kot d'Fer, an irrigated area on the mountainside not far from the Hamlet. Surprised, because I know there is no clinic there, I contacted Lance and asked him about his clinic. He responded telling me that he had not actually established it yet, but that he had already collected a full container load of equipment and medicines and a Haitian woman, a member of his church in Fort Meyers, Florida, had donated land on which to build the clinic.

"All we got to do is get there," Lance assured me.

Lance did eventually get there, and on the day when he and his wife Mary arrived from their clinic site reconnaissance in a place called Kot d'Fer, I just happened to be visiting the mission where they were sleeping over.

Lance and Mary came into the house and Mary headed straight for the bathroom. Lance clumped his body down in a chair by the kitchen table where I was sitting. "You would not believe what we have been through," he sighed.

It turned out that the Fort Meyers woman who had donated the land for Lance's clinic was a Dubois, one of the wealthiest families in the Jean Makout area, including among them several doctors and a senator—all, of course, living in Port-au-Prince, Paris, Florida, and New York.

It also turned out that she was a little crazy.

"I always thought she might be off her rocker," Lance said. "She walks around Fort Meyers wearing a napkin on her head."

"The land for the clinic," Lance went on, "is nothing but a pile of rocks and it appears she doesn't really own it anymore." A peasant had taken over the land and was farming it.

"But now I have a different problem," said Lance. "Some of this Dubois woman's family have formed a committee to run the clinic and it's pretty clear they're setting me up to be swindled."

"I've had it," he said. "Maybe we will just try to give the stuff away."

Then Lance started telling me that he spent the day in the Hamlet where the Dubois woman's cousin had assured him he could off-load the container of clinic supplies.

"I could probably do it," Lance said. "I've unloaded boats in worse places. Ain't my first rodeo you know." Lance added that he had been in the "mission business" for over thirty years. "Some of the places I off-loaded containers in Africa you wouldn't believe. And actually, that beachhead is a good spot. Water's deep."

So I asked him, "Lance, why did you want to set up a clinic here?"

Lance looked right at me, paused for a moment, as if he were in deep thought about the question. Then he began, "Once," he said, "I was visiting this place in the south of Haiti. I was at a baptism. There was this woman and she was holding a tiny baby. She held that baby up next to the basin of baptism water and as she held it there I looked at it, and then I looked closer, and you would not believe what I saw." Lance looked at me, letting the suspense build, then continued. "That baby's entire skin, underneath, it was just crawling with worms. It just moved." Lance makes a creepy-crawling motion with his fingers and let the image sink in. "I've never seen anything like it in my life. Right then and there I said to myself, 'Lance, buddy, we're going to do something for the poorest people we can find in Haiti.' And that's how it began."

"Lance," I said, "you saw the people in the Hamlet where you were at today?"

"Yeah," Lance said, "that place is awful."

"Well, they're just about as poor as any you're gonna find. Why don't you open the clinic down there, land wouldn't cost you dime and…"

I didn't get to finish because Lance was howling with laughter. He called out to his wife in the bathroom. "Mary, Mary, you gotta hear this. Come out here. Tim wants us to open the clinic down at that beachhead."

And then, looking at me, he half shouted. "You gotta be outa your mind! I saw the looks on those people's faces. They would just as soon kill you as give you the time of day."

"Did you talk to any of them?"

"I didn't have to." Lance was still half-shouting. "I could see it on their faces."

"But Lance, half of the people down there are children."

"Forget it! Don't even talk to me about it. My wife would never go for it. Mary, come out here. You gotta hear this!"

And so that was it. I had come to the realization that there wasn't any hope for the people of the Hamlet. I sure as hell couldn't do anything for them. I had no money. And no one else was going to do it.

Then one night the voice of Moise, a DJ on the Jean Makout radio station, breaks in between songs.

"*Bagayyyy blanch Tombeeee*," he shrieks over the air. "The white stuff has fallen. True to their promise to make all Haitians rich in three years, the Columbians have seeded the coastal area with thousands and thousands of kilos of cocaine. Go to sleep poor and wake up rich. Halleluiah! And now, a little number from Sweet Mickey."

Chapter Fourteen
Colombia and the Drug Trade
to the Rescue

It was noon, Sunday in the dusty Village of Jean Makout. Among the decaying wooden houses and corroding tin roofs, the sound of Creole music blared out of battery powered radios and mingled with the chatter of children and the resolute slapping of dominoes on rough hewn wood tables. The scent of roasting coffee wafted through the air and mixed with the smell of sewage and charcoal. On the village soccer field, where grew not a single blade of grass, a group of young boys played marbles in the dirt. In the yards, up under canopies of mango and avocado trees, men sat around domino tables and passed bottles of white rum spiced with roots and herbs. Girls sat on the porches braiding one another's hair. Behind the homes, scrawny dogs lounged outside smoky thatch-roofed kitchens; inside the kitchens women tended pots of rice and sauces that simmered over charcoal fires.

On the dry desert knoll above the village, the sun glinted off a windshield. The vehicle crested the hill and made its way slowly down toward the village. Behind it another vehicle appeared, crested the knoll, and began the descent. Two more followed. As the caravan rolled into the village, a hush fell, Women peeking out from the kitchens and shopkeepers stepping out onto their porches. Radios were silenced. The only sound as the strange vehicles rolled single file through the village was that of gravel crunching beneath their tires, and the occupants of the first two vehicles were hidden behind dark tinted windows. The third and fourth vehicles were vans, big, white, with clear glass windows through which the villagers could see uniformed policemen holding assault rifles. The villagers pretended to mind their own business. Men concentrated on their dominoes. Mothers pulled children into shabby houses, shutting the doors behind them.

The caravan made its way slowly through the Village, passing the old stone cathedral, the market in the center of the village, and then on to where the village houses degenerated to thatch-roofed peasant shacks. The vehicles disappeared through the crumbling stone walls of an 18th century fort and then reappeared on the other side, soon making their way along the spectacular blue-green bay where cliffs lined the desert shores and the rays of the afternoon sun penetrated the water in deep silver streaks. The vehicles inched along. One mile down the shoreline road lay the Hamlet, hidden from sight on the beach head below. Another mile and the vehicles arrived at a remote and seldom used seaside airfield.

The doors of the first SUV opened and out stepped three large-bellied, older black men dressed in loose, untucked cotton shirts and cotton slacks. The doors to the other SUV opened and from the front seat stepped two young Hispanic men holding Israeli-made Uzi assault rifles. A dozen Haitian police officers and several armed Haitian civilians clambered out the side doors of the white Toyota vans. From the front seat of one van stepped the regional police chief. A half dozen of the men were directed to begin clearing the airfield of rocks and brush. The rest of the policemen and armed civilians fanned out into the desert brush surrounding the airstrip. Several took positions among the cacti and thorn bushes bordering the road, where they spent the entire day. Whenever a local woman or child approached looking for firewood or on their way to the salt pans on the coast, an armed man hidden in the brush barked out *"Tounen!"* (Go back!)

The Hamlet, the Village, and the surrounding countryside buzzed with excitement, as they always do when anything unusual disrupts the rhythm of daily life. But this time was different. Young men, locals, who had been away at school in Port-au-Prince had mysteriously begun arriving the day before. Several young men, notorious local toughs had come from the Village. The word was that there would be a cocaine drop, a *djeal* as Haitians call it, and the news had spread among the curious peasants and fisherman. The locals knew about cocaine and they knew that it is valuable. And so while the police and the armed civilians sat in the brush warning peasant women and children away, and while the big pot-bellied Haitian men and the two long-haired Hispanics stood around their vehicles waiting, whiling away the day in conversation of soccer games and sexy night clubs, other men, impoverished and hungry men who spend their days and nights sweating for a pittance, crept through the bushes and crawled among the rocks, through terrain they'd known since they were children, spying on the strangers and speculating in hushed voices.

Haiti for years had been a transshipment point for Columbian cocaine. But with a repressive military that strongly controlled trade into and out of Haiti, it had been a monopoly reserved for a few of the powerful and politically connected. During the latter Duvalier era it had been Jean Claude Duvalier's father-in-law who reputedly monopolized drug trafficking. After the fall of Duvalier the monopoly fell to military officers. Then with the coup d'etat and ouster of Jean Bertrand Aristide by the CIA trained military junta, cocaine became rampant.

The United States under the Bush administration appeared to have sponsored, or at the least not initially objected to, the ousting of Aristide in 1991. And why not? As a radical left-wing priest he was interfering with their programs to make Haiti hospitable to foreign capital investment, to agro-industry and Trade Free Zones. U.S. politicians, urged on by lobbyists and Haitian elites whose interests were threatened, believed that the military junta was going to facilitate the emergence of a regime more amenable to the U.S. political and economic agenda. But the junta, reportedly already engaged in the cocaine trade, had other ideas. And they were not the only ones. The embargo cut off all legitimate trade and so all trade became contraband—cars, fuel, stereos, music CDs, mattresses, bicycles, and televisions.

Overnight, hitherto legitimate businessmen, if they wanted to keep their livelihoods, became smugglers. And soon many discovered they could smuggle much more lucrative cargoes than used junk from Miami.

When threatened with an imminent multinational invasion, the officers who made up the military junta agreed to leave. They went with their cocaine millions into lush exile in Panama. Aristide came back to find that he was faced with hundreds if not thousands of millionaire narcotraffickers. Many had their own security forces, artillery,   visas,   planes,   boats.   They   controlled neighborhoods, towns, cities, and they wasted no time controlling the new politicians. The hitherto pro–United States elites who had traditionally thrived on monopolizing imports and exports—a monopoly that Aristide had broken—had also found a new livelihood: They were now monopolizing banking and gasoline distribution, operations that facilitated the laundering of enormous sums of money. Aristide found himself boxed in. From one direction the United States and the international community were pressuring him by withholding foreign aid, a source of income that made up some 80 percent of the Haitian Government's budget. From the other direction, the new drug lords and the traditional elite checked him. They wanted no deals with the United States, not if they hurt business. No deals with the DEA. No deals with the military. Aristide could do nothing. With the army disbanded and replaced by a fledging police force he could neither control the drug lords nor accept U.S. demands for drug treaties and interdiction within Haiti. According to many credible accounts, if not Aristide than at least many of his associates reacted by simply joining the drug trade (House of Representatives, 2004).

Early on in my field work I had been largely oblivious to the creeping effect of the drug trade.

Then I began to hear stories.

In a remote fishing outpost called Cap-a-Fou, the cops, no doubt inspired by the possibility of a payoff, beat a group of fisherman from the Hamlet who were pestering a broken down cigarette boat.

A plane crashed at Bord Mer and impoverished Haitian conch divers fetched up several hundred kilos of cocaine.

Givme's brother guarded a broken down cigarette boat that, unbeknownst to him, carried thousands of kilos of cocaine. It was a favor that got him a free ride to the United States.

Lavish houses then began to sprout up around The School of Jesus Christ of America, gas stations and fancy banks in dirt street towns, ice factories that produced no ice. Ships in the Baie-de-Sol harbor multiplied, one to dozens. Sharon and her parents told me stories told to them by parents of children at their school, people who were so certain that there was nothing wrong with what they were doing that they would sit down at dinner and tell American missionaries about their smuggling operations.

I was naively oblivious to much of this. I thought that it was a few big shots, people who lived in both Baie-de-Sol and Miami. I thought—to the extent I thought about it at all—that most cocaine coming into Haiti entered through the southern coast and went out over the Dominican border. I also believed it didn't really concern me. I wasn't there to study drugs.

Then there was an incident in Baie-de-Sol. The day before I was supposed to hitch a ride aboard a Haitian freighter bound for Florida so that I could finish my doctoral dissertation, a small plane touched down on the city airstrip. Two SUVs waited on the muddy road by the airfield. Before they could drive out to meet the new arrivals, a policeman approached the plane. Inside was a Hispanic man, a Haitian man, and several hundred kilos of cocaine. The Hispanic handed the policeman two kilos of cocaine. The policeman took his prize and began to walk away. But apparently thinking he should have gotten more, he turned around and walked back to the plane. BLAM! The Hispanic man shot him in the chest. SUVs rolled out and frantically unloaded the cocaine. But the people, *pep la,* were watching. Road blocks of burning tires and boulders went up. One SUV escaped. *Pep la* got the other. Whether there was a connection or not, the next day my boat didn't leave. That week the DEA and customs officials in Miami seized five freighters from Haiti with cocaine packed in their hulls.

It was the beginning of a major campaign against Haitian narcotraffickers. My boat didn't leave.

A few days later, waiting for another boat to leave so that I could hitch a ride, I drove my motorcycle through the Northern city of Cape Haitian. It was a drizzling, overcast day. I rode down out of the mountains and through the streets, past the harbor where some thirty ships were moored, a harbor where only a five years before there would have been no more than half a dozen ships. I stopped the motorcycle and asked a man, "why so many ships?"

He laughed. "They're waiting for things to cool off."

So while I was doing surveys for the Germans and CARE, who were supposedly developing the country, another transformation was taking place.

The people with money, skills, and contacts, those who would normally have left the country, migrated to Miami or Canada and never returned, they were finding a way to profit from Haiti's instability.

I was away in the United States for most of the year, but then I was back and Moise's announcement and what happened next made me realize at last the extent of what was really going on around me.

The men and their vehicle were on the airstrip and the peasants and toughs from the village secretly watched from the brush. The entire day passed and nothing happened. Night began to fall, and by 7:00 it was pitch black, with no moon. At 7:15 the first plane came in. Minutes later another one. No one could see them, but everyone heard. People in the Hamlet were listening, and some ran out of their houses and tried to see the aircraft. Others only poked their heads out the door. Some crouched in their little hovels, pulled their children close, and prayed to spirits, to Jesus, to God. The planes had no running lights. They came in low over the Hamlet, flashing an occasional signal as they approached. On the landing strip, flashlights and headlights came on and outlined the dirt runway. The first plane touched down. Its seats had been ripped out to make way for the cargo, 4,500 kilos of Columbian cocaine, a huge shipment, worth at least $100 million on the streets of Miami or New York. The other plane followed. The planes were twin-engine, made to carry sixteen passengers.

On the airstrip,p men ran to the planes and quickly unloaded the crates. Once the first plane was unloaded, it was abandoned. The pilots boarded the second plane and took off. The first vehicle, a large SUV, was loaded and began winding its way back down the rocky seaside road to the Village. It crept around the first bend, but then stopped. There were boulders in the road. The men were not sure what to do, and then the decision was made for them as rocks flew from the bushes, pelting the sides of the vehicle. The passenger side window cracked. The driver slammed the vehicle in reverse and worked his way back to the airstrip. Five minutes passed. The vehicle returned, accompanied by the other vehicles. All the windows were down, pistols and rifles poked out, and dim shadows scurried in the bushes. Then came the rocks, like hail. There was shouting, "*bay pa nou.*" (Give us ours).

The men in the vehicles sat low in their seats to avoid the rocks, but a shadow came up from behind the last vehicle, a pistol in hand. A tire was shot out. Another shadow came from the other side. A shotgun, Boom! Another tire deflated. The men in the first vehicle climbed out, firing guns in the air and the shadows retreated into the brush. The men with the guns rolled the boulders out of the way, climbed back in the vehicles, and drove on.

One after another, the four vehicles passed the first barricade. Then there was another barricade. The men got out of their vehicles, firing into the air, and removed the boulders. At the third barricade, the first vehicle got through. The second vehicle passed. The third vehicle. But as the crippled fourth tried to limp through, a barrage of rocks came sallying from the bushes and smashed the windshield. Then the driver's side window cracked, a third tire was blown out, the back window smashed in. The chief of police and his sergeant scampered from the front seat and ran into the brush. The other policemen in the vehicle ran off behind them and the shadows covered the vehicle like hungry rats. They pulled out boxes, loaded them onto their shoulders, and fled into the brush. Other men armed with machetes and stones ran along behind them and stopped them, forcing them to split up the contents of the boxes. By the time the cocaine was fully divided, two thousamd kilos were dispersed into the hands of hundreds of peasants and fisherman.

Buyers began arriving almost immediately and many peasants sold their *keys*, as in "kilos"—which they did not understand is a unit of measure—for as little as fifty Haitian dollars (about US$10 at that time). A lot of money to them, but, of course, nowhere near the true value. Nor did they understand initially that the *keys* of cocaine were wrapped in tape so that what seemed like a single *key* was really two compressed kilos of cocaine.

Two days later the feared special police, the SIMO, arrived from Port-au-Prince. Two truckloads of thirty-six big muscular men dressed in tight black t-shirts, black pants, and black steel-toed boots. Hunting knives strapped to their legs, clubs strapped to thighs, nine-mm semiautomatics holstered at hips.

First they went to the Village, where they searched houses and intimidated people. They stopped short of beatings and abuse. Then they came to the Hamlet where they terrorized and beat people.

When the police arrived, Givme, Alsibien, and Robè were on the beach preparing to launch a rowboat. They could see the thugs coming, loaded in the back of the two trucks, bouncing down the rocky road among the cacti. They saw them spill out of the trucks and disappear jogging down the trail toward the Hamlet. Givme, Alsibien, and Robè needed no urging. They all dove into the water and swam around to cliffs on the back side of the beachhead where they climbed up into the desert *kadas.* Squatting in the bushes above the Hamlet, they watched as the thugs rounded up the few men they could find and ransacked the houses. The SIMO were wasting their time. Most people in the Hamlet who had gotten cocaine had already behaved like wily peasants anywhere else in the world: They had hidden it under the sea in their fishing weirs or in caves in the *kadas* and then literally headed for the hills.

The night of the cocaine hijacking almost every male in the Hamlet left for "a relative's funeral on the mountain." The SIMO thugs found mostly people who did not participate in the attack or who had gotten nothing for their efforts. But they forced the eight men who were still present to lie down under the big oak tree in the middle of the Hamlet and there they beat them with rifle butts, saplings, a shovel, rocks. When one thug slapped eleven-year-old Lonise as she sat next to her father on the sand, Givme, crouching among the scrub bushes above, could take no more. He grabbed a rock, stood up, and, hurling the rock down toward the thugs, screamed, "Your mother's ass stinks." Neither he nor Alsibien nor Robè waited to see where the rock landed. Instead, they all took off running through the *kadas*.

Not all the police were malicious. There were humorous incidents. One thug was ransacking the house of Dinel, who was already off selling his cocaine in the next fishing hamlet. The thug tore through boxes, dumping the contents on the ground and kicking them out the door. Manmin and six of her eleven children, huddled together in terror on their bed as the thug pulled items down from the rafters. He came across a sack of dried fish that Manmin had prepared for market. He dumped the contents of the sack on the ground, then, picking up a string of dried fish, he said: "Momi," a polite way to address a mature peasant woman, "how much you want for this?"

Manmin forgot her fear and immediately assumed her role as market woman. "Ten dollars."

"I will give you six."

"*Non, non*, my son." Manmin climbed off the bed and pointed defiantly at the thug. "Are you crazy? The cost of living has been going up." She paused for a moment and then counteroffered. "Give me eight and you can take it."

"Ahh, Momi, you're killing me. You know we don't get paid well. Here," the thug pulled out a small wad of bills, "I got seven dollars."

"Okay, It's a deal, *oui*." Manmin snatched the money.

Only one person in the Hamlet gave in. After being rapped on the knuckles for several minutes, Jayjay told only on himself and only that he had one kilo—he had two—which he retrieved from the *kadas* for the thugs. They found nothing in the Hamlet itself.

In the Village they recovered over one hundred kilos. One man I know lost an entire case of twenty-four doubles, meaning forty-eight kilos. Another was Rachel. When the police came to search her house she stood outside raving that they had no right. The police became suspicious and proceeded to uproot a series of recently planted palm saplings under which they found a total of eleven double kilos.

But then the police were gone and people who had cocaine came back down from the hills. In the Village, judges, school teachers, *bokor*, and pastors gathered their citizens, flocks, constituents, students, and disciples around and asked—sometimes nicely and sometimes with threats of prison, failing grades, or black magic—for their cut. By that point, buyers from the city were arriving in force. They had heard about the incident on the radio, from friends and family, and so they came on motorcycles, in SUVs, on boats and on ships. Two of the SIMO thugs returned in civilian cloths and bought kilos—they fooled no one, but such is the materialistic Haitian understanding of life that the locals forgave them for performing their job and sold them kilos of cocaine anyway.

Before the SIMO experience, the buyers were purchasing the two kilos wrapped up together as one for no more than a couple hundred Haitian dollars per unit (at that time one Haitian dollar was worth twenty-five cents). A single kilo at the time would sell for about US$23,000 in Miami and US$6,000 to US$7,000 on Haitian city streets. The people wised up quickly and the price soon hit US$2,000 and ultimately US$5,000. It was enough to make some peasants rich by local standards. There was much jealousy and stealing, and one guy, a buyer from Baie-de-Sol, got stoned to death when, pushing hard on several peasants, he pulled out a pistol and fired it in the air. Peasants poured out of the brush and came running from neighboring houses, showering the man with rocks.

Eventually everyone came to understand what had happened, how much the cocaine was worth, that they had really been selling doubles and for much less than the cocaine was worth. There was resentment. There were also peasants who began making fake kilos. Using the same type of brown tape in which the *keys* had been wrapped, they packed them full of baking soda and peddled them to overeager buyers from the city.

On the fourth day after the hijacking of the cocaine, Alsibien came to my hut and told me someone wanted to see me.

"There is a boat anchored outside the bay," he says. "Com'on."

"It's not the first boat to anchor outside the bay."

"*Oui,* but it is the first time that Jenson's boat has been anchored there and he is asking for you."

Jenson was a *gran neg* or political boss in Jean Makout and he had become very rich in a very short time. Five years earlier he was in Canada working as a warehouse supervisor. When he returned to Haiti, he lived in a small tin-roofed house in the Village, on property owned by his mother. All he had of any value was a Toyota SUV. But he used his SUV to pick up cocaine air drops made by a Columbian he met in Canada. At the time of the hijacking, only five years after he had returned, he owned the largest house in Jean Makout, a four-story mansion on a mountain overlooking the county. He had a similar house in Baie-de-Sol, one in Port-au-Prince, a house in Fort Lauderdale, and one in Montreal, Canada. In the city he also now had an ice plant, a gas station, a water delivery service, a laundromat, a fleet of SUVs, and three ships, including an 850-ton freighter. He usually was accompanied by several bodyguards.

"You go, Alsibien. I'm staying here."

"You have to go."

"I don't even know the guy."

"If you don't go, it's going to be a problem for all of us." Alsibien, myself, and Robè borrow the fishing cooperative's seldom-used motor boat and take off on the three-mile trip. Arriving outside the bay, Alsibien, the cook who used to pass out drunk and drool on the floor of the survey office, is standing proudly behind the wheel of our skiff, a cigarette dangling from his mouth, as he makes straight for the big three-story wooden trawler, a type still made of hand-hewn boards on the island of La Torti and powered by diesel truck engines. As we approach I expect that Alsibien will kill the engine or put it in neutral, turn the skiff, and gently come up alongside the trawler. It never occurs to me that in all probability this is the first time he has driven anything other than a rowboat. Alsibien keeps the skiff pointed directly at the trawler, full throttle, him standing tall, cigarette dangling from his mouth, and when we are about ten feet away he suddenly loses his composure, lets go of the steering wheel, and disve to the deck. Robè and I, momentarily astonished, dive after him and cover our heads as the skiff slams directly into the side of the trawler.

We recover from our crash with a lot of cursing. The trawler crew are standing on the ship's deck above us, looking down, shaking their heads. Alsibien announces he had to go to shore to shit. Robè announces he is going with him to help. So I board the trawler alone.

I climb up the rope ladder. A crew member greets me on deck and then leads me through the empty passageways of the boat, a vessel with a lot of unfilled space, reminding me of the large, ghostly old wooden houses one finds in Haitian cities and villages. There is no furniture, and the bulkheads are unpainted. We climb a creaking ladder to the third deck and there in a cabin waiting for me is Judge Similus and Jenson.

The cabin is large and there is an open hatch that gives out onto the upper deck. Built into the center of the cabin against one bulkhead is a king-sized wooden bed frame with an exposed and dirty mattress. Jenson is sitting on the mattress, huge, like a bear, dark black skin and a big pudgy baby-face. Judge Similus is sitting in a chair against a wall. He rises to greet me and introduce Jenson.

"I won't waste your time, *non*," says Jenson. "What I want is for you to round up all the cocaine you can. We will pay you for it. Price is $5,000 and that's a hell of a lot more than anyone is paying now."

"Why me? Why not Alsibien or Robè?"

"Because everybody trusts you."

"Everybody trusts money. Just give Alsibien and Robè the money and they can buy all the cocaine you want."

"I am having a little cash flow problem. I don't have much on hand. I can give you some money, but it is not enough. So I want you to give everyone a little cash and then promise to pay the rest later. They trust you. You're a *blan*."

"I can't be involved in anything like this."

"It is a U.S. politic. It is only against the law because the U.S. says so. What do you care."

"It's illegal. That's enough for me. I can't help you."

After turning Jenson down, I walk out to the deck. Alsibien is not back yet so I lean against the rail feeling very uncomfortable and wishing like hell Alsibien would get done taking a shit. And just how is it that Robè is helping him shit? I begin to wonder if they could be in on this.

"Judge," I say to Judge Similus who leans on the rail next to me, looking displeased that I won't help, "I thought you guys believe I am CIA?".

For years the police and everyone else in the Village believed I was a CIA agent. They were sure of it, for several reasons. When I first showed up in Haiti it was immediately after the first election of Aristide. I showed up again one year later, in the middle of the coup d'etat when the military had shut the country down and was shooting slum dwellers in Port-au-Prince. Then I showed up again during the junta, when most Americans had abandoned the country and the U.S. government had warned its citizens not to go there. I also spent much of my time in a tiny port town called St. Pierre which, although today it is little more than crumbling ruins inhabited by goats and half-naked fisher folks, was known during the colonial era as the Gibraltar of the Caribbean and in the past century had been the one time object of U.S. military interest as an option to Quantanamo Bay. The suspicion that I was CIA was also encouraged by two incidents in the village. Once in 1995, on the day of the first postinvasion presidential elections, a team of high-ranking U.S. military men flew in on a helicopter. They landed on the soccer field just on the outskirts of the village. Hundreds of people went down to see them, including a delegation of police and upper level village administrators. I happened to be nearby. Dressed in flip flops, torn swimming shorts, and flanked by two barefoot fishermen, I stood off to one side of the field watching. The general and his staff stepped down out of the helicopter, looked around, and headed straight for me. The general shook my hand, waved off the police and toured the village with me at his side. The reason I suppose he headed for me was because I was white, and once he realized that I was not an official he, having no translator and none of the Haitians being able to speak English, simply decided to have me take him around. But it must have looked like I had been waiting for the general and no matter what I said there was no one to back me up on the fact that I had not. Two weeks later a team of U.N. officials flew in on another helicopter and the scene was repeated. So everyone including the police was sure that I was a U.S. agent of some kind. And besides, what the hell else would a *blan* be doing living with impoverished fishermen; it was clear from my drinking and the cigar usually hanging out of my mouth that I was no missionary.

But the notion that I was CIA was, to me, absurd. Beyond high-level politics, the U.S. intelligence community seemed to care little and know even less about what was going on in Haiti. In 1994, as the U.S. was preparing to lead a multinational invasion force into Haiti, I was teaching a university class in which one of the students was an active member of an elite U.S. military unit. He came to class one day and told me they had briefed his unit and he would probably go into Haiti on the first wave. He was concerned because his unit had been told that the Haitians had heavy artillery, some planes, and a relatively large military. I know little about military hardware. But from simply having walked by military bases and hung out with soldiers, I was able to tell him what any CIA agent could have told him, if he wasn't sitting in Port-au-Prince getting his information from the newspapers or from chatting up elites at cocktail parties: Little if any of Haiti's heavy artillery functioned, having been left in the rain for years; tanks were piles of rusting, immobile junk; planes and helicopters were strewn about in pieces; and most soldiers were equipped with WWI single-shot Mausers for which they didn't have more than a couple of bullets, if any at all.

"No shit!" was all he could say.

"*Non, monchè*, we don't think you're CIA any more," Judge Similus says, perking up. "We think you're DEA."

"Then you ought not to be talking to me about drugs."

"DEA or not, you're on our side, *oui*. You're our *blan*. You're one of us."

"The answer is no."

Some people who read previous drafts of this book expressed surprise that I did not feel that I was in danger turning down the request of a drug lord, someone whom the popular notion would presume to be a cold-blooded killer. I was not eager to go meet Jenson. But there was never any reason to expect, nor did I expect, to be in any danger. Since some people thought I might be CIA or DEA, they did not want to risk the wrath of the U.S. law enforcement people. What was more, Jenson was a friend of Sharon's, one of his children went to the School. He knew full well that Sharon and I were close.

There was also the fact that there is little killing in Haiti over drugs. The people in the trade like Jenson aren't going to kill someone for knowing. Everybody knows. They may kill you for getting between them and their money, but not always. There is in Haiti a general sentiment that if you are dumb enough to get taken by a failure to pay or deliver that's tough luck. Most violence over drugs occurs in explosive incidents such as an argument over price that suddenly gets out of hand, as with the man whom the peasants stoned to death, or during an outright attempt to rob. I should also clarify that the reason the smugglers had not opened fire on the mob that was robbing them was because it would have been suicide. There have been many similar thefts in Haiti and never to my knowledge has anyone opened fire on *pep la,* not for drugs—killing impoverished people appears to be fall in the nobler realm of politics. The peasants in the incident I described did not hit the smugglers or the police with rocks; they hit the vehicles. And the smugglers aimed over the heads of the peasants. The one exception was the chief of police. According to the people who were there, he leveled his gun at the people and fired. Miraculously no one was hit, but the peasants and villagers were furious. There was widespread talk about killing him, and he had to leave the Village secretly that very night. He never returned. Such is anarchy.

So I felt no fear in Jenson's presence. As a matter of fact, during my ten years in Haiti, living among an alien people in abysmal conditions, walking the dangerous streets of Port-au-Prince, witnessing explosive mob violence, I may have occasionally felt apprehension, but seldom fear.

In any case, Alsibien and Robè finally came back for me.

"You could have made a lot of money," Jenson said to me as I started down the ladder to the skiff.

That same week, it's a Sunday morning, I am on the beach where I encountered Pastor Sinner. He has come to the beach to say good-bye to a visiting French missionary and his family who had brought in a load of schoolbooks on their sailboat. The Pastor, his wife, and several of his flock are standing on the beach waving goodbye. The Frenchman has pulled anchor and is motoring away. Looking over at Pastor Sinner waving, I can't help but think about how he is such a different man than when I met him ten years before.

Back then he was a struggling pastor, humble and sincere, simply dressed.

Today he operates a large school in the Village of Jean Makout. An Arkansas church donated his three vehicles, built his three story cement house and school, his out buildings and church. They also donate all the school supplies as well as medicines and food, all of which he promptly sells. And they give him $70,000 a year to educate 190 children. The children have to pay for their tuition, books and uniforms and his teachers earn only US$30 per month.

I look at him standing there next to me on the beach, waving. Gone is any trace of humility. He is boastful and haughty and standing there waving he looks like a televangelist. He wears a white silk shirt, a silk tie, and a tailor-made white blazer. White powder cakes his neck and he appears to have makeup on his face.

While the Pastor, his wife and the members of his flock continue what has become a very long wave goodbye, Ti Tonton from the Hamlet speeds by on a boat powered by a brand new

Yamaha 9.9 outboard motor, every Third World fisherman's dream. It's an efficient motor that, unlike the gas-guzzling Johnson 25-horsepower motors bought by the U.N. for the fishing cooperative boats, lasts for decades. These motors hardly ever break down, and when they do, you don't have to go to Miami to buy the parts, because they are available in Port-au-Prince. *Lucky Ti Tonton,* I hink, *maybe his life will finally change.* Watching Ti Tonton in his boat, Pastor Sinner brings up the cocaine.

"They'll be poor again," he says. "Then they will be right back where they were. *Non,* won't last. They don't know what to do with money. They've never had any."

As I listen to the Pastor I wonder about his own background, whether he was dirt poor or if his father had been one of the better off peasants. I think about how much money the US$70,000 he gets from the Arkansas church is worth here in rural Haiti. *Christ, that's like having a million or more in the States.* As I decide that his father must have been a relatively wealthy peasant, Sinner, still waving, is saying, "When you don't work for money it just passes right through your fingers."

At US$5,000 per kilo, the Haitian street value of the hijacked cocaine was about US$10 million and while much of that money surely ended up elsewhere, plenty was visibly spent in the Hamlet and the Village. The amount can be compared to the $1 million (U.S.) spent in Jean Makout County by the government during a six-year period in the 1990s and the $34 million in aid provided to the area during the same period by two NGOs, CARE and PISANO, expenditures that arguably made matters worse, not better, for the poorest of the poor.

Dozens of motorcycles were bought with the cocaine money. Many people bought cars and trucks, electric generators, outboard motors and new fishing boats. Jiji built a new store. Dozens of fresh block houses went up. School and university tuitions paid were paid. Families moved to the Village, some moved to Baie-de-Sol, some to Port-au-Prince, and in the two months after the cocaine incident, at least fifteen people emigrated illegally to Miami. Most were subsequently to send regular gifts of money back to their families, and over the years their efforts and contacts would lead to the migration of many more.

Some people, like Judge Similus, made hundreds of thousands of dollars. The judge, born and raised in the Village, found out from family members and confidants which people had gotten cocaine and he went around and personally visited them. If he could not find them, he spoke with their family and insisted that he be given a cut in exchange for, as he explained it, "protection."

Most people complied and the judge reputedly made over US$500,000 before he was relieved of his judgeship by Baie-de-Paix superiors who were unhappy at not getting their cut. The judge put his new fortune to work on an intensified campaign to have sex with young women. Included among his objectives was my girlfriend Arnaud. He literally chased her down the street in his new Jeep, cornered her behind a building in Tierre Bleu, and threatened to have her jailed if she did not cooperate and go out on a date with him. She pointed out he was not judge any longer. He pulled a pistol from inside the jeep and said that he would shoot her instead. To my knowledge she never complied, but who knows.

Another guy who made a fortune was Abraham, a pastor/entrepreneur from the village. His entrepreneurial instincts triumphing over any inkling of morality, he arrived in the Hamlet the day after the cocaine was stolen and bought two kilos for 2,500 goud (about US$100). Because the kilos were bundled up in packages of two, he really had four kilos. He took them to the city, sold them for US$20,000, and was back the next day to buy twenty more keys at the new price of H$1,000 per kilo. The people still not having figured out that they were double kilos meant that he actually was able to buy forty kilos. When it was finally over, Abraham made, by his own claim, at least US$600,000. But maybe more. Within a month he transformed himself from a small Village pastor and petty businessman to an export-import mogul who was flying off to Miami to purchase vehicles and other goods and ship them to Haiti for resale.

To be sure there were some who actually ended up right back where they started, or worse. Son was a big, muscular young man, twenty-three years old at the time of the cocaine incident. He had the distinction of being one of the most obnoxious men in the entire area, constantly haranguing people, and he had been kicked out of the Village high school for a fist fight with the principal. Son made off with an entire case of kilos, forty-eight of them, something made possible no doubt by his aggression and strength.

He turned out, to my surprise, to be generous. He handed kilos out to family and people he liked. He gave one to his grandmother, one to his mother, one to his sister, several to special friends, his favorite preacher, his favorite ex-teacher, a girl he liked. Alone, Son, by virtue of his generosity, was responsible for at least three people I know reaching Miami.

Overnight he became a big man and Son was very cool about it. Several weeks after the night of the cocaine, Judge Similus sponsored a *gombo* (festival), the first of many, to thank the *lwa* (the spirits) for the cocaine. People from the Hamlet and the Village came together in a yard on the outskirts of the Village. I sat on a porch drinking rum with Givme's uncle and across the street, Son sat in a chair, freshly bathed. He was wearing brand new clothes, a young woman knelt beside him trimming his nails and another stood over him trimming his hair.

A couple weeks later, he and his best friend, Nennen, the only professional tire repair man in the area and one hell of a nice guy, boarded a boat for the Bahamas. They were going to Nassau where they would board another boat for Miami. But the boat didn't make it. It smashed against a reef near one of the Bahamian outer islands in the exact spot where, a few years before, the pilot of a small airplane had recounted to a journalist his experience of circling overhead watching schools of hammerhead sharks attack a shipwrecked boat full of terrified Haitian refugees. Son could swim and he managed to make it to shore. But Nennen did not. Three years later, Son was still hanging out around the Village, playing cards and dominoes and hoping that one of the friends he had helped send to Miami would one day remember him.

A similar story is that of Pol, who also got away with an entire case of cocaine: Twenty-four packages, forty-eight kilos. Pol and Tito, my former chauffer—the one who threatened to kill the supervisor—were two of the principal organizers of the hijacking. The illiterate Pol was a local tough who had lived on the streets since the age of eight years. He worked as a porter loading and unloading buses and trucks and he trusted a guy who owned a freight truck he used to ride on, Macandal, a *gran neg*. Afraid that someone would steal his cocaine and not knowing enough about the business to sell it himself, Pol put his faith in Macandal. Macandal gave him $100,000 Haitian dollars—about US$20,000 at the time—more money than Pol had ever seen in his life. Macandal sold the lot for US$200,000. Over the next year Pol spent half his money drinking, dancing, and engaging in relationships with a series of women who before the cocaine incident would not have so much as spoken to him. He did some good things. He gathered up his wife and five children and put them in a house that Macandal loaned him—and later took away.

Pol blew most of the money on drinking and women but before it was all gone, he put the last US$5,000 in the government Cooperative Savings Plan. That was the money that was going to keep his family going. The Cooperative Savings Plan was a program launched by the Aristide government. In 2001 the head of the program came on the radio promising peasants that if they took their money to the local government agricultural cooperative and left it there, they would receive a guaranteed interest rate of 23 percent per month. At first many people didn't believe it. How could it be? Only a few people put any money with them. But then the government paid the first month's interest. The poor throughout Haiti flocked to the Cooperatives with their meager savings, some even mortgaging their land to raise money. Pol was one of them. Pol put all of his US$5,000 in the Government Cooperative. The next month, government officials absconded with all the funds—US$250 million. Among them was the last of Pol's cocaine money and so, one year after the hijacking, Pol was right back where he started, loading and unloading trucks.

Then there was Jean-Paul, a slick business-minded guy. He was a grandson of Saint Pierre, founder of the Hamlet, and one of the most successful fisherman in the area. But he didn't know anything about cocaine and he trusted a *gran neg,* big Rigobert, who promised that if Jean-Paul bought cocaine on credit for him he would buy him a car and give him 25 percent of all the profits he made. Jean-Paul's respect and trust among peasants got him thirty-four kilos on credit. When it was over, Rigobert paid the money Jean-Paul owed for the kilos and gave Jean-Paul US$4,000. No car. No 25 percent. For his efforts, which were none because Jean-Paul got it all for him on credit, Rigobert made US$150,000, in profit.

The cocaine incident bothered me in a personal way. On the one hand, I was happy to see that some people of the Hamlet and the Village had gotten a chance to ease their poverty. On the other hand, it deeply disturbed me that the people of the Hamlet were involved in the drug trade and it concerned me that they might begin to use the drug. I knew that cocaine, especially crack, had increasingly become available in the cities. In many of the little stores, *boutik*, where Haitians have traditionally purchased smoked herring, salt, dried beans, and flour, where they purchased their spiced rum and cigarettes, one could increasingly purchase crack cocaine.

When I spoke to the people of the Hamlet and Jean Makout about the temptation to use cocaine, they unanimously dismissed it, *sa pou vakabon yo*, "That's for bums," they would say.

But it was nevertheless clear where things were heading. Drug trafficking and the profits that could be made were on everyone's lips. "The Columbians have promised to make us all rich in three years," was the rumor. "They are going to drop kilos of cocaine everywhere," a young man, a neighbor living next door to my house on the mountain, assured me. "They are going to sprinkle the entire mountain with kilos of cocaine."

The thirst for money and the enormous sums that could be made had, in one night, transformed the people's outlook and their behavior. Shortly after the cocaine incident, a rumor began circulating that there would be another *djeal*, this time the drugs were coming by boat. The night of the supposed *djeal*, hundreds of people hid in the bushes waiting in ambush. A boat did in fact enter the bay and approach the beach where the people were waiting. It was a rare event, a boat entering at night, and it lent some credibility to the rumor. But whether the boat was loaded with drugs or not, none of the fisher folk or peasants in the area will ever know because a trigger-happy peasant began shooting at the boat before it ever got to shore.

My faith in development had been destroyed. I no longer had any will to be an anthropologist and I planned to leave Haiti soon. I lingered in the Hamlet for a while, watching as people I had known for years, pastors, businessmen, police, schoolteachers, people who I had never suspected could be involved in drugs, came and bought kilos of cocaine.

I learned how the cocaine trade works in Haiti, how with the disbanding of the military in 1994 it had become democratized so that littler people could make money too. I learned how at first, with the military no longer monopolizing the drug trade, the Columbians had used local Haitian ship owners and businessmen. Haitians picked up the drugs when they were dropped from a plane or brought in on a go-fast boat and stored them, tasks for which the Columbians would give the handler 25 percent of the load. Soon the people who were receiving it were selling kilos to other Haitians. Ship captains, from the largest megaton steel freighters to the small wooden sailing vessels that plied the channel between the Bahamas and the North Coast of Haiti, began making a trade of hauling dope. By the time I became aware of it, the price for hauling a kilo to Miami was $3,000. Welded shut in a steel hull or nailed shut in a wooden one, a captain might have three hundred kilos from one hundred different people. He would sell the cocaine right off the dock in Miami or Nassau, take his cut, and then bring the money back to his clients, who could triple an investment with every trip.

It went on with almost complete impunity. Everyone knew when a ship left and when it arrived, when the coke had been sold and when the captain was on his way back to Haiti.

After most of the "fallen" cocaine had been sold, I left and went up the mountain to see Arnaud. When I arrive and explain to her what had happened, she is furious: "You didn't get any of it? Are you an idiot?"

"It's against the law. It's dangerous."

"You're a fucken idiot. An international fucken idiot."

I ignore her. I bath, eat supper, and go to bed. But early in the morning shortly before dawn, we are both lying awake talking. She seems to have gotten over her anger and now I am telling her that I want to write a book about development and perhaps about cocaine and how it has impacted Haiti.

"Won't you ever do anything right?" she snarls. "Look at you, you can't even get a job. You're the only *blan* I know who can't afford a decent pair of shoes."

Well, she was right. But the difference between me and her, and the other Haitians I had lived with, was that I had chosen to live poor. I could get out anytime I wanted. And I had a hell of a lot more to lose than they did by getting involved in the drug trade. Nevertheless, I felt anger welling up inside of me. She continued.

"My cousin Nicolas has already made it and he's only sixteen. He has twenty-four kilos. He's set. And you, you're pathetic. Write a book? You can't even start an orphanage for me. I've wasted four years of my life with you."

Shortly before I left Baie-de-Sol, I was occupying the empty house that I once shared with the Nanny, Albeit, and Tobe. The girls are gone. I could no longer afford to care for them. Albeit has moved in with an aunt she barely knows, a sister of her dead mother, and Tobe is living with her eighteen-year-old brother. Sharon is helping to support and care for them. So I am sitting in the house, thinking about all that has happened, feeling a little lonely and wondering what I am going to do with my life when a car horn honks outside. I go out and lean over the balcony to find Jenson down below standing by a Toyota Land Cruiser.

"*Mon Ami*, we are having a party tomorrow night and I want you come." He held up two tickets, "These are for you and your girlfriend."

I no longer have a girlfriend. But I find Sanya, a girl who worked at a hotel in Baie-de-Sol and with whom I have a shallow and intermittent relationship. We go to the party together.

Jenson's house in Baie-de-Sol looked very much like his house in Jean Makout, a four-story cement and tile monstrosity with many balconies, banisters, turrets, and steeped roofs. Jenson is greeting people at the door and he welcomes us. Inside we find that on each of the first three floors there are tables set up everywhere. On the tables are vases of flowers, bottles of Hennessy cognac and Babancourt rum. Guided by the guitarist for Jenson's personal jazz band—a guy who once stole H$10 from me—we make our way through each of the three stories set up for the party. The representative for the German embassy sits at one table. At another are a half dozen UN officials. I shake hands with the Guyanese crewmembers from Jenson's freighter. I see dozens of parents from The School of Jesus Christ of America, a gas station owner and his wife, several ship owners, the assistant chief of police. Sanya and I sit for awhile with two School parents. I know them both. The wife is a good friend of Sharon. I met her husband in the Hamlet when he was there buying kilos of cocaine. He owns a two-hundred-ton ship and five houses in Baie-de-Sol. He spent twenty years in Miami and speaks a clear if imperfect English. We talk as we watch people dance. Bodyguards mingle with the diners and dancers, pistols bulging in their waistbands. Naturally, we talk about cocaine. My presence in the Hamlet seems to have convinced him that I am alright.

"You see that guy over there?" he confides.

"Yeah."

"He was the first guy to make contact with the Columbians."

My new friend also talks about himself. He tells me he was arrested in Miami for shooting his cousin. To prove it, he lifts his shirt, turns, and shows me the scar from a bullet wound where the cousin had shot him back. Eventually I say: "You know, a lot of people think I am CIA?"

"Yeah," he says. "You know it used to be that none of *us* knew who was working for whom. It was so confusing at first."

I met a lot of people that night. Sanya and I spent hours sitting with Jenson and the assistant chief of police, and with the owner of an ice plant and several visiting businessman from Port-au-Prince. Sanya danced and I talked with the dealers and drank. We talked about politics and where Haiti was headed. About Aristide and the U.S. government. The week before, Aristide, in dire need of promised foreign aid money, had been publicly considering an accord with the U.S. government. If he signed it, the Coast Guard and the DEA would be able to enter Haiti in pursuit of drug traffickers.

"If he does that," said Jenson, "he's through."

"I'll kill him myself," said one of the Port-au-Prince businessmen.

"You won't have to," said the assistant chief of police. "One of us will have already done it."

Later that night I lay in bed with Sanya and she talks about cocaine. My reception among the *djealers* at the party has convinced her that I am one of them, that I have been secretly masquerading as an impoverished anthropologist when really I am a drug trafficker. She tells me about her cousin.

"I was holding forty kilos of cocaine for him and the bastard didn't give me a dime." She tells me about boyfriends she has had who are policemen and how some have made it and some have not. "It's just a *sol*," she says.

"What do you mean '*sol*'?" I ask.

"You know what a *sol* is? Where people throw money in a pot every week and one person gets it all one week, then the next week it's someone else's turn?"

"Yeah."

"Well, the cops say they are just waiting their turn in the *sol*. It's a joke. They are just waiting for their turn to steal cocaine or get hired to pick up a load. Then they're gone. That's the only reason most of them stay on. Just waiting for their turn to get rich."

Then she tells me about the assistant chief of police.

"He is a *tret*. He's dangerous. Don't have anything to do with him. My uncle left fourteen kilos in the house one time and he showed up at three in the morning and stole them all, at gunpoint."

The next morning I am sitting at the table that Sharon has loaned me, the only furniture left in the house besides a mattress that she has also loaned me. There is a knock at the door. It is the assistant chief of police. He comes in, sits down at the table with me, unclips his pistol and clunks it down on the table.

"I would like you to make a little trip out to Jean Makout with us."

"Who is us?"

"Just me and some of the guys you met last night."

"Why?"

"We heard there's some people still holding cocaine and we'd like you to help us locate them, talk to them about buying it."

"When do you want to go?"

"Tomorrow."

I take the development expert way out. "Sure," I lie, "of course, anything for you guys, come by and pick me up in the morning."

I immediately book a flight to Port-au-Prince for 6:30 the following morning. I don't tell anyone I was leaving, not even Sharon.

On the edge of Baie-de-Sol, right before you get to the Big River that marks the end of the city, there is long bare runway enclosed by a six-foot chain link fence and surrounded by shanty towns. The actual "airport"—if you can call it an airport—is a small, single-story, two-room building scrunched between the outside of the fence and a shanty town. To get to it, you must drive down a muddy lane that parallels the edge of the chain link fence. When a plane has landed, you often can't get there at all because of all the cars and motorcycle taxis that clog the little road. You have to walk.

I get off of my motorcycle taxi, pay the driver, take my bag, and walk up the lane toward the airport. I get no more than ten steps. Parked on the roadside in front of me is a green Toyota 4-Runner with tinted windows. Just as I get along side of it the passenger door swings open.

Out steps the assistant chief. My heart stops.

"*Monchè.* I thought we had a date."

"Yeah, sorry," I say. "I had a call from USAID. They want me in Port-au-Prince. I figured we could work this out when I get back."

I don't know where I found those words. But they worked.

"Ah, *monché.* You promised. When will you be back?"

"Day after tomorrow," I say.

"Okay. You're important to us. I'll meet you when you get in. *N'ap ba-ou sikirite.*" (Police escort).

By evening I am on a plane out of Port-au-Prince bound for Miami. We fly over Haiti and although it is dusk, I can still see the countryside and the cities below. We pass over St. Mark and then Gonaives, over the mountains that separate the north coast from the interior. I can see the county of Jean Makout in the distance, disappearing into darkness. We are flying over Baie-de-Sol and I look down at the city. On the outskirts I see a new five-story hotel rising up by the sea. It isthe biggest building down there—built by a guy who can barely read, a *nouvo riche*, a *djealer* who did not even own a car ten years ago.

I can see the extravagant houses built around the School of Jesus Christ of America. I see the spaceship-like water tank rising above the mission complex. It doesn't look so alien anymore, not with all the big new houses around it. I remember when I first came to Haiti more than a decade before The neighborhood didn't exist. It was nothing more than a large beachhead with a few thatch-roofed houses, no running water or electricity. It was like the Hamlet. But now I can see the lights coming on in more than two hundred new houses, any one of which, if it were located in Miami, would be worth hundreds of thousands, if not millions of dollars. I can see the island of La Torti outlined by glowing lights. I remember several years before when I sat with the Direktor looking out at the sea as he told me about short-term development. How black the island was; I couldn't even discern its outline. Now it is lit up like a Christmas tree. *It sure as hell isn't the state providing that electricity*, I think to myself. No, it is hundreds of privately owned household generators being cranked up all over the island, generators bought with profits from the drug trade. I think about the irony of it all. The development I am looking at below did not come from the United States, or Germany or France. It is not a product of the billions of dollars they poured into Haiti. It came from Columbia, another poor country and from an industry seen by those countries as a threat to their survival. Haitians are getting their cut of wealth from the vices of people in the countries that had set out to engineer their servitude. I think about how drug trafficking had allowed some Haitians to escape the clutches of the sweatshops or emigration to cane fields of the Dominican Republic, how it had helped Haiti to survive. And I think about the greatest irony of all: How the people of the Hamlet and the Village, many of whom really are the poorest of the poor, had done more in one day to better their lives than the Haitian government and all the foreign NGOs had accomplished during half a century...by hijacking a cocaine shipment.

"What's going to happen to Haiti?" Jenson had asked me rhetorically as we sat looking out from the balcony of his lavish home in the deforested hills of the Province.

"I will tell you what's going to happen," he said, answering his own question. "Nothing. *Pa gen benefis nan chanjman anko.*" (There is no longer any profit in change.)

Appendices:

Discussions, Additional Notes, Recommendations,
and Chapter by Chapter Citations

Appendices

APPENDIX A

REFERENCES

Chapter One
The Hamlet: Witch Doctors and Sorcery

All other data and accounts in this chapter were obtained from individuals in the field or from representatives or records of the respective NGOS.

Chapter Two
The Village: Crime, Corruption, and Vigilantes

Population size for the county of Jean Makout is based on the Jean Makout Survey discussed in the text.

All other data and accounts in this chapter were obtained from individuals in the field or from representatives or records of the respective NGOS.

Chapter Three
The Survey and Chaos in the Court

All data and accounts in this chapter were obtained from individuals in the field or from representatives or records of the respective NGOS.

Chapter Four
Gutless Wonders: The Windmill Fiasco and the History of Aid in
Jean Makout County

Estimates on county export revenue for 1997 were made by me, based on interviews with merchants and farmers in the region. For details see:

Schwartz, Timothy T. 2000. "Children are the wealth of the poor:" High fertility and the organization of labor in the rural economy of Jean Makout, Haiti. PhD diss., University of Florida.

Information regarding income garnered from

CARE. 1996. A baseline study of livelihood security in Northwest Haiti. Tucson: The Bureau of Applied Research in Anthropology, University of Arizona.

CARE. 1997. An update of household livelihood security in Northwest Haiti. Monitoring Targeting Impact Evaluation/Unit. Tucson: The Bureau of Applied Research in Anthropology, University of Arizona.

UNOPS. 1997. Ministère de la Planification et de la Coopération Externe (MPCE) Direccion Departmental du Nord-Ouest July. Éléments de la Problématique Déparetmentale (Version de Consultation) Programme des Nations Unies pour le Développement (PNUD), Centre des Nations Unies pour les Établissements Humains (CNUEH-Habitat), Projet d'Appui Institutionnel en Aménagement du Territoire (HAI-94-016).

USAID. 1977. Haiti: Rural community development. Washington, DC: Agency for International Development.

Data for health status comes from interviews with doctors, nurses, and clinic administrators, as well as NGO reports. Readers interested in this data can consult:

Schwartz, Timothy T. 2000. "Children are the wealth of the poor:" High fertility and the organization of labor in the rural economy of Jean Makout, Haiti. PhD diss., University of Florida.

Schwartz, Timothy T. 2004. "Children are the wealth of the poor": Pronatalism and the economic utility of children in Jean Makout, Haiti. *Research in Economic Anthropology* 22: 61–105.

EMMUS-II. 1994/95. Enquete mortalite, morbidite et utilisation des services. Eds. Michel Cayemittes, Antonio Rival, Bernard Barrere, Gerald Lerebours, Michaele Amedee Gedeon. Institut Haitien de L'Enfance Petionville, Haiti. Calverton, MD: Macro International.

PISANO (Theis, W, S. Lund, and T. Janssen). 1990. Rapport relatif aux resultats de l'enquete de donnes de base de Juillet. Hindenburgring: Istrupa Consulting.

All other data and accounts in this chapter were obtained from individuals in the field or from representatives or records of the respective NGOS.

Chapter Five
CARE International

All data and accounts not specified below were gathered by me or obtained from the respective NGOS.

CARE Haiti. 1990. Long range strategic planning (LRSP) report for 1990–1995.

CARE Haiti. 1995. Long range strategic planning (LRSP) report for 1995–2000.

Data on world agricultural yields from:

Food and Agricultural Organization of the United States, Agriculture and Economic Development Analysis Division. 2006. The state of food and agriculture 1995. At www.fao.org/docrep/v6800e/V6800E00.htm (accessed May 2, 2006).

Data on price changes with ID corn sales were from an Unpublished ID Report, 1993.

Nutritional data from:

CARE. 1996. A baseline study of livelihood security in Northwest Haiti. Tucson: The Bureau of Applied Research in Anthropology. University of Arizona.

CARE. 1997. An update of household livelihood security in Northwest Haiti. Monitoring Targeting Impact Evaluation/Unit. Tucson: The Bureau of Applied Research in Anthropology. University of Arizona.

PISANO (Theis, W, S. Lund, and T. Janssen). 1990. Rapport relatif aux resultats de l'enquete de donnes de base de Juillet. Hindenburgring: Istrupa Consulting.

Schwartz, Timothy T. 1998. Nutritional, Health, Agricultural, Demographic and Socio-Economic Survey: Jean Makout, Haiti, 1st June 1997–11th June 1998. On behalf of PISANO, Agro Action Allemande, and Initiative Developpment. Available at the University of Florida Library, Gainesville.

CHAPTER 6
The American Plan:
How to Destroy an Agricultural Economy

Alphonse, Henri. 1996. Haiti-Agriculture: Last battle of the coffee planters. Amsterdam: InterPress Third World News Agency.

Augustin, A. Dans. 1997. USAID strategy to improve food security in Haiti: A proposal.

Agustin A. 1999. La Sécurité Alimentaire En Haiti Groupe d'Etude et de Réfexion. At www.ht.undp.org/UNDAF/CD%20PNUD/Bilan%20commun%20 de%20pays/Services/7e%20texte-%20securitealimentaire.htm (accessed November 13, 2007).

Augustin A, R. Van Bokkelen, M. Josué, and M. Occénad. 1993. *Haiti: Nutrition and food security.* CAPS: Editions de l'Enfance, Port-au-Prince.

Barr, Jane, Myriam Mansour, and Alan Nash. 1993. Immigration Research Project. Concordia University (Projet de recherche sur l'immigration Université Concordia).

BiblioMundo. 2006. Haiti la diaspora. At www.bibliomonde.net/pages/fiche-geo-donnee.php3?id_page_donnee=293 UN/POP/EGM-MIG/2005/01 (accessed April 19, 2006).

CELADE (Centro Latinoamericano y Caribeño de Demografía). 2000. América Latina: Proyecciones de población urbano [Rural Latin America: Projection of urban–rural population 1970–2025]. Santiago, Chile: CELADE/CEPAL. At www.eclac.cl/ Celade/publica/bol63/BD63.html (accessed April 30, 2006).

Chomsky, Noam. 2004. U.S. & Haiti. Third World Traveler. At www.thirdworldtraveler.com/Haiti/US_Haiti_Chomsky.html (accessed February 3, 2007). Reprinted from Z *Magazine.*

Central Intelligence Agency. 2006. World fact book. At https://www.cia.gov/cia/publications/factbook (accessed April 15, 2006).

CIAT (Centro Internacional de Agricultura Tropical). 2005. CIAT, United Nations Environment Program, Center for International Earth Science Information Network, Columbia University, and the World Bank Latin American and Caribbean Population Database. Version 3. At www.na.unep.net/datasets/datalist.php3or gisweb.ciat.cgiar.org/population/dataset.htm.
Christian Peacemaker Teams. 1998. At www.corrystuart.com/slavehaiti1.html (accessed April 23, 2006).

Corbett, Robert. Haiti: Miscellaneous topics. At www.webster.edu/~corbetre/haiti/misctopic/misctopic.htm (accessed April 6, 2006).

DeRienzo, Paul. 1994. Haiti's nightmare: The cocaine coup & the CIA connection. *The Shadow* 32, April/June. At www.globalresearch.ca/articles/RIE402A.html.

DeWind, Josh and David H. Kinley III. 1988. *Aiding migration: The impact of international development assistance in Haiti.* Boulder: Westview.

Driver, Tom. 1996. USAID and wages (contribution to a dialog on Bob Corbett's Haiti list).

Food and Agricultural Organization of the United States, Agriculture and Economic Development Analysis Division. 2006. The state of food and agriculture 1995. At www.fao.org/docrep/v6800e/V6800E00.htm (accessed May 2, 2006).

Dupuy, Ben. 1999. The attempted character assassination of Aristide. Third World Traveler. www.thirdworldtraveler.com/ Global_Secrets_Lies/Aristide_CharacAssass.html. Reprinted from Project Censored.

Food for the Hungry International. 1999. P.L. 480 Title II Institutional Support Assistance Program "Improving Food Security Programming And Resource Management." Haiti Food Security Needs Assessment. Gettysburg, PA: Author.

Georges, Josiane. 2004. Trade and the disappearance of Haitian rice. Ted Case Studies Number 725. At www.american.edu/TED/haitirice.htm (accessed April 4, 2006). Globalis. 2006. Global methodology for mapping human impacts on the biosphere. At globalis.gvu.unu.edu (accessed April 20, 2006).

————. 2007. Globalis—An interactive world map. At globalis.gvu.unu.edu/doc.cfm?page=info (accessed February 3, 2007).

Grossman, Zoltan. 2001. A briefing on the history of U.S. military interventions. At academic.evergreen.edu/g/grossmaz/ interventions.html#anchor1469361. Reprinted from *Z Magazine*.

Haiti Progres. 1995. Boycott threatens Lavalas "election" win. Vol. 13(17).

Hallward, Peter. 2004. Option zero in Haiti. *New Left Review* 27, May–June.

Heinl, Robert Debs, and Nancy Gordon Heinl. 1996. *Written in blood: The story of the Haitian people.* Boston: Houghton Mifflin.

International Monetary Fund. 2005. Haiti—2005 Article IV consultation statement by IMF staff. March 16. At www.imf.org/ external/np/ms/2005/031605.htm (accessed April 12, 2006).

Jensen, Carl, ed. 1994. *Censored: The news that didn't make the news and why, the 1994 Project Censored yearbook,* pp. 79-81. NY: Four Walls Eight Windows.

Lenaghan, Tom. 2005. Haitian Bleu: A rare taste of success for Haiti's coffee growers. DAI, Development Alternatives Inc. At www.dai.com/daideas/pdf/developments/HaitianBleu-DAIdeasDec05.pdf#search='usaid%20haitian%20bleu%20coffee%20exports (accessed April 20, 2006).

Library of Congress. 2006. Haiti foreign trade. Country Studies. At www.photius.com/countries/haiti/economy/haiti_economy_foreign_trade.html (accessed April 15, 2006).

Lundahl, Mats. 1983. *The Haitian economy: Man, land, and markets.* New York: St. Martin's.

McGowan, Lisa A. 1997. Democracy undermined, economic justice denied: Structural adjustment and the aid juggernaut in Haiti. Washington, DC: Development Group for Alternative Policies.

Mortished, Carl. 2005. News: Highly Subsidized U.S. Rice Destroys Haitian Farmers. *Times Online—Business.* At business.timesonline.co.uk/ (accessed May 11, 2006)

Naval, G. 1995. Evaluation of the crisis program of the Catholic Relief Services in Haiti. Final report.

Oxfam. 2005. Food aid or hidden dumping? Separating wheat from chaff. Oxfam Briefing Paper. At http://www.oxfam.org/en/policy/food-aid-or-hidden-dumping (accessed May 1, 2006).

Reidl, Brian. 2002. Still at the federal trough: Farm subsidies for the rich and famous shattered records in 2001. Research

Agriculture Backgrounder #1452. Washington, DC: The Heritage Foundation.

———. 2004. Another year at the federal trough: Farm subsidies for the rich, famous, and elected jumped again in 2002. Research: Federal budget and spending. Research Agriculture Backgrounder #1763. Washington, DC: The Heritage Foundation.

Richardson, Laura. 1997. Feeding dependency, starving democracy: USAID policies in Haiti. Boston, MA: Grassroots International.

Roberts, Ivan, and Frank Jotzo. 2001. 2002 US Farm Bill: Support and agricultural trade. ABARE Research Report 01.13. At www.agobservatory.org/library.cfm?refID=30357 (accessed May 3, 2006).

Rocheleau, Dianne. 1984. Geographic and socioeconomic aspects of the recent Haitian migration to South Florida. In *Caribbean Migration Program.* Gainesville: University of Florida, Center for Latin American Studies.

Rotberg, Robert I., and Christopher A. Clague. 1971. *Haiti, the politics of squalor.* Boston: Houghton Mifflin.

Saint-Louis, Loretta-Jane Prichard. 1988. Migration evolves: The political economy of network process and form in Haiti, the U.S. and Canada. PhD diss., Boston University Graduate School.

Swanson, Richard A., William Gustave, Yves Jean, Roosevelt Saint-Dic. Report: Farmer needs assessment exploratory surveys: CARE Northwest Region 2, 3 & 4. South-East Consortium for International Development and Auburn University. USAID contract No. 521-0217-C-0004-00.

Schwartz, Timothy T. 1992. Among Those Left Behind: Impact of Emigration on Haiti. Master's thesis. University of Florida: Gainesville.

————. 1998. Nutritional, Health, Agricultural, Demographic and Socio-Economic Survey: Jean Makout, Haiti, 1st June 1997–11th June 1998. On behalf of PISANO, Agro Action Allemande, and Initiative Developpment. Available at the University of Florida Library, Gainesville.

————. 2000. "Children are the wealth of the poor:" High fertility and the organization of labor in the rural economy of Jean Makout, Haiti. PhD diss., University of Florida.

————. 2004. "Children are the wealth of the poor": Pronatalism and the economic utility of children in Jean Makout, Haiti. *Research in Anthropology* 22: 62–105.

Shah, Anup. 2005. Food aid as dumping. At www.globalissues.org/TradeRelated/Poverty/FoodDumping/Intro.asp (accessed May 5, 2006).

Simmons, Alan Dwaine Plaza, and Victor Piché. 2005. The remittance sending practices of Haitians and Jamaicans in Canada. At www.un.org/esa/population/migration/turin/Symposium_Turin_files/P01_ASimmons.pdf.

Stepick, Alex. 1982. Haitian refugees in the U.S. Report No. 53. London: Minority Rights Group.

————. 1984. The roots of Haitian migration. In Charles R. Foster and Albert Valdman, eds., *Haiti—Today and tomorrow.*, pp. 337–50. Lanham, MD: University Press of America.

Tayler, Letta. 2006. U.S. exports killing Haiti's once thriving rice industry. *Newsday*, February 12.

Treco, Ria N.M. 2002. The Haitian diaspora in the Bahamas. Florida International University, Department of International Relations.

United Nations. 2005. World population prospects. The 2004 revision population database. At esa.un.org/unpp (accessed February 3, 2007).

UNICEF. 2006. Fertility and contraceptive use: Global database on contraceptive prevalence. At www.childinfo.org/eddb/fertility/dbcontrc.htm (accessed May 3, 2006)

USAID. 1977. Haiti: Rural community development, HACHO United States. Agency for International Development.
USAID. 1998. CDIE impact evaluation. Team Leader Robert G McClelland.PN-ACA-932.

————.2006.USAID/Haiti
www.usaid.gov/ht/economicgrowth.htm (accessed May 3, 2006).

U.S. Department of Commerce. 2006. Haiti country reports on economic policy and trade practices—1998 key economic indicators. Assistant Secretary of Commerce for Market Access and Compliance, Trade Compliance Center. At trade.gov/mac (accessed April 13, 2006).

WHO. 1995. Special issue report about the U.S.-owned Rice Corporation of Haiti, whose parent company has a virtual monopoly on rice imports. Washington DC: Washington Office on Haiti.

Wikipedia. 2006. Economy of Haiti. At en.wikipedia.org/wiki/Economy_of_Haiti (accessed April 5, 2006).

World Bank. 1998. Haiti: The challenges of poverty reduction. Volume I: Poverty Reduction and Economic Management Unit and Caribbean Country Management Unit—Latin America and the Caribbean Region. Report No. 17242-HA. Washington, DC: Author.

Chapter Six
Orphans with Parents and Other Scams that Bilk U.S.Churchgoers

All data and accounts in this chapter were obtained from individuals in the field or from representatives or records of the respective NGOS.

Chapter Seven
Medical Treatments of Choice: Rudeness, Cruelty, and Death

The story of Yvonne was taken from:

Maternowska, Catherine. 1996. Coups d'etat and contraceptives: A political economy analysis of family planning in Haiti. PhD diss., Columbia University.

All other data and accounts in this chapter were obtained from individuals in the field or from representatives or records of the respective NGOS.

Chapter Eight
Disconnected Directors and the Arrogant Haitian Elite

Readers interested in Plantation Dauphin are directed to Bob Corbett's Haiti Page: www.webster.edu/~corbetre/haiti/misctopic/dauphin/dauphin.htm.

All other data and accounts in this chapter were obtained from individuals in the field or from representatives or records of the respective NGOS.

Chapter Nine
A Boy's Mysterious Death Evokes Troubling Thoughts

For Aristide see:

Chomsky, Noam. 2004. U.S. & Haiti. Third World Traveler. At www.thirdworldtraveler.com/Haiti/US_Haiti_Chomsky.html (accessed April 20, 2004). Reprinted from *Z Magazine*.

Clara, James. 1997. Haiti: The roof is leaking. *Z Magazine*. At iticwebarchives.ssrc.org/Z%20Mag/www.zmag.org/ZMag/articles/june97james.htm (accessed May 11, 2006).

DeRienzo, Paul. 1994. Haiti's nightmare: The cocaine coup & the CIA connection. *The Shadow* 32 (April/June). At globalresearch.ca/articles/RIE402A.html.

Farmer, Paul. 1997. *The uses of Haiti*. CITY, STATE: Common Courage Press.

————. 2004. Who removed Aristide? *London Review of Books* 26(8). At www.lrb.co.uk/v26/n08/farm01_.html (accessed May 15, 2006).

Heinl, Robert Debs, and Nancy Gordon Heinl. 1996. *Written in Blood: The story of the Haitian people*. Boston: Houghton Mifflin.

Ives, Kim. 1994. The unmaking of a president. NACLA Report on the Americas, Vol. 27, 1994.

All other data and accounts in this chapter were obtained from individuals in the field or from representatives or records of the respective NGOS.

Chapter Eleven
Anger, Disillusionment and Despair

All data and accounts in this chapter were obtained from individuals in the field or from representatives or records of the respective NGOS.

Chapter Twelve
Colombia and Its Drug Trade To The Rescue

For readers interested in background on the drug trade in Haiti see:

Bernstein, Dennis. 1993. "What's behind Washington's silence on Haiti drug connection?" and "A Haitian call to arms." Pacific News Service, October 20 and November 2.

Bernstein, Dennis and Howard Levine. 1993. The CIA's Haitian connection. *San Francisco Bay Guardian*, November 3.

DeRienzo, Paul. 1994. Haiti's nightmare: The cocaine coup & the CIA connection. *The Shadow* 32 (April/June). At globalresearch.ca /articles/RIE402A.html.

Jensen, Carl, ed. 1994. *Censored: The news that didn't make the news and why, the 1994 Project Censored yearbook*, pp. 79-81. New York: Four Walls Eight Windows.

Mann, Jim. 1993. CIA's aid plan would have undercut Aristide in '87–88. *Los Angeles Times*, October 31.

Weiner, Tim. 1993. Key Haiti leaders said to have been in the CIA's pay. *New York Times*, November 1.

Note: Whether Aristide himself was to blame for his decline in popularity or he really became corrupt and involved in the drug trade is a mute point. Aristide, a priest who grew up with not a cent to his name, reportedly became extremely rich as president and he did very little if anything to dispel that rumor or, if it was not a rumor, to dispel the popular suspicion that he got the money through corruption. At the end of his first full term as president he refused to account for his income before congress, as was called for in the constitution. Instead he borded a UN helicopter and flew to the States.

Perhaps the most damaging incident leading to the loss of popular support for Aristide came with the Cooperative scandal. As recounted in the main text, government officials hatched a plan whereby anyone putting money in the Governments Agricultural Cooperatives was promised some 23 percent interest per month. Aristide reportedly promoted the cooperatives and then when what seemed to enlightened observers to be such an obvious scam proved to indeed be a scam he did not effectively distance himself from it. There were no convincing speeches nor was there any forth coming remuneration. He reportedly did promise to pay peasants back but the fact that he did not made matters even worse.

For readers interested in accusations that he was involved in narcotrafficking, or at least enjoying profits from the industry see:

Adams, David. 2004. U.S. history in Haiti: Hands-on or hands-off U.S. policy changes to fit the crisis in the turbulent nation. This time, though, it may have been caught by surprise. *St. Petersburg Times*, January 29.

APPENDIX B
The Market
(or lack thereof)

To understand the impact of food aid on Jean Makout, one must remember that over 99 percent of people living there were and still are directly dependent on farming. Moreover, sacks woven from palm thatch and gourds from trees are the principal storage containers and as a result, corn and beans, when stored for longer than three or four months, become infested with insects and molds and infiltrated by rats and mice, problems reflected in the fact that rather than conserving seed from the previous harvest to be used in future plantings, 94 percent of Jean Makout farmers purchase seed for each planting from *marchanns,* specialists in seed storage (see Table B1). This means that farmers must sell their produce within a few months of the harvest, causing cyclical gluts in the market and a fluctuation in crop prices by factors as high as 300 percent (see Figure B1 and Table B2). It also means that when food aid is delivered during harvest seasons, it helps crash local produce prices, something that, as seen in the main text, was not a mystery to the NGO workers themselves.

Table B1: Source for all seeds and cuttings
(responses from persons interviewed)

Source	Count	Percent	Cumulative percentage
Purchased	3,362	92.4	92.4
Last harvest	150	4.1	96.5
NGO	68	1.9	98.4
Gift	55	1.5	99.9
Other	3	.1	100.0
Total	3,638	100.0	100.0

Table B2: General price ranges estimated
by Jean Makout merchants, 1993
(goudes per pound)

Crop	Measure	Price Low	Price High
Corn	Mamit	3.6	15.0
Millet	Mamit	4.0	15.0
Beans (*rache*)	Mamit	16.0	33.0
Pigeon peas	Mamit	8.0	25.0
Plantains	Regime	17.0	27.0
Sweet potatoes	Sack	8.0	25.0
Peanuts	Mamit	5.0	15.0
Cow peas	Mamit	10.0	32.0
Coffee	Mamit	12.5	25.0
Tomatoes	Each	.7	1.0
Cabbage	Each	1.3	2.0

SECID and Auburn University 1993

Figure B1

Corn Prices for a Good Harvest Year

January 1998 to January 1999

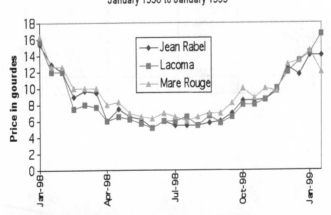

Food Aid in Jean Makout

Table C1: Food relief distributed in Jean Makout by ID, PISANO, AAA and CARE, September 1996 to April 1999 (in metric tons)

	Total wt	Kcal per kilo	Total kcal (in 000s)[3] Person Food/days	(based on 2,200 kcal per day)
Wheat	2,958	3,400	10,058,560	4,572,072
Sorgh	4	3,500	14,700	6,682
Corn	709	3,400	2,410,940	1,095,882
Rice	1,316	3,350	4,406,925	2,003,148
Peas	346	3,200	1,105,920	502,690
Beans	1,671	3,200	5,348,480	2,431,127
Oil[1]	659	8,000	5,273,600	2,397,091
Total	7,663	24,850	28,619,125	13,008,692

The food was definitively not delivered with the welfare of the peasants in mind. In the six months from November 1998 through April 1999, a period that, according to many farmers, included the most bountiful harvest in thirty years, AAA, PISANO, and ID distributed an average of 15 percent more food per month than was disbursed during the 1997 season.

Table C2: Distribution in Jean Makout for thirteen months, September 1996 to October 1997: Crisis

	Date	Srgh	Corn	Rice	Bean	Oil[1]	Total
AAA	09/96-10/97	4.2	9.1	1,050.0	499.8	170.5	1,733.6
ID	09/96-10/97	0	350.0	0	0	0	350.0
PISANO	09/96-10/97	0	0	0	0	0	0
Total wt	09/96-10/97	4.2	359.1	1,050.0	499.8	170.5	2,083.6
Per month	09/96-10/97	0.3	27.6	80.8	38.5	13.1	160.3

Table C3: Distribution in Jean Makout for four months, December 1998–March 1999: No Crisis

	Date	Srgh	Corn	Rice	Bean	Oil[1]	Total
AAA	12/98–02/99	0	0	115.5	29.4	18.5	163.4
ID*	02/99–03/99	0	350.0	0	0	0	350.0
PISANO	01/99–03/99	0	00.0	150.0	75.0	0	225.0
Total wt	11/99–03/99	0	350.0	265.5	104.4	18.5	738.4
Per month	11/99–03/99	0.0	87.5	66.38	26.1	4.63	184.6

CARE also gave the most when it was needed the least. Note in looking at the charts below that 1992–1993 and 1996–1997 were the most severe drought years; 1993–1994 as well as 1998 were bumper crops.

Table C4: CARE distribution in northwest and and northern Artibonite for FY 1993–1997

Type of food	July 1992 June 1993	July 1993 June 1994	July 1994 June 1995	July 1995 June 1996	July 1996 June 1997	July 1997 June 1998	Total
SFB	1,784	16,045	26,904	19,971	10,135	9,419	
WSB	5,380	4,901	3,233	2,189	24	0	
Peas	1,679	0	0	0	0	23.3	
Beans	645	3,779	10,550	9,373	2,036	1,857	
Fish	1,062	1,225	440	346	0	0	
Veg oil	1,306	2,346	3,570	2,189	1,453	1,425	
Total	11,856	28,296	44,697	34,068	13,648	12,724	145,289
Rain (mm)	133.6	1,477.00	562.4	868.7	399.4	752.8	770.4

Table C5: CARE centers and recipients in northwest and northern Artibonite for FY 1993–1997

Fiscal year		FY 1993	FY 1994	FY 1995	FY 1996	FY 1997	FY 1998
Schools	Date	7/92-6/93	7/93-6/94	7/94-6/95	7/95-6/96	7/96-6/97	7/97-6/98
	Centers	560	552	580	609	1,215	1,287
	Recipients	111,960	105,610	112,048	119,850	198,659	210,476
Canteens	Centers	394	867	907	0	0	0
	Recipients	74,373	137,540	193,955	0	0	0
Dry Distrib	Centers	---	92	92	36	48	68
	Recipients	---	465,050	465,050	130,100	228,181	256,685
Total	Centers	954	1,511	1,579	645	1,248	1,319
	Recipients	186,333	708,200	771,053	249,950	426,840	467,161

Note: Food for work and Mother/Child nutrition programs for fy 1997 and 1998 are included in "Dry Distribution."

To calculate the total food AAA distributed in Jean Makout, I have approximated the number of people living there at 115,000 people, roughly halfway between the official estimate for the population (104,000 people) and NHADS for local population (130,132 people). Then the total food distributed was multiplied by .70 because only 70 percent of AAA project falls within the confines of the commune of Jean Makout. Note: 4/15ths of food distributed for project Hai 70-96/NH (22.1 metric tons of beans and 8,800 liters of oil) was subtracted from the total because four of the fifteen months of this project fell outside the time frame for which the calculations were made).

Table C6: AAA food distribution 1995–1997

		Sept 1996 Sept 1997	Oct 1996 Oct 1997	May1997 Aug 1997	Nov 1997 Fev 1998	Total
Seeds (metric tons)	Corn		13			13
	Beans	100	55			155
	Sorghum	6				6
Food (metric ton and liters)	Rice	500	1,000			1,500
	Beans	200	200	99	83	582
	Oil	80,000	95,000	58,000	33,000	266,000
Value (Dutch- Mrks)		1,000,000	1,300,000	200,000	2,000,000	4,500,000

Table C7: AAA food distribution within Jean Makout

	Total ((metric tons)	Recipient population in Jean Makout (70%)	Total distribution in Jean Makout (metric tons & liters)
Corn	13	.70	9.1
Beans	714	.70	499.8
Rice	1,500	.70	1,050
Sorhum	6	.70	4.2
Oil	266,200	.70	186,200

APPENDIX D

Food Aid as Deliberate Undermining of the Market

United States overseas food aid began in 1954 with the passage of Public Law 480. It was not principally meant as a humanitarian gesture. Rather, it was intended to promote U.S. foreign policy, business, and agroindustry. Until very recently there was no effort to conceal this objective. In 2000, three of the five reasons USAID gave on its website for foodaid were, 1) expand U.S. trade, 2) develop and expand export markets for U.S. agricultural businesses, and 3) foster and encourage the development of U.S. overseas enterprise. The website also boasted having used food aid to transform Egypt from an exporter and competitor of U.S. agricultural produce to a net consumer while at the same time creating an industrial sector with some of the lowest wages in North Africa, i.e., urbanization and vast slums of impoverished workers. Since then, however, USAID has come under heavy fire from organizations such as Oxfam and the rhetoric has been carefully purged from the USAID website. Now the focus is on the humanitarian aspects of food aid (www.usaid.gov/pubs/cp2000/pl480ffp.html) (accessed 5th May 2006).

Nevertheless, critics of food aid and its use as a tool of foreign policy are no longer rare nor are we radical. Indeed, it is safe to say that whether or not food aid has been destroying agricultural economies is no longer an argument. It has. The issue now is how to stop the governments and charities from continuing to deliver it irresponsibly and in areas where and at times when it is not needed. USAID and what are called "cooperating PVOs" (Private Voluntary Organizations), such as CARE, have made great efforts to reinvent themselves and food aid as if they were changing the outcome of flooding agricultural markets. An example of one of these agencies admitting food aid distorts development and then trying to defend it is on World Vision's website:

Bibliography

www.worldvision.org/resources.nsf/main/FoodAidBriefing_Dec20
05.pdf/$file/FoodAidBriefing_Dec2005.pdf.
Readers interested in an excellent summary of sites and articles
about food aid should chcek out Anup Shah's website:

Shah, Anup. 2005. Food aid as dumping. At
www.globalissues.org/TradeRelated/Poverty/FoodDumping/Intro.a
sp.

APPENDIX E

Agricultural Production in Jean Makout

After fifty years of development activity, not one of the four major international intervention agencies working in Jean Makout at the time of the research had a statistically reliable estimation of average yield for any of the major regional crops. To rephrase the problem: No one knows to what degree Jean Makout farmers fall short of producing for local needs or if they fall short at all. And to be even more specific about this neglect: Initiative Developpment has no data regarding crop yields and they are the least likely organization working in the region to have such data because, although they participate in food distribution, they do not have programs targeted specifically at helping farmers in their fields. Agro Action Allemande (AAA), who does specialize in agriculture and has been doing so at least since 1994, never measured crop yields and it is not clear if they believe the task is important. AAA directors, three of whom I have befriended over the years, responded to my requests for data with a stone "no, we do not have that information." CARE, after fifty years of being the biggest NGO in the region, should be more embarrassed than any organization about not knowing crop yields, and when I visited with USAID, the two directors then responsible for food distribution said that they too did not know how much farmers in the region produced—one director cited CARE. PISANO, which has been around since the 1980s in the form of Fonds Agricol and is in fact the German government as represented by GOPA consultants, is the only development organization that could come up with data on yields and they would have done better not to. Below are PISANO's data for crop yields that PISANO agronomists sheepishly assured me are the best they have been able to come up with after five years of effort. At the risk of talking down to the reader, I will remark on two things about the data that stand out most: 1) there is very little of it, and 2) the range of estimates, even within the same geographical and ecological zones are so extreme that one has to wonder whether the data is reliable. In the *habitasyon* of Fond Ramadou (referred to elsewhere as Famadou), for example, the range of five reports on corn yields, all from the same year (1998) and from the same mountainous zone, is 349–1,395 kg/ha; the three reports on corn yields for Fond Ramadou bottom land vary from 744 to 1,860 kg/ha. To the credit of PISANO agronomists, they do not think the data is reliable either.

Table D1: PISANO crop yield data

Township	Crop	Type of soil	kg/ha
FR	corn	Mountain	930
FR	corn	Mountain	695
FR	corn	Mountain	1395
FR	corn	Mountain	349
FR	corn	Mountain	744
FR	corn	Bottom land	744
FR	corn	Bottom land	1860
FR	corn	Bottom land	930
FR	corn	Ravine	1302
FR	corn	Ravine	1395
Lcm	corn	Ravine	698
Lcm	corn	Ravine	485
Lcm	corn	Ravine	698
Lcm	corn	Bottom land	651
Lcm	corn	Bottom land	1395
Lcm	sorghum	Ravine	558
Lcm	cow peas	Bottom land	2093
Lcm	arachide	Ravine	898
Lcm	arachide	Mountain	1395
Lcm	arachide	Mountain	248

When asked, farmers seemed confident that they know the production yields they can expect in a normal year. Production figures reported in the Livestock and Gardens Survey (n = 104) appear low at first glance. Yields on the plain of Jean Makout are about 1/5th the world average for corn, 5/6ths the world average for beans, and about 1/2 the world average for sorghum and millet (see Table D1). But this image of production is obscured by the fact that farmers in Jean Makout intercrop. This means that the same low-altitude hectare that yields 1,116 kilograms of corn is planted in pigeon peas, lima beans, pumpkin, manioc, sweet potatoes, and okra (see Appendix F).

Corn and beans do not grow well in the mountains and farmers there reported expecting yields lower than the lowest country average in the world. But mountain farmers only marginally depend on corn and beans. Instead, peanuts are the premier income-generating crop in the mountains and farmers enjoy yields respectably close to the world average (1,273 kilograms per hectare, see Table D1 above). Furthermore, peanuts are also intercropped with a variety of other plants, including tobacco, castor beans, sorghum, melons, squash, okra, pigeon peas, sweet potatoes, and sesame. Thus, if Jean Makout farmers can be believed, it would appear their gardens are not so unproductive. Furthermore, agriculture intervention specialists—foreign agronomists working in Jean Makout—unanimously report that local farmers could increase garden crop yields, and some estimate by as much as 300 percent, if only the farmers would use fertilizers and pesticides.

APPENDIX F

Funding Institutions, Lobbysts, and Corporations

For Haiti, indeed for much of the developing world, the biggest and most important financial institutions are the World Bank (WB, established 1945) and the International Monetary Fund (IMF, established 1945). Also important for Haiti and Latin America is the Inter American Development Bank (IDB, established 1959). These lending institutions are controlled principally by the United States and secondarily by the E.U. and, in the case of IDB, Brasil and Argentina. The way this works is through ownership of shares. Here's a breakdown.

The World Bank (WB)

As of November 1, 2006, of 184 member countries the United States held 16.4 percent of total votes, Japan 7.9 percent, Germany 4.5 percent, and the UK and France each held 4.3 percent. As major decisions require an 85 percent super-majority, the United States is capable of blocking any major decision (Wikipedia.org, accessed January 3, 2007).

International Monetary Fund (IMF)

Votes   US 17 percent
Japan 6.1 percent
France 5 percent
Germany 6 percent
Canada 3 percent
China 3 percent
Russia 2.7 percent
Saudia Arabia 3.2 percent

IMF http://www.internationalmonetaryfund.org (accessed April 18, 2005).

Inter American Development Bank (IDB)

> Of 47 members, the US controls 30 percent of the votes, three times greater than the voting power of the nearest other members, Brazil, having 10.752 percent of the votes.
> http://www.iadb.org/ (accessed 18-04-06)

Perhaps more important with regard to impact of the lending institutions, are the business interests of the people who staff these institutions. That means multinational corporate power, something that cannot be gainsaid. Comparing corporate year 2000 sales versus GDPs, fifty-one of the largest one hundred economies in the world were corporations; the combined sales of the world's two hundred largest was greater than the combined GDPs of all countries in the world excluding the ten most powerful (Anderson and Cavanagh 2000). Moreover, it is precisely the governments in the most powerful countries, particularly the United States, Germany, Japan, and France, that promote international development policies hospitable to corporate interests. With regard to Haiti, corporate influence over government development agencies and the lending institutions are manifest in three sectors: the offshore assembly industry, corporate agricultural, and the charitable institutions, such as CARE, that execute these development plans.

Works Cited (for Appendix F)

Anderson, Sara, and John Cavanagh. 2000. The rise of corporate global power. Institute for Police Studies. At www.ips-dc.org (accessed May 5, 2006).

APPENDIX G

Crops and Resistance to Drought in Jean Makout

The crops planted in Jean Makout are those that are best adapted to the harsh environment. Relatively high yields of these crops can be produced with minimal effort in a wide range of soil pH conditions, and prove to be resilient in the face of unpredicatable rainfall patterns, and most importantly, periodic drought. The five principal crops planted by Jean Makout farmers are corn, beans, sweet potatoes, cassava, and peanuts, the very same five crops most important to the Taino Indians who inhabited the area in pre-Columbian times. To this basket of Taino domesticates, early colonists added three of the most drought resistant crops on the planet: sorghum, millet, and pigeon peas, crops that continue to be of great importance to Jean Makoutiens. The lima bean is a quick-growing, high-yielding legume that has also become popular among farmers in the region (Newsom 1993; Rouse 1992; St Mery 1797).

Table H1: The most commonly planted crops

Crops planted	Origin	Percent farmers	Crops planted	Origin	Percent farmers
Corn	Americas	87.9	Yam		2.6
Beans*	Americas	70.8	Okra		2.5
Sweet potato	Americas	59.1	Taro & a. root	Americas	2.0
Cassava	Americas	44.9	Castor bean		1.8
Peanuts	Americas	39.1	Egg pant		0.9
Millet	Africa, asia	32.1	Carrot		0.5
Sorghum					
Pumpkin	Americas	20.6	Tomato	Americas	0.4
Plantain	Phillipines	8.7	Echalot		0.3
Sugar cane		7.2	Squash	Americas	0.3
Melon		6.0	Other		5.6
Sesame		3.4			

Table illustrates the percentage of Jean Makout respondents (n = 1,539) mentioning a crop when asked to report the five crops they most commonly plant.

*All beans and peas were lumped into a single category during the baseline survey this was a mistake and the distinction between beans *rache*—beans harvested at one time which are known in French as Haricot—and pigeon peas, cow peas, and lima beans is made elsewhere.

Sweet Potato (*Impomea batatas*)

In calories per square meter, sweet potatoes are the most productive tropical cultivar on earth. They have few natural pests, and from planting to first harvest, they can produce as much as twelve metric tons per acre on as little as four inches of rainfall. In Jean Makout there are at least thirty-six varieties of sweet potatoes, which are recognized for features ranging from the ability to resist drought to the tremendous size of the potato. All varieties begin yielding in from two to six months. Cuttings must be planted when the ground is moist, but thereafter provide a continuing year round harvest, *yon manje tout tan* (a food at all times). After the initial planting, the vine itself becomes drought resistant; it withers during long dry spells, and its fruit degenerates. But the vines go into a state of dormancy and come back vigorously when it rains and the more it rains the more the vine produces. When harvesting sweet potatoes, a farmer need only re-bury the remainder of the vine for it to continue growing. Patches of sweet potatoes endure for several years and would endure indefinitely if hungry children did not help themselves, digging the sweet potatoes up and roasting them whole in small fires (see Bouwkamp 1985; Onwueme 1978).

Cassava (*Manihot utilissima*)

Cassava is a close competitor with sweet potatoes for the most productive tropical food plant in terms of calories produced per square meter. It needs more rain than sweet potatoes to grow, but it is more tolerant of drought, easily surviving dry periods longer than six months. Further, unlike sweet potatoes, cassava has the unique ability to be stored in the ground and it is hurricane proof because it can lose all its leaves and its branches may break, but the root, which is where the food is, will not die. After drought or hurricanes, the plant draws on carbohydrate reserves in the roots to rejuvenate itself. Cassava is propagated by cutting short lengths of its branches, and these sticks can be stored for as long as five months.

In Jean Makout there are least five varieties of bitter cassava and five varieties of sweet cassava. Cuttings can be planted at any time, even in the dry season, and will remain until the rains come.

Depending on the variety of cassava, the type of soil, and the frequency of rainfall, the roots are ready to harvest anywhere from six months to one and a half years but can be left in the ground for up to four years. After the tree has reached maturity (at one and a half to two years), farmers will often trim branches, allowing for the planting of other crops and the harvesting of the cassava roots as needed over a period of several years. When harvesting, portions of the roots are commonly left in the ground to grow back (see Toro and Atlee 1980; Cock 1985).

Pigeon peas (*Cajanus cajan*)

Pigeon pea roots reach six to seven feet beneath the surface, deeper than cassava, making the plant highly drought resistant. When drought does strike, pigeon peas shed all their leaves and go into a state of dormancy just like cassava, coming back to life when the rains return. The peas are a high source of protein (20 percent) and provide all but two of the thirteen amino acids necessary for protein synthesis in humans. The leaves provide animal fodder superior to most grasses and mature stalks are burnt as cooking fuel. There are at least seven varieties of pigeon peas in Jean Makout. They are planted with corn—good for the corn because pigeon peas are nitrogen fixing—and after a year the plant provides a continuous yield for six to eight months and can survive for up to five years., yielding for 6-8 months every year (see Nene et al. 1990).

Sorghum (*Sorghum vulgare*) and Millet (*Pennisetum gluaucum*):

Both crops yield with minimum rainfall. The roots reach more than eight feet beneath the surface, enabling the plant to withstand over two months of drought. When the crop is entirely lost to drought or has been harvested, the stalks can be cut back and the plant will begin growing again. The primary strain of sorghum planted in Jean Makout is called *bout ponyet* (known elsewhere as guinea corn) and yields every three months at a rate higher even than nine months millet. Millet and sorghum have a special status as a subsistence grain crop because it has a very hard, pest, and mold-resistant kernel that can be stored for over two years (see Nzeza 1988).

Corn (*Zea mays*) and Cowpeas (Phaseolus vulgaris)

Farmers reported planting corn and beans more than any other crops, probably a reflection of the fact that they are high-status cash crops, particularly on the plains. Corn and beans are not highly drought resistant although the cultivars planted in Jean Makout have traditionally been short season varieties like those originally planted by the Taino Indians. Beans and corn are among the few plants Jean Makoutiens harvest all at once and even though about 50 percent of the crop is consumed by the household, they make up one of the most significant sources of income available to farmers. They are planted on the plains and corn is the most productive domesticated nontropical plant species on earth in terms of calories per square meter (Newsom 1993; Prophete 2000).

Peanuts (*Arachis hypogaea*)

Peanuts are even more drought resistant than sorghum and in Jean Makout they are planted in sandy soil and in the *kadas* where only cacti and xerophytic plants are found. It is also the premier high-yield cash crop in the mountains, taking over the role that corn and beans fill on the plains (see Nzeza 1980).

The other lesser but still important crops all fit into an agricultural strategy that is clearly selected more for eking out a living in the face of an unpredictable market and natural environment than for participating in the world economy. Lima beans, which are intercropped with corn, are nitrogen fixing and begin to yield two to three months after harvest and continue to yield for as long as there is sufficient rainfall. Pumpkins and squash also yield continually as long as there is rain. The most popular yam in the mountains of Jean Makout (*yam reyal*) can be planted during dry spells and will begin to grow with the first rains. Like manioc, it can be stored in the ground indefinitely serving as an important food during droughts and other crises. Sugarcane endures for years, propagates itself without human intervention, can be harvested at any time after it is mature, and will grow back after being cut. Perhaps most importantly with regard to sugarcane, the hard fibrous exterior locks in water while the roots extend some eighteen feet underground, making it a completely drought-resistant source of water and high-energy food for both people and animals.

Another aspect of the Haitian peasant subsistence strategy that should be emphasized here is that the crops planted by Jean Makout farmers do not require simultaneous harvesting but yield slowly over a period of several months, even year round. The cropping strategy adopted ensures that several staples will be available in the garden in every month of the year.

Crop harvesting cycles are complemented by the availability of produce from at least nineteen types of fruit and nut trees, most of which are not planted deliberately but rather selectively permitted to grow and the harvests of which conveniently fall during the some of the leanest months for garden produce. Fruits are sold in the markets for local consumption, they are given away freely among friends and neighbors, and are consumed in abundance by everyone, especially by children, and mangos are the unrivaled favorite fruit in Jean Makout.

Table H2: Planting cycles on plain of Jean Makout (H = harvest)

	Jan	Feb	Mar	Apr	May	Jun	Jul	Aug	Sep	Oct	Nov	Dec
Beans		H	H	H								
Cow peas	H	H	H	H	H	H	H					
Lima beans	H	H	H	H	H	H	H					
Pigeon peas	H	H	H	H	H	H	H					
Corn		H	H	H								
Peanuts			H	H						H		
Millet		H	H									
Manioc	H	H	H	H	H	H	H	H	H	H	H	H
Sweet potato	H	H	H	H	H	H	H	H	H	H	H	H
Plantains	H	H	H	H	H	H	H	H	H	H	H	H
Squash	H	H	H	H	H	H					H	H
Sugarcane	H	H	H	H	H	H	H	H	H	H	H	H
Yam	H	H	H	H	H	H	H	H	H	H	H	H

Table H3: Regional tree cycles

	Jan	Feb	Mar	Apr	May	Jun	Jul	Aug	Sep	Oct	Nov	Dec
Avocado							H	H	H	H	H	
Mango				H	H	H	H	H	H			
Bread Nuts	H	H	H				H	H	H	H	H	H
Bread Fruit	H	H	H				H	H	H	H		
Kenep							H	H	H	H		
Sweet Oranges	H	H	H	H				H	H	H	H	H
Gratefruit	H	H	H	H	H	H	H	H	H	H	H	H
Lime	H	H			H	H	H	H	H	H	H	H
Sour Oranges	H	H	H	H	H	H	H	H	H	H	H	H
Coconut	H	H	H	H	H	H	H	H	H	H	H	H
Papaya	H	H	H	H	H	H	H	H	H	H	H	H
Korosol	H				H	H	H				H	H
Grenadine				H	H	H	H	H	H	H	H	H

Works Cited
(for Appendix G)

Bouwkamp, John C. 1985. *Sweet potato products: A natural resource for the tropics.* Boca Raton, FL: CRC.

Cock, James H. 1985. *Cassava: New potential for a neglected crop.* Boulder, CO: Westview.

Nene, Y.L., Susan D. Hall, and V.K. Sheila, eds. 1990. *The pigeonpea.* Andhra Pradesh, India: International Crops Research Institute for the Semi-Arid Tropics.

Newsom, Lee Ann. 1993. Native West Indian plant use. PhD diss., University of Florida, Gainesville.

Nzeza, Koko. 1988. Differential responses of maize, peanut, and sorghum to water stress. Master's thesis, University of Florida, Gainesville.

Onwueme, I.C. 1978. *Tropical tuber crops.* New York: John Wiley.

Prophete, Emmanuel. 2000. personal communication, Vegetal Production Specialist MARNDR.

Rouse, Irving. 1992. *The Tainos: Rise and decline of the people who greeted Columbus.* New Haven: Yale University Press.

St Mery, Moreau. 1797. *Description de la Partie Francaise de Saint-Domingue.* Paris: Societe de l'Histoire de Colonies Francaises, 1958 v. 2.

Toro, Julio Cesar and Charles B. Atlee. 1980. Agronomic practices for cassava production: A literature review. In *Cassava cultural practices: Proceedings of a workshop held in Salvador, Bahia, Brazil, 18-21 March 1980.* Ottawa, Canada: International Research Development Research Centre.

APPENDIX H

What Should be Done?

(Tim Schwartz and Stephane Grandvaux)

"We don't have any problems with the NGOs, but I've always said we need to know what they are doing and with what money and where."

Jean-Max Bellerive:
Prime Minister & Minister of Planning, Haiti

The Problem

Sometimes called the "Republic of NGOs" (United States Institute of Peace 2008), with the single exception of India, Haiti is said to have more NGOs and charities per capita than any country on the planet (Clinton 2009).

NGOs first began arriving in Haiti after WWII but their presence significantly increased three decades later, in 1981, when USAID began bypassing what U.S. officials defined as an extremely corrupt Haitian government. Aid dollars were subsequently delivered directly to international NGOs. Germany, Britain, and France followed suit and, in the words of Robert Lawless (1992), "Haiti soon became everybody's favorite basket case."

But while individual NGOs have educated children, drilled wells, planted trees, and saved tens of thousands of lives through vaccination and clinic programs; they have accomplished little detectable change in the country as a whole. Haiti remains the most underdeveloped nation in the Western hemisphere and over the past three decades, precisely when NGO activity flourished, it has sunk further into abysmal poverty.

Putting aside the politics, the principal reason for this failure is the lack of transparency, feedback, accountability and coordination. While most aid workers in Haiti are sincere and well intentioned, the NGO sector as a whole is best described as an uncoordinated mass of organizations *de facto* unaccountable to any governing or regulatory institution, i.e. no accountants, no auditors, no verification or review of projects, no mechanism for systematic feedback from recipients, and no publication of poor or dishonest performance. But it is not because no one ever tried to impose order on what Robert Maguire (1981:14) calls, "a wave of development madness."

In 1981, the same year the U.S. decided to redirect aid from the government to the NGO sector, USAID financed the creation of an NGO umbrella organization called HAVA (Haitian Association of Voluntary Agencies). But instead of helping, HAVA itself became a prime example of the need for accountability.

> The HAVA story begins in 1981 when, with its then 24-year-old French director at the helm, its chartered *raison d'être* was defined as, "an organism of coordination to sustain and reinforce the activities of NGOs working in Haiti." Its first task was to create a database of NGOs working in Haiti (see Mathurin 2008).
>
> In 1985-- after a full five years of effort, and financing-- the only thing HAVA had to show for itself was being 'on the verge' of inscribing on microfiche the data for 100 member NGOs (Fass 1990).
>
> In that same year, 1985, the organization won its first Inter-American Foundation (IAF) contract; a contract, not to 'coordinate, sustain and reinforce the activities of NGOs working in Haiti,' but rather for the provision of training, microcredit and legal services to the poor.

Over the next 10 years HAVA was given at least $1,149,353 of IAF funds, and perhaps money from other sources as well – no one really knows because, bolstering my point, there is no place to find out.

Meanwhile, in 1989, a point in time when most estimates of NGOs in Haiti were in the 1,000's, HAVA still had less than 100 members on its list.

In year 2000, an IAF investigator reported to the Senate Committee on Foreign Relations that HAVA "only existed on paper" – no word on what happened to the microfiche.

The story does not end there.

In 2004, with HAVA still listed on the Internet as a viable entity, a new United Nations funded NGO umbrella organization was chartered: it was called CLIO, 'Le Cadre de Liaison Inter-ONG'.

CLIO was created with the same charter as HAVA, 'to act as an organism of coordination to sustain and reinforce the activities of NGOs working in Haiti.' It also had as its director the same French national, now 47 years old (Mathurin 2008:13).

Perhaps not a surprise, CLIO has done little to nothing to make the NGO sector more accountable. After five years its membership has declined. Out of the thousands of NGOs in Haiti, it currently has 26 members.

In 2008, Concern Worldwide gave CLIO the money to conduct a study to try to figure out why it was unsuccessful in pulling the NGO community into a coordinated whole. What it discovered was that most NGO directors did not even know that CLIO exists.

The lesson to be learned from the failure of HAVA and CLIO has to do with the same lack of accountability that is rife throughout the NGO community in Haiti.

First off, HAVA and CLIO focused on "long-term strategic accountability" (five year plans, distant goals, coordination meetings), They forsook "short-term functional accountability" (verifying that projects exist and are serving the intended beneficiaries). In the process, they depended on the second major ingredient for failure: the disposition of NGOs to self-regulate and self-evaluate (Mathurin 2008).

HAVA itself was never held accountable for not following up on the creation of an NGO database. The failure in this regard was such that 29 years after HAVA was charted and 5 years after CLIO was founded, the same director/president was still at the helm, of both organizations, the same one.

Post-earthquake

Following the earthquake that struck Haiti on January 12th, 2010, sympathetic individuals, companies, church congregations, schools, and governments pledged or donated an estimated 10 billion US dollars to help the Haitian people overcome the tragedy and reconstruct the capital city and surrounding areas. More than 50% of the donated money has already gone or will go directly to NGOs and UN agencies. Veterans of the Haitian NGO sector such as CARE International, World Vision and CRS massively expanded their programs and a vast number of new NGOs also arrived in Haiti for the first time, leaving observers no doubt that the total number of both NGOs and projects have significantly increased.

Since then, new and more earnest attempts to count the foreign funded NGOs working on the ground in Haiti have been launched. As of June 2nd-five months after the earthquake – OCHA listed 961 independent NGOs and United Nations sub-organizations working in Haiti. The UN Office of the Special Envoy has accumulated a directory of 832 of what they call Haitian Civil Society Organizations.

While these might be useful first steps, these directories fall far short of the number of NGOs that was estimated prior to the earthquake. Moreover, the directories tell donors nothing about the effectiveness and efficiency of *specific projects*. In effect, they do not address accountability.

The issue of accountability is now at center stage. It has been mentioned in at least 36 major news articles and is a major topic at Haiti donor's conferences. Attempts at accountability include the traditional background checks and financial audits that go with money given by State donors such as USAID; *self*-evaluations and *self*-monitoring schemes are still firmly in place as well; so are declarations of sincerity and eagerness to particpate in spending the billions of dollars donated, such as a pledge signed by a consortium of the largest NGOs to cooperate with government reconstruction efforts; and at least one independent group, Haiti Aid Watchdog, has vowed to track the aid.

But there is virtually nothing of substance to these efforts: No hard data; no independent and systematic evaluation of the actual work done (the projects rather than simply the NGOs); no comprehensive program to address the issue of project accountability, nor a definitive plan on how to go about evaluating transparency, efficiency and, more importantly than anything else, on-the-ground effectiveness and recipient satisfaction of the mass of projects operating throughout the country.

Accountability Project

What is needed is an independent and impartial ranking and evaluating agency. The agency should have three divisions: A Project Monitoring Group, Aid Map, and the Report Repository

The **Project Monitoring Group** should be an independent and impartial ranking and evaluating team that verifies the existence of all foreign funded projects in Haiti, rates them on a basis of transparency and efficienc--i.e. is the parent organization disposed to disclose information about the project, does the project in fact exist, is it reaching the intended beneficiaries and how efficiently (see TA&A below)—and then publishes the information to a publicly accessible internet site .

The Project Monitoring Group should not be another voluntary cooperative alliance or a medium for NGO self-evaluation and self-monitoring. It should be an independent company that hires, trains, and manages physically capable, committed, and educated tri-lingual Haitian development workers to collect information on current foreign funded aid projects.

The objective is not to detract from NGO efforts to alleviate poverty and suffering; the objective is to make the sector more efficient and effective.

The **Haiti Aid Map** should illustrate NGO overlap, cooperation, and progress, meaning that the Aid Map should be available for organizations such as USAID (United States), CIDA (Canada), GTZ (Germany), EU, the UN, and most importantly, the GOH (Government of Haiti) in their efforts to coordinate development activities. Geographical Information System (GIS) technology should be used to maximize the efficiency and accuracy of the Mapping and make the information easily accessible on the website (as per InterAction and the UN Special Envoy's office who have made project maps but have not implemented a rigorous *project evaluation* component).

The **Haiti Report Repository** should be a system similar to academic peer review to help agencies determine the quality and usefulness of reports, evaluations, as well as academic treatises that can be drawn on to make development in Haiti more effective. The Repository sector should include a Wikipedia type of interactive and editable encyclopedia regarding Haitian history and development topics, and could be linked to an online Haitian Development Journal, development news, and online discussion groups where ideas can be shared.

Institutional Affiliation

The type of accountability project proposed here should be conducted in cooperation with a Haitian and a U.S. University, facilitate the development, publication, and maintenance of an online Journal of Haitian Development, and involve student internships, field schools, and graduate programs.

The long-term objective is to expand the agency to evaluate NGO overlap, cooperation, and progress, meaning that it will be a resource available to organizations such as USAID, the UN, and GOH to coordinate development efforts.

Summary

A list of overlapping benefits would include,

- Close the feedback loop between NGOs, donors and recipients
- Give NGOs an unbiased media for reflexivity, feedback, and improvement
- Give recipients a means of voicing their opinions and recounting their experiences
- Provide pressure for honesty and effectiveness
- Demonstrate the credibility of sincere NGOs
- Help expose fraudulent NGOs
- Help channel funds to NGOs that are honest, efficient, and effective
- Eliminate waste
- Guide resources where not only they are most effective but most needed
- Create the institutional foundation for certification and accreditation

- Create the institutional foundation for a system of data gathering and regional monitoring
- Create the institutional foundation for future planning and coordination
- Assure that standards are being met
- Inform public officials, journalists, and other NGOs of important field developments
- Share information between NGOs and other sectors
- Train and encourage Haitian students to enter evaluation, monitoring, and coordination.

Rating Systems for Haiti Monitoring Group

Short Term Functional Ranking System
(TA&A= Transparency, Arrival, & Accuracy)

Ranking could be on a 3 point rating scale called TA&A (Transparency, Arrival, and Accuracy): Note that this is significantly different than the Evaluation and Monitoring procedures of prior USAID and UN criteria in that it focuses on the basic aspects of functional accountability.

Transparency: does the parent organization honestly allow the evaluators to look at project income and expenses, assets, tasks, and lists of recipients? Rated with six stars, extent to which,

1) Organization provides information for the project (two stars),
2) Information is complete and organized (two stars),
3) Information appears consistent (two stars),

Arrival: how much money gets spent on the project versus overhead? Rated with six stars (based on ratio).

1) Ratio of money devoted to project to what actually gets spent on activities that directly benefit recipients (six stars)

(Evaluator will base conclusions on recipients by average cost for similar programs)

Accuracy: Is the money accurately and honestly spent on what it is supposed to be spent on? For example, if it is a project for orphans, are they really orphans and are there as many as claimed; if it is for educated poor children, are they really poor children and are they educating as many as claimed; if it is to buy food to feed hungry children, are the recipients really hungry children and are they feeding as many as claimed; if it is for latrines, are they really building latrines and are they building as many as they claim. Rated with six stars.

Rating should be based on a system of sample interviews with staff, recipients, informal community focus groups and community leaders. Standardized questions/instruments will be developed during first phase of project. Published ratings should be accompanied with explanation of merits and deficiencies.

Long-Term Planning and Accountability
I&R (Integration, and Results) and N&O (Needs and Overlap)

In the third phase of the project TA&A evaluation should be expanded to include data that can be used by organizations and governing bodies for long term strategic planning. The criteria used should be refined in collaboration with the monitoring and evaluation consultants. But two variables that could be included are I&R (Integration, and Results).

Integration: rated with six stars

1) Degree to which the evaluated project is integrated with other projects. (purchasing from them, using their resources, reinforcing them)
2) Degree to which the project uses local resources (this includes such factors as training and employing local workers, purchasing food from local farmers, purchasing services)

Results: this is an evaluation of the project's impact. Rated with six stars

3) Material evidence, such as alleviated malnutrition, number of people educated, patient visits (three stars)
4) Opinion of recipients (three stars)

As stated above this third phase should be elaborated with experts in Monitoring and Evaluation. For the present purposes I&R is expressed in the form of what we will call N&O (Needs and Overlap).

N&O provides the basis for the long term planning resource sector of the project. The Goal is to provide an annually updated **needs** assessment database that also indicates **overlap** of projects and the degree to which they are functionally **integrated** with one another as well as the local and national economy and how well they produce **results**.

Needs: to what extent the regional problem(s) are being addressed, as for example, educate children in an area where 50,000 children do not have access to a primary school or providing primary medical care to a population of 50,000.
Overlap: the number of other projects in the same area addressing the same problem and the overall degree to which the needs are being met.

Bibliography

Charles, Jaqueline 2009. Haiti at a crossroads as donations dry up and upheaval looms Miami Herald. Thursday, January 15, 2009
http://www.miamiherald.com/news/americas/haiti/v-fullstory/story/849297.html

Clinton, Bill 2006. Clinton to NGOs: With Great Power Comes Great Responsibility Finding Our Collective Voice – President Clinton 4/12/2006

Farmer, Paul 2009. Interview by Mediahacker. October 4th 2009 (http://www.mediahacker.org/2009/10/interview-un-deputy-envoy-to-haiti-dr-paul-farmer/).

Fass, Simon M. 1990. Political economy in Haiti: the drama of survival. Transaction Publishers, New Brunswick, N.J.

Global Development Research Center, NGO Codes of Conduct. http://www.gdrc.org/ngo/codes-conduct.html. (Accessed July 24, 2006)

Global Development Policy Forum, NGO Accountability. http://www.gdrc.org/ngo/accountability/index.html (Accessed May 26, 2006)

Laurent, Marguerite "Ezili Danto" 2009. (August 16) What U.N. Special Envoy Bill Clinton may do to help Haiti Haitian Lawyers Leadership Network

Lawless, Robert 1992. Haiti's Bad Press. Rochester, Vt: Schenkman Books, Inc.

CPSIA information can be obtained
at www.ICGtesting.com
Printed in the USA
LVHW040716280722
724561LV00001B/26

9 781419 698033